MAD-DOG
PROSECUTORS
AND OTHER HAZARDS OF
AMERICAN BUSINESS

MAD-DOG
PROSECUTORS
AND OTHER HAZARDS OF
AMERICAN BUSINESS

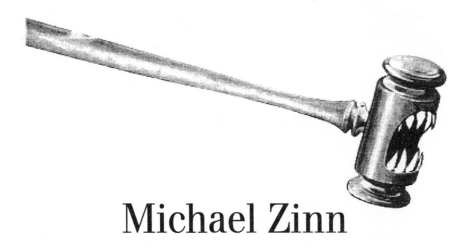

Michael Zinn

STATION HILL / BARRYTOWN, LTD.

Published under the Station Hill imprint of Barrytown, Ltd., Barrytown, New York, 12507.
Distributed in the United States by Consortium Book Sales & Distribution, Inc., 1045 Westgate Drive, Saint Paul, Minnesota 55114-1065

Text typesetting and design by Susan Quasha
Jacket design by Paul Bacon
Project editor: Charles Stein

Online catalogue and purchasing: http://www.stationhill.org

Library of Congress Cataloging-in-Publication Data

Zinn, Michael, 1952-
    Mad-dog prosecutors and other hazards of American business / Michael Zinn.
        p. cm.
    ISBN 1-58177-056-1 (alk. paper)
    1. Zinn, Michael, 1952- 2. Besicorp—History. 3. Solar energy industries—United States.

HD9681.U62Z569 1999
338.7'62147'092—dc21
[B]
                                                                99-045817

Manufactured in the United States of America

Contents

ACKNOWLEDGMENTS

I would like to thank those friends, family, and business associates who reached out during the dark days with letters and phone calls expressing support and encouragement to my wife and myself. Without your support we would not have made it. For Jim Waleur, Charlie Brown, Chuck Zwickel, Larry Fisher, Evan Meltzer, Steve Trast, and, of course, cousin Fred Zinn, who took it upon themselves to watch over my family while I was gone, a special thank you.

I would like to thank those who assisted me with developing this manuscript. Carol Charles, my trusted friend, received my phone calls, transcribed dictation, and typed my handwritten scribbles, all to keep me motivated and connected. Terri Nickolich, my trusted assistant, faithfully assisted with transcription, editing, and general organization of my writing effort. Without them I would not have been able to complete this book.

Chuck Stein, Associate Publisher at Station Hill Press, gave my first draft manuscript his insightful and incisive criticism, and then we worked side by side to edit my revisions, helping me become an "author," for which I will be eternally grateful. Sara Blackburn gave us the finishing touches, with her flair for drama and delicate touch. Sharon Van Ivan helped me with early manuscript review and editing. And many friends along the way, too numerous to mention, gave me constuctive input and commentary.

PREFACE

I began the first draft of this book while serving a six-month term in federal prison for a crime that, at worst, was a minor technical violation of an obscure campaign finance regulation. I wanted to tell the story of how this happened to me. But there is more to it than that. I want to expose some dangerous realities of life in American business today—realities that, far from the attention of media headlines, are quietly ripping apart the fabric of our system of laws and government.

I founded Besicorp in the mid-1970s. Besicorp is not an ordinary corporation, concerned only with "the bottom line." It is dedicated to the development of solar energy and efficient, clean power generation and has earned an impressive track record as an innovator in environmental technologies. My story and the story of Besicorp begins in the turbulent 1960s. Many of the ideals of that time have affected me profoundly and I adhere to them to this day.

My business life has revolved around bringing risky, cutting-edge, environmentally beneficial technologies and projects to life. Besicorp made its fortune developing clean-energy power plants that sold power to larger public utilities. It has been my belief that the only way to save the natural environment is through the development of new technologies that are both environmentally sound and economically competitive. Driven by market forces, the economy itself might thus become the means by which we save the natural world.

But the creation of such technologies requires time and careful nurturing. As the precarious beginnings described here dramatically illustrate, these efforts do not produce huge profits overnight; the business of creating them can never cater to the short-term demands of stock speculators seeking a quick return on their investment. Our approach made Besicorp a prime target for corporate raiders. They organized a clandestine campaign to oust me from the company, and this campaign resulted in my being unjustly incarcerated by the federal government. I have learned that such tactics are not unusual in corporate take-over battles. Why not use the power of the government to force your prey into submission? The government is only too willing to comply, with an army of agents and investigators standing ready to ferret out real or manufactured wrong-doing. This extravaganza cost the company, its stockholders, and American tax-payers millions of dollars. And it cost me my freedom.

Early one morning in May 1996, a week after the celebration of Besicorp's twentieth birthday, there was a knock at my door, and I was accosted by a team of federal agents. The United States Government had declared war on me, determined to find grounds on which to indict me. My life was ripped apart, my family and friends were terrorized, and finally I was sent to prison.

My criminal "offense" stemmed from my role as chief fund-raiser for the 1992 Congressional campaign of New York Representative Maurice Hinchey. I was accused of having illegally traded company bonuses for campaign contributions. Though such irregularities are usually punished by civil proceedings and fines, in my case the federal charges brought by the prosecutor were so severe, and the mandated minimum sentences I was subject to were so stringent, that my lawyers insisted I enter into a plea-bargain agreement rather than go to trial. As a result, I never had my day in court. One of my reasons for writing this book is to present a true account of the events that led to my plea-bargained conviction and incarceration. Depending on how you interpret the relevant statutes, I may in fact have inadvertently violated certain regulations. But I never intended to do so. And I strongly believe that in America, nobody should be harshly prosecuted for unintentional, technical violations of bureaucratic regulations. Yet it happens every day.

Americans have only recently begun to note the way our system of justice is spinning out of control. Under increasing scrutiny, apologists for the criminal justice bureaucracy hide behind the flag, repeating the mantras of "law and order" and deterrence while defending the excesses of individual prosecutors and federal agents as insignificant aberrations. Yet record numbers of citizens are being investigated into bankruptcy or incarcerated for technical violations and "white-collar" crime. At the same time billions of dollars are being plowed into new prison construction. The criminal justice system has become one of America's hottest growth industries, with giant companies seeking to capitalize on a seemingly irreversible juggernaut that produces ever-burgeoning numbers of prisoners—more prisoners per capita than any country in the world.

The relentless pursuit of convictions by the justice bureaucracy is gradually undermining our constitutional safeguards and destroying America's freedom. The lack of criminal intent or the actual innocence of an accused person gets lost in the process, whether the criminal is a first-time minor drug offender or a white collar "criminal" who has made a mistake in filing a federal form. Even when wrongdoing has actually occurred, mandated sentences for first-time offenders and other excesses of the process too often assure that the punishment is shockingly out of proportion to the crime. The knock on the door can come to anyone, at any time.

It is well recognized that the health of our essential economic institutions depends not only upon a fair and free market for goods and services, but a similar standard in the buying and selling of securities. Back in the 1980s, it seemed that federal intervention was going to address abusive practices in the stock market when the U.S. Government broke the back of a massive, insider-trading ring at the highest echelons of American financial markets. People like Ivan Boesky made billions of dollars in ill-gotten riches, casting a tangled web of clandestine intimidation over their corporate targets. (Their story has been well documented in *Den of Thieves*, the book by Pulitzer Prize-winning reporter James B. Stewart.) But despite the attention that these prosecutions brought to illegal insider trading and predatory takeover tactics, similar illegal raids are still being conducted by traders, stock brokers, financial agent-provocateurs, and their attorneys, though usually on a smaller scale. The present-day raiders target vulnerable businesses with predatory litigation and demands for cash settlements that amount to extortion. They are rarely exposed or held accountable for their actions: most corporate boards faced with such litigation buy off the claimants to avoid costly and invasive litigation. Sometimes they are forced to put their company on the auction block.

In this book I expose the methods of those who tried to destroy my business—people who had no interest in Besicorp either as an environmentally sensitive energy company or as a business with enormous potential for long-term growth.

For almost ten years, I have fought a legal "war of attrition," first in defense of my business, and then in defense of my freedom. When I emerged from prison, I had to heal the trauma that in many ways affected my family even more terribly than it did me.

As this book goes to press, the story continues to unfold. I hope that its complex drama will serve as a wake-up call to our country, and will be a revelation to those who can still protect themselves from making the same mistakes I did.

LEARNING LIFE'S LESSONS

I was born in 1952 and grew up on the fifth floor of a six-story apartment building in Brooklyn, New York, surrounded by aunts, uncles, and cousins. I had at least one family of relatives living on every floor of the building and several more in the neighborhood. We were a typical working-class extended family living a very modest lifestyle. My parents rented a three-room apartment where my brother and I shared a converted alcove off the kitchen as a makeshift bedroom. The whole family congregated in my parents' apartment to play cards, eat, smoke cigarettes, and engage in boisterous discussions. Many a night I'd lie in bed listening to the sounds of their talking, shuffling cards, and clinking glasses. It would be hard to imagine a closer family or people more generous with what little they had than my mom and dad.

Some might have found growing up in that environment oppressive, but I did well among the tumult, and when my time came to spread my wings, I left the nest without anger or hostility. I fondly recall telephoning my mother from Toledo when I was just fourteen, and I'll never forget her disbelief when I told her that I was hitchhiking cross-country with only twenty dollars in my pocket. So I experienced the sixties first hand, traveling the country and returning to open arms. The streets of Brooklyn were not so nurturing, however, and all around me people overdosed on drugs and died. Kings Highway was a hangout for thugs and junkies, and they cruised the neighborhoods looking for trouble. I moved with a gentler crowd and never associated with the ones who were violent or into hard drugs. Our big challenge on the streets was to avoid the gangs and hitters and find safe places to hang out.

My family's single luxury was a cottage in the foothills of the Catskill Mountains that my parents purchased for $5,000 when I was about three. The setting was idyllic, with a wide year-round stream running behind the house. Each summer we would depart for the country, and Dad would commute back and forth on weekends from whatever job he had then. Mom was a very hard worker in her career as a top-drawer legal secretary and she worked all her life, but somehow she managed to talk her bosses into giving her the summers off. Otherwise she commuted from Brooklyn to midtown Manhattan every day and also bore the burden of shopping, cooking, and housekeeping for the entire family. We boys weren't much help around the house.

My dad struggled hard to try to be the breadwinner, but he never earned more than $7,500 in any one year. It was painful to him that my mother always made more than he did. She was good-looking and accomplished and the law firms she worked at were loaded with bright and talented attorneys, but she told me one day that she had never succumbed to the interest many of them expressed in her. One thing is certain—Mom hadn't married Dad for money, and she stayed with him all those years out of devotion and loyalty. She remained faithful to him through a long marriage, which at the time of Dad's passing in 1995 had lasted for sixty-three years.

Dad was wiry and spare, and practiced a deep-rooted work ethic. A printer by trade, he tried all his life to become successful in business, going from job to job and venture to venture. He worked very hard in order to provide greater comforts for Mom, but he struggled against a severe hearing impairment that made it especially difficult for him to succeed. (Despite his deafness, we had many wonderful conversations and we enjoyed a very affectionate and loving relationship. The feeling of holding hands with him is indelibly etched in my soul.)

My father's last job before he retired was as a non-union printer in a one-man sweatshop in South Brooklyn, to which he commuted two hours each way. Dad ran a letterpress, a technology from the 1920s that had gone by the wayside. He never learned modern offset printing, and that cost him his career as a printer. Only the most marginal businesses still operated antiquated letterpress equipment, so Dad was relegated to a sweatshop when he needed to work a salaried job in between his attempts at business ventures, which always seemed to fail. At his last job, he suffered extreme abuse and indignity at the hands of the sweatshop owner.

One day, when I was about twelve, my brother and I traveled to South Brooklyn to meet Dad at the print shop. From there we planned to pick up Mom in Manhattan and continue on upstate to the cottage for the weekend. That day had been particularly brutal for Dad. He showed us an angry bruise on his leg that he'd sustained at the hands of the sweatshop owner. He had been standing by the press, he told us, just doing his work and minding his business, when out of nowhere the owner pushed a giant paper cart down the aisle directly at him, deliberately injuring his leg. This was the owner's method of trying to force my dad to quit so he wouldn't have to fire him and thus pay out unemployment insurance.

"How can you continue to work here?" I asked my Dad.

"Son, I need this job," He said. "I can't quit because then I won't be able to collect unemployment."

I was so enraged that I wanted to burn the building down. I vowed then and there never to take such abuse from anyone, and never to allow my father to suffer again. That experience shaped my life.

I advanced into my teenage years assimilating the idealism and social awareness of the sixties. I was yearning to find a way to help usher in the "Age of Aquarius," determined to be a force for good in the world.

I also had a wild side and hitchhiked around the country a few more times, once traveling cross-country in an old silver Volkswagen bus with a Zig-Zag man painted on the side. (The Zig-Zag man was the logo from my favorite brand of rolling paper.) Though I was fun-loving and rebellious, I was also quite determined, and from an early age knew how to commit productively to serious projects and endeavors. I had my first job as a busboy at the age of fourteen, and while I was still a teenager, I dismantled and reassembled several Volkswagen engines just for the experience. After spending most of an entire summer rebuilding the engine of an old beat-up "bus," I was elated when I put it in and it started up. I proudly took it for a test drive, and the engine I'd worked so hard to rebuild quickly and violently seized into a solid block of metal. My guru on the project was the book *Zen and the Art of Volkswagen Bus Maintenance*, or some such nonsense. Needless to say, this was not my path to enlightenment. I decided not be an auto mechanic.

After a solid education at Brooklyn Technical High School, I began my higher education at Brooklyn College at the start of "Open Admissions," a well-intentioned policy that quickly encumbered the City University colleges with many more students than they could reasonably handle. Overwhelmed by the crowds and ignored by my overburdened professors, I was bored stiff and dropped out, determined to blaze my own trails.

I soon became involved with an activist environmental organization called Citizens for a Better Environment. Its modus operandi was to enlist crews of college students and ship them out by the carload into suburban communities where they used encyclopedia sales techniques to canvas door-to-door, raising money for environmental causes.

I was rapidly promoted to crew chief and then to "sales" manager, and in time took over the operations of the New York office. This was no half-hearted effort. The money we raised door-to-door funded the first lawsuit against the Shoreham Long Island nuclear power plant before the first shovel was even put into the ground. Unfortunately for the people of Long Island, that lawsuit was unsuccessful, and the plant was built. It would take another decade of opposition to defeat it, but the plant was never placed into service. In fact, it has become an environmental fiasco, a folly that has driven Long Island Lighting Company into bankruptcy. Partly as a result, Long Islanders now pay the highest electric rates in the nation.

I had great fun while contributing to a cause I deeply believed in. When the organization folded, I was still in my early twenties and decided to move out of New York City. I winterized the family's upstate New York summer cottage and lived there for a year or so until my parents gave up the apartment in Brooklyn and retired there.

Thankfully, I was able to afford to support my parents generously in their old age. Dad became wheelchair-bound and then bedridden, and eventually needed twenty-four-hour care at home. With his hearing impediment, he would have been given less than adequate care if he had been confined in a nursing home.

We preserved our family unit until the very end—gathering at the dinner table, watching TV together at night, sharing affection. Basic insurance and Medicare don't reimburse for in-home care, even though it costs far less than a nursing home. This harsh reality has separated many less fortunate families.

I had been very frustrated by the inability of the environmental movement to stop major nuclear and coal-fired power projects, and I decided to devote my work to pursuing the production of alternative energy. With that in mind, I started job-hopping in a variety of technical positions, soaking up experience like a sponge.

After a few years, I was hired as project director by a local organization called Community Action Commission to Help the Economy. Funded by a federal grant, I would be addressing the problem of the chicken manure that was being produced in copious amounts at dozens of large egg farms in upstate New York. Hundreds of thousands of caged layer chickens produced a most outrageous byproduct that was just being dumped in open fields. The manure was a major environmental problem, contaminating ground water and stinking like crazy. Our goal was to explore the development of economically viable uses for chicken manure.

After researching state-of-the-art methods of converting animal waste to energy, I designed and built a system for the anaerobic (airless) digestion of the chicken manure, which included employing giant tanks and creating a means of moving liquefied manure. Working at the rear end of a chicken farm was no joy—in fact, the clouds of flies were so thick that I occasionally found myself inhaling them. I learned to catch flies in mid-air with my hands, and to this day, I can amaze my friends with my expertise. (The trick is anticipating their next move.)

The system generated huge amounts of methane by the action of invisible bacteria. Methane is the primary component of natural gas and, though explosive, is a very clean and desirable fuel. The gas was collected and used to run a generator; hot water was extracted from the generator for egg washing, and the electricity was used to power all of the farm's equipment. Built in 1976, before "cogeneration" became a buzzword, this was one of the first renewable energy systems. (I'll explain more about cogeneration later.)

After two years, the grant ran out and my employment terminated. In the absence of federal funding, the bacteria continued to generate profuse amounts of explosive gas, and I couldn't just walk away. I stayed involved for several months without pay, and eventually I found a horse farmer to take over the project. He was able to move the plant and successfully re-install it, and it continued to operate for several years until the new owner passed away.

While the project was still operating, a team of Cornell University scientists came to the site and studied my work, which I proudly displayed and described to them in great detail. They subsequently applied for, and received, a multi-million dollar grant from the U.S. Department of Energy to duplicate the work I had already done. It seemed at the time to be an injustice of a sort, but now I look back with fond memories and see that experience as a wonderful stepping stone. My departure from that project gave me the kick-in-the-butt I needed to start my own business.

2

A Publicly Traded Solar Business

It was 1976 and I had just passed my twenty-third birthday. The time was right to start an enterprise of my own.

I launched Bio-Energy Systems, Inc. (the predecessor of Besicorp) in Ellenville, New York in an unheated garage on a mountain road two miles from the nearest town, where the closest neighbor was a mile away. I purchased the entire property, where all of us involved both lived and worked, for $13,500, using a $3,000 loan from my parents as the down payment. The rundown buildings were totally dilapidated; the house contained torn-out walls, a smelly old couch that itinerants had used as a bed, and a wood and coal stove that provided the only source of heat. Next to the house was a large unheated garage made of concrete block, with no running water. For several exciting years, this house and garage would provide a home for the business.

Bio-Energy's original mission was to take chicken manure digester technology to the market, but it quickly became apparent that the farm economy of New York State was dying, and I turned my attention to developing solar energy technologies. I survived by retailing energy products of all kinds, from energy-saving showerheads to wood-burning stoves.

My team embarked on a project to develop unique solar water-heating products based upon roll-up mats of extruded rubber tubing; the water circulated through the rubber tubes and was heated by the sun. At the time, the state-of-the-art solar collectors were made from aluminum framed copper sheets, with water circulated through copper tubing covered by glass. These solar collectors were heavy and expensive. We succeeded in creating a highly marketable and elegantly simple product and obtained patent protection for our invention. Our product was dubbed SolaRoll, and it became one of the most widely used (and copied) solar heating products in the world. In 1979, the noted researcher William Shurcliff wrote about

SolaRoll in his book, New Inventions in Low-Cost Solar Heating: 100 Daring Schemes, Tried and Untried, and then a feature article on SolaRoll in Popular Science magazine appeared as a result. That single event put Bio-Energy Systems on the map. Our phones began to ring off the hook, the orders followed, dealers signed on, and a business was launched.

Bio-Energy Systems was a hand-to-mouth enterprise, a proverbial garage operation. It was an eclectic group, ex-hippies, long-haired scientists, and engineers, the best of New Age entrepreneurial capitalism. Although I've been burned by my idealism over the years on many occasions, I was able to bridge the gaps between the "revolution" and the business world.

During this period, I also had the good fortune to meet my future wife Valerie. She never knew what she was getting herself into. To this day, she finds me a bit difficult to handle, and I give her great credit for sticking it out with me through thick and thin. When she became pregnant with our daughter, she put her foot down and demanded that the employees move out of the house and into the workshop. They did, but since there was no plumbing in the workshop, they entered the house through our kitchen to use the bathroom. Later in Valerie's pregnancy, we put a portable toilet in the yard for the employees to give her a small bit of privacy, but after a time this became intolerable for them, especially in winter. To solve the problem, we cut a door into an outside wall of the house so they could use the bathroom without coming through our living space. Our phone "system" was similarly make-shift, and it was a slapstick comedy scene whenever the phone rang as we tried to figure out which line was ringing by saying "hello" on each one and turning the home-made knob while other people's conversations were in progress. This was still the late 1970s, before one could own one's own phone system, and we couldn't afford to pay New York Telephone for commercial service.

We went to extraordinary lengths to bring in money. My buddy Ron Leonard and I went peddling energy-saving showerheads to bungalow colonies all around Sullivan County in the nearby "Borscht Belt." We personally installed fifty showerheads in a large bungalow colony, and after we completed the installation, the colony's owner decided not to pay us. We were running around like mad idiots, enjoying every minute of our relative starvation.

We were part of a new age of environmental entrepreneurs, Woodstock graduates who brought a sense of mission to the business world. Nothing was impossible, and no deprivation or cash flow reality would knock us down. We didn't know what the term cash flow meant!

By 1980, the solar energy revolution was in full swing, pumped up by the federal tax credits promoted by President Jimmy Carter. Companies went public, and the market was hot for new solar energy stocks. Initial public offerings were snapped up, and money flowed copiously into the stock market. Our local celebrity was Harold Harris, one of the creators of Channel Master Corporation, the region's entrepreneurial success story at the time. Harold had helped build Channel Master into a worldwide antenna and electronics company and merged it into AVNET, a New York Stock Exchange-listed conglomerate where he went on to work in mergers and acquisitions. Harold also developed oceanfront real estate and was a highly regarded sculptor. His striking contemporary home was a showcase.

Harold Harris put fifty thousand dollars into Bio-Energy, becoming its first outside investor. Fifty thousand dollars was a significant sum in those days, especially for a hand-to-mouth garage operation. Over the years I cajoled, begged, and pleaded for Harold to put in more, but he was extremely disciplined and had set his limit. He gave freely of his advice and his time, but not a penny more did he ever invest in Besicorp.

It was time to raise some real money for Bio-Energy, and we learned that one of our best options would be selling our stock to the public. This was a new world to me, but I was up for it. As a first-time public company, we would do what was known as an Initial Public Offering of common stock (an "IPO") and would need an investment banking firm to act as an "underwriter" or intermediary in the process of selling the stock to investors. Billion-dollar companies that do IPO's get to choose from among the largest and most well known of the investment banks; we were at the small end and didn't have that luxury.

Harold's nephew worked for John Muir & Co., a hot-shot investment banking firm in the IPO market. John Muir & Co. was run by the famous Ray Dirks, the man who, in 1973, had exposed the Equity Funding scandal, one of the biggest insurance scams in history. The market was hot and Ray was taking public some outlandish deals. These were go-go days on Wall Street, and it seemed that almost anything could get done. When Harold and I first went down to John Muir, we were amazed at the frenetic pace of their business. What we saw was a boiler-room operation, with terminals and telephones lined up in endless rows, a public address system blaring important news on offerings, and countless brokers working the telephones in an intensely paced attempt to rake in the dough while the market was hot. Those who had been there before knew that the window could slam closed at any time.

Bio-Energy's birth as a public company was itself not without pain, and our success as a business was many years in coming. As with many over-the-counter IPO underwriters, Ray Dirks was not a blue-chip player, and most of the companies he took public went nowhere. One of the ironies of the IPO business was that an operation like Ray's made money whether or not the companies whose stock he sold even survived. He was in the fee-and-commission business and, as such, churned out offerings from many less than exciting companies. But things were hot for Bio-Energy stock. John Muir was receiving tremendous interest in our company, and people were excited about it, especially with the Popular Science article propelling us forward. Underwriting is a volatile business, driven by the unpredictable elements of market timing, fads, telemarketing, and syndication. In hot markets, the most absurd deals get done, and companies with virtually nothing going for them can raise large amounts of money. In the bull market of 1980, we set out to capture our piece of a hot IPO underwriter's business, and the forces we rode spun out of control. It was the first of what would be many difficult times in the future history of Besicorp.

Jack Silver was Ray's deal manager for Bio-Energy's stock offering. When Jack arrived to do his "due diligence" (the process of kicking the tires on a new deal), he pulled up in front of our ram-shackle office building in a stretch limousine and emerged in a black cape. We were a backwater company, and I wasn't sure whether to be intimidated or to laugh. Jack Silver remained involved with the company for several years. He was smart and had a very good touch for picking horses in business. The dog-and-pony shows we con-ducted for Bio-Energy in cities all over the nation were well received, and the business environment all around was generating greater and greater momentum: morning sales meetings, the deal of the day, bring in the checks. The IPO market was a money machine!

I was about to begin a long process of learning about the pitfalls of dealing with lawyers. Those who are uninitiated in the ways of the legal profession may not understand the murky decision-mak-ing procedures that larger law firms use to avoid taking on risks and responsibility. The "lawyer's lawyer" practices with a high de-gree of formality and loyalty to a set of standards that function tightly to protect him and his firm from liability or conflict. I have learned from hard experience the value of a practical street-smart business attorney, one who follows high ethical standards but works hard to help the client avoid pitfalls and solve problems.

The practice of law is just like any other business or profession, with successes and failures, villains and heroes. A bad lawyer can put you out of business, ruin your life, drive you crazy, and other-wise do untold damage. If you are unfortunate enough to go through the trauma of a criminal investigation, even an excellent attorney may not keep you out of jail, but with a poor attorney a criminal defendant has little chance. It is up to the client to know the differ-ence, and the difference can be difficult to discern.

The heat of the market was overwhelming at the time we signed the underwriting agreement, and the relentless quest for money oozed out of every pore in the offices of John Muir. Though the window of opportunity could slam shut at any moment, the gravy train for gullible investors was rolling ahead at full speed. Row after row of desks, computer monitors, telephone banks, and men and women were employed to capacity and beyond, working the

phones, yelling, doing deals, flinging paper. Everybody was pushing to get his or her deal done. It seemed unstoppable, and perhaps for a time it was. But all bull markets eventually come to an
end. I was about to experience the first of many hard lessons about
the rough and tumble business world.

∽

Once I made the decision to sell stock in an IPO, I went to our
local legal counsel to see if they could help get the process going.
They, in turn, were hooked up with a Wall Street law firm, and we
put the team together and were off and running. Everyone was excited. Bio-Energy was going to be a winner, and all of us were thrilled
that calls were coming in for our stock. We knew we had an opportunity that couldn't be missed.

The first order of business was the creation of a prospectus, which
required getting through a maze of lawyers and accountants. A prospectus is the "offering" document that describes the company and
its financial condition, discusses its business prospects, and notes
the risks associated with the investment. A prospectus has to follow
guidelines prescribed by the Securities and Exchange Commission
("SEC") in order to satisfy their disclosure requirements. I would
come to learn that there are wide variations in how the content is
presented. The lawyers told me that a prospectus for sale of stock is
designed to protect the company and is not a promotional brochure.
This helped me to understand why our prospectus seemed to be
written specifically to scare away even the most aggressive potential investors.

I came to learn, however, that not all companies are presented in
such a negative light. Other companies filled their prospectus with
beautiful color photos of their products, rosy financial projections,
and optimistic descriptions of the business, all placed right up front;
buried in the back were the fleetingly described risk factors. But I
was ignorant about how to make the presentation satisfy the legal
requirements regarding disclosure while still presenting an attractive investment opportunity, and depended entirely on the attorneys. The result: all that was missing from our prospectus was a

mirrored surface on the inside cover with a translucent silk screen that said "Schmuck—"don't buy this!"

It took a long time and lots of effort by these super-conservative expensive lawyers and accountants just to get the prospectus to a first draft. Then the fun began. Prior to a stock offering being sold, a draft is circulated to the brokers. This is called a "Red Herring" because the lettering on the front page is red, just like a piece of bloody bait. While the Red Herring is being promoted, the SEC is reviewing the document and providing comments to which a response is required. Each time a modification is made in response to the SEC's comments, another version has to be printed, and when the offering of stock is finally cleared, the document is printed in black.

Our first Red Herring seemed to be a decent deal: We were going to sell one-third of the company for seven million dollars, or $7.00 per share for one million shares—not bad for a garage operation that had $50,000 in invested capital. The phones were still ringing off the hook at John Muir. Bio-Energy was in demand. The 1979 Popular Science article was still generating the demand, and it appeared that the offering was going to be oversubscribed.

I just wanted to get the prospectus done, but due diligence, writing, and re-writing were taking up endless time. I knew we needed to strike while the iron was hot; even garbage deals were being sold. I wanted to get our deal done, but it wasn't my show. Out of the blue, I was called into a meeting with Ray Dirks and Jack Silver. The Bio-Energy deal was in so much demand that they had unilaterally decided to forego forming a syndicate with other brokerage firms and were going to sell the Bio-Energy offering entirely through their own boiler-room operation.

"But wait!" I said. "What about the other brokerage firms that are supposed to help get the deal done?"

"Don't worry," Ray said, "This is just as good. And we decided to re-price the deal. Instead of a million shares at $7.00, we'll offer seven million shares at $1.00. That way we can sell it all retail, because our clients like low-priced stocks. So get the lawyers going on it."

There was nothing I could do, I thought. But the absence of syndicate participation was to have a devastating effect.

~

The lawyers did a seven-to-one stock split and re-priced the deal; we understood that we would get the same amount of money, $7 million, for the same percentage of the company. It was back to the printer to produce another "Red Herring." Everyone said that another $50,000 or $100,000 in costs was nothing.

Things have a way of dragging on, and by the time the Red Herring was ready, the market was starting to slow. Ray and Jack decided to cut the deal back to $5 million. More dithering. Meanwhile, Harold Harris and I were camped in New York City, walking the floors at John Muir, trying to keep the brokers pumped so the offering wouldn't lose momentum while we waited for the lawyers to finish.

Then, from California, a missile was fired, and I was about to become initiated into an ugly side of the legal profession. Just as we were struggling to complete our public offering, a former customer served Bio-Energy with a multi-million dollar lawsuit. He and his attorneys had decided to take a crack at our money by timing their suit to hit at our most vulnerable time. They made a bogus claim for damages to the tune of millions of dollars, and everything ground to a halt. I learned my first hard lesson in the world of finance. The Wall Street law firm that was representing Bio-Energy became petrified and paralyzed. Legal bills were mounting up, and the company had no money. The lawyer for the California customer claimed that we had given his client the exclusive rights to distribute our solar energy products west of the Rocky Mountains. In fact, we had given him the opportunity to distribute our products only nonexclusively. These guys were visionaries in having figured out the game of predatory law, the advance guard of a new generation of disreputable raiders and legal practitioners who would make their living by targeting any vulnerable person or business with money.

Our underwriters were not about to raise public money to pay off a big-dollar lawsuit for a start-up company. Larry Fisher, outside counsel for John Muir, came up with a proposed solution. In order to go forward with the underwriting, we were to obtain a legal opinion that the claim was without merit. But no matter what documentation I provided, or how much I pleaded, our attorneys were not willing to provide such a legal opinion, even if it meant that we would go out of business. Their primary consideration was to protect themselves from any potential liability. Despite my arguments that their opinion would contain all kinds of disclaimers about their lack of certainty about the outcome, they just wouldn't budge. I couldn't believe that they were so unwilling to take any risk at all. I began to search for whatever legal resources I could muster, but there weren't many places to turn. I had only been in business for a few years and didn't have many chits to call in.

Charles Brown was a top-drawer patent attorney. He and I had spent countless hours drafting specifications and claim language to obtain patent protection for our solar energy inventions. Charlie had moved out of New York City several years before, giving up a position as a star patent attorney with the firm of Penney Edmonds to establish a country law practice and live the good life. I called him in a panic and told him what was up. We were on the verge of going belly up, all the lawyers were heading for the hills, and the finger-pointing had already started. They were actually sitting around conference tables analyzing how much money there might be to go around, all while the victim was still very much alive.

Like a true White Knight, Charlie came in as if on a beautiful horse, regal in appearance with gray hair and glasses, his steady, reassuring voice taking quiet control of the situation. Like a country doctor diagnosing a child's sick doll, he examined the patient and found that there was life to be preserved. For a person with such character, it seemed simple: In a matter of hours, Charlie reviewed the California lawsuit and decided that it wasn't even necessary to give an opinion as to whether we would win or lose; with a quick calculation on the back of an envelope, he determined that the net profit that the distributor could make and therefore the maximum award they could obtain if they won the suit was $50,000. Charlie's practical problem-solving had escaped the dozen highly paid lawyers who had been agonizing over how to avoid putting their own necks on the line. They were so worried about being sued themselves that they had been looking at the problem from the wrong end of the telescope.

The stock offering was back on track, and the lawyers were happy that someone else had stuck his neck out and that they were going to get paid. (The bills for lawyers and accountants kept running up, and we still had NO MONEY). We were again in what appeared to be the home stretch, and the next Red Herring was hot off the press. The market was still fiery enough, but danger signs were mounting as deals were seemingly harder to get done. I began to notice a level of nervousness at John Muir that I hadn't seen before, but I was reassured that things were going to be fine now.

At the next meeting with Ray Dirks and Jack Silver, a new bomb was dropped: they had cut the underwriting back to $2.4 million and had reduced the price from $1.00 to 75 cents per share. This meant we would raise just a fraction of the money that we had intended to raise, and at a substantially lower overall valuation for the company. Bio-Energy would be a "penny stock," with all the implications this carried for our future market as a public company. I was very upset, but there was no choice but to go forward. We had hundreds of thousands of dollars in expenses already committed, and no possible financing alternatives.

And so it went. Each time we were forced to go back to the printer to produce another Red Herring, there were more delays, along with the inexorable clock-ticking on the lawyers' and accountants' fees. The offering company pays the fees on both sides of the transaction, whether or not the deal closes, and rooms full of people were endlessly deliberating over our business, arguing obscure points, all at our expense. I realized that even if our company went out of business, it wouldn't much matter to the Wall Street guys. They made so much money that an occasional non-collectible was just written off. At this point our audited financial statements were going stale, and if the deal was not completed, it would have been certain death for the company; we couldn't afford the accounting fees for a re-audit, and we certainly could not afford any further delay. Harold Harris and I kept the deal alive by camping in New York at the office of John Muir. We kept moving around the office from desk to desk, reminding the brokers that we were still there, trying to keep them pumped on the deal. Not only were our audited numbers going stale, but we were as well. To our enormous relief, however, our in-your-face strategy worked: we were able to create personal loyalties and sustain the commitments that kept the company alive.

With the new pricing structure, it was back to the printer again, and all of the prior printings were put in the wastebasket. Another Red Herring was produced, and yet another $50,000 in expenses were incurred. Another week went by and it was now 1981. We were just waiting around for lawyers, accountants, and printers, while things were getting increasingly dismal at John Muir & Co. No matter how Ray and Jack tried to pump everyone up, the sales force was just running out of steam. Investors weren't buying and the expressions on everyone's faces were getting more depressed and depressing. Tension was high, and deals were dying on the vine left and right.

At last, the SEC ordered our last deal "effective" and yet another prospectus was printed, with all BLACK letters (indicating clearance by the SEC to sell!). There were to be no more Red Herrings, but it turned out that things were far from done. Ray and Jack motioned me into their office with solemn expressions. The firm was going out of business and they couldn't finish our deal. I was floored. Oh my God. We were out of business.

In a panic, I begged Ray to finish the deal, pleading with him and trying to penetrate his armor. He then informed me that if they didn't sell the whole offering out, they couldn't close at all because the deal required all or nothing to get to closing. They could sell more, but not less. The only alternative was to place a printed sticker on the prospectus to inform investors that we might close with less money than was sought. The lawyers were consulted yet again and the door to Ray's office was closed. Harold and I were waiting, still pacing, when the door opened and Ray and Jack came out to tell us they had decided to use their own funds to purchase whatever Bio-Energy stock was unsubscribed. They had made a decision that they would not let our company go out of business if they had any ability to save it.

We were the last IPO for John Muir. Immediately after our closing, its doors closed and its brokers all began looking for other jobs. At the end of that grueling public offering process, we took our smaller than expected pile of marbles and began to evaluate what we actually had: a public company with a penny stock and net proceeds after expenses of less than $1.9 million out of a gross of $2.4 million. We had survived.

Ray Dirks held a closing party at the home of Peter Yarrow (of Peter, Paul & Mary), and among the happy attenders, we listened to Peter sing a song about the sun.

Thankfully, there are good people in the business world, just as there are predators. You just have to find them and hope the predators don't find you. Now we were on our own—a public company without enough money, but at least it was alive.

3

Saving a Struggling Company

The decisions that Ray Dirks made regarding the structure and pricing of our public offering had negative consequences for our company for many years. Bio-Energy stock had been sold only through John Muir's internal brokers, which depressed the price of the stock for a long time. The lack of a marketing syndicate made Bio-Energy an orphan, depriving it of the market reach and diversified investors that syndicates attract to a company's stock. Syndicators also support each other's transactions. Small pieces of a company's offering are placed through multiple channels and engage numerous brokers and potential investors in a company's future. Each firm that places some of the offering takes at least a small interest in following the stocks in which they have placed their clients. With our underwriting firm out of business, the lack of a syndicate meant guaranteed oblivion for us. We had no research reports, no recommendations, and no ability to place secondary public stock offerings. We were relegated to the backwater of the stock market, a small, weak company with a penny stock and inadequate access to the capital markets.

I turned my attention to building the business. Taking advantage of relationships I had built in the investment community, Bio-Energy placed a private stock sale in 1983 and raised an additional $1.2 million. This was the last equity the company ever raised.

During the early 1980s I continued to build our network of solar energy dealers. Our solar energy products, based upon our inventive SolaRoll rubber solar collectors, were selling well, and I began to look for growth opportunities with which to diversify the business.

Keeping my ear to the ground, I had observed that other companies in the solar energy market had begun riding a wave that was propelling their stocks to all-time highs. A company called American Solar King began packaging "tax shelter" offerings for sale to wealthy investors. The investors purchased interests in partnerships that owned large industrial solar energy projects and enjoyed large tax savings based upon the lucrative tax credits that the federal government was offering to promote solar energy.

We jumped on the bandwagon, and after a couple of years of languishing, investors discovered our company. Beginning in 1983, Bio-Energy stock began a run up to a degree that defied rational explanation. Before we knew it, the company had a market capitalization approaching $100 million. This remarkable turn of events took place long before there was any intrinsic value in the business, and illustrates how crazy the stock market can be.

The opportunity was not to be missed, and nobody was going to talk me out of selling some of my own Bio-Energy shares into that crazy market. I was warned not to sell any stock by a variety of well-intentioned people and threatened by stockbrokers who argued that I would be sending a negative signal to the market. "Think of the public investors and hold your stock," I was told, but I would not be dissuaded. I began selling stock on the way up and I continued selling on the way down, until the stock had returned to a more reasonable value. That period in 1984, lasting but a year, changed my personal financial picture from flat broke and living hand-to-mouth to having some real money in the bank. I had been in business almost ten years, but until that moment, I hadn't earned a nickel beyond a paltry salary which barely paid my bills.

With cash in the bank and a high stock price, it didn't seem urgent to raise money for the company. But the high stock price for Bio-Energy was unsustainable. With no earnings and minimal assets, inevitably the stock began to drift down. I never realized how low a stock could go; on the way down, I watched with amazement as it hit each new plateau. The bottom dropped out of the market for Bio-Energy stock, and by the time it stopped dropping from its high of $5.50, it was being bid at five cents per share. By the mid-1980s, Bio-Energy had gone into a period of decline that seemed irreversible.

Dark days were ahead, and only my newfound personal net worth allowed me to inject the business with continuing life.

∾

As the mid-eighties rolled around and oil prices collapsed, the solar business became dormant. Adding to the malaise was a radical change in market conditions brought about by the expiration of the federal tax credit program for solar energy installations. Virtually all of the other solar energy companies folded their tents, but Bio-Energy survived that radical change in the market by using what I can best describe as street smarts.

I don't mean to sound pious and self-righteous, but my involvement in solar energy has been sustained for over two decades by my conviction that it's the most sensible energy source for the planet and its people. Even when pundits said that it was a fad that should be relegated to the past, I continued in the business. I believe that the world will eventually come to grips with the growing demand for an improved quality of life by the people of the developing countries, and those needs can only be met with renewable energy.

We "pioneers" in the solar field have been aware of the severe environmental impact of fossil fuel consumption for decades before the issue of "global warming" brought solar energy back into the public eye in the 1990s. But in the 1980s there was still a long way to go before this would happen. Unless there was a radical change in strategy, I knew I could not survive in business.

The company was continuing to develop solar energy projects and had begun to dabble in the electricity generating business. In 1984, I decided to move more aggressively into the development of cogeneration plants.

Cogeneration was the wave of the future. In the cogeneration process, small power stations cogenerate electricity together with useful thermal energy in the form of steam or hot water, operating at very high efficiencies and using clean fossil fuels like natural gas. Cogeneration fit my environmental vision for the company as an "alternative" source of energy for such institutions as hospitals. Without a cogeneration plant, institutions would have to continue purchasing electricity from nuclear and coal-fired utility plants and would continue generating steam in their own old, dirty coal- or oil-fired boilers.

It was in this market that the company began to cut its teeth and become a more mature enterprise with real potential. The name Bio-Energy didn't seem broad enough to describe a diversified energy company, and I came up with Besicorp: B.E.S.I. was an acronym for Bio-Energy Systems, Inc., and Bio-Energy continued on in the solar business as a subsidiary of Besicorp Group, Inc.

At the time, our people in the solar business were uneasy about the change and didn't understand why I would divert hard-earned cash flow into a different business. It turned out to be a very sound decision. The market for solar technology was dormant; energy prices were down and looked like they were going to stay down for a long time to come. As a solar business, the company was dead, but as a power and energy business, at least we had an uncertain future. There was one major problem: lack of funds. By 1985, Besicorp had run through all the cash we had raised from sale of stock. The company's publicly traded stock was worthless, so another offering was impossible. The board of directors considered the company's death spiral to be irreversible. No bank would finance our business in what had become a negative financial trend. Even Harold Harris, my first investor who was so dedicated to the success of the company, wouldn't put a nickel more into the business. He flat out told me, "I don't see how you can turn this business around." It was just what I needed to get me fired up.

I had been telling the board that I was going to move Besicorp aggressively from the solar energy field into the electric power generation business. They were unanimously opposed to going in that direction; their consensus was that I should wait out the recession and stay in the business we knew. Unwilling to accept that defeatist attitude, I suggested that board members who didn't support my position should resign.

I wanted to keep the company alive, and I made a decision that I would put myself at personal financial risk if it was necessary to ensure the company's survival. If I was going to bankroll the company with my personal funds, I didn't need a board whose lack of support was siphoning energy from the future prospects of the business. Regretfully, and reluctantly, I accepted the resignations of all of the outside board members; I appointed several executive employees to the board and began a journey into the uncharted territory of running a publicly traded company without an independent board of directors.

I was proud of my accomplishments and certain I could overcome virtually any adverse situation. I personally identified with the company and would not allow it to go out of business. I had a resounding determination to protect the interests of all the "stakeholders" of Besicorp. Aware of my responsibility to the public shareholders, I was also keenly concerned about the employees whose interests needed to be protected. I also did not want the stigma of being associated with a company that went into bankruptcy, which I considered to be the easy way out. I am proud of my battles and the personal risks I undertook, and the results speak for themselves.

I didn't waste time trying to maximize my own position or even taking basic measures to protect myself if things went awry. I look back on that time and see that I displayed an amazing lack of foresight in terms of protecting my own interests. But it was precisely that focus and dedication in the face of what seemed almost insurmountable difficulties that enabled me to bring the company through those years of financial turmoil.

It would have been far more pragmatic to let the business go into liquidation and start a new company using my own money, but I assumed that if I did the right thing, the public shareholders would be appreciative. By the late 1980s my ownership interest in Besicorp had dropped to less than 35% of the company's common stock. I had given stock to the founding team, and over the years had extended stock options and grants to various management employees. Forty percent of the company had been sold to the public and to various private investors over the years. I never viewed my reduced ownership position as a dilution in my personal stake: I believed that a rising tide lifts all boats.

As I look back and contemplate the battles that still lay ahead, my decision seems just plain dumb. I could have bypassed all of it by allowing the company to fail and then continuing on in business.

4

Launching the Power Business

Although I founded our company as a solar and alternative energy business, its fortune was made as a developer of cogeneration projects.

I've often been troubled about the ethics of developing fossil fuel-burning power plants of any kind on this overburdened planet. I've had to evolve my thinking about environmental issues to realize that building clean-burning, fossil fuel-powered plants makes environmental sense.

The fact is that most of the electricity consumed in the United States comes from coal, with oil playing a major role as well. Burning coal and oil to generate electricity produces acid rain, which is killing the forests and lakes of the northeastern United States. As a developer of clean-burning and economical natural-gas-fired power plants, Besicorp is part of a transition to more environmentally benign technologies. I can honestly say I'm proud of the environmental record we have developed, even while making a ton of money.

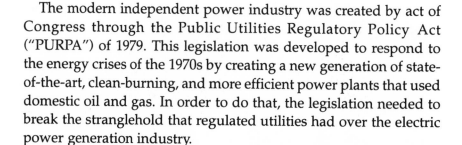

The modern independent power industry was created by act of Congress through the Public Utilities Regulatory Policy Act ("PURPA") of 1979. This legislation was developed to respond to the energy crises of the 1970s by creating a new generation of state-of-the-art, clean-burning, and more efficient power plants that used domestic oil and gas. In order to do that, the legislation needed to break the stranglehold that regulated utilities had over the electric power generation industry.

Before PURPA, the United States was experiencing brownouts in some major metropolitan areas, and it was forecast that increasing electricity demand was going to make matters worse. Utilities couldn't seem to get off the treadmill of trying to build giant nuclear plants. The Three Mile Island catastrophe of 1979 was a turning point in the retreat from nuclear power as an energy source.

PURPA spawned a new industry by requiring regulated electric utilities to enter into contracts to buy electricity from independent power producers. This industry presented unusual opportunities for those who could move quickly and nimbly. It was a true entrepreneur's dream. But it was not all a bed of roses.

Utilities were required to pay higher electric rates at the front-end of the contract so that the independent power producers ("IPPs") had sufficient cash flow to service their debt, which was generally of a ten- or fifteen-year duration. In exchange, utilities demanded that the independent power producers enter into gas contracts at fixed prices for as long as fifteen years. These were out-of-market contracts that required payment of substantial premiums to the gas companies. This structure was supposed to guarantee that the IPPs would be able to sell electricity at the fixed contract prices for the duration of the gas contract.

What seemed like an excellent strategy turned into a nightmare. Energy prices in the late 1970s appeared to be heading straight up, but in the 1990s they were at historic lows. IPPs were stuck with their gas contracts, and utilities were stuck with their IPP contracts, and the IPPs were stuck with billions of dollars in borrowings.

The clean, modern cogeneration plants were attacked by the regulated utilities as parasites. In a bit of hypocritical double-speak, utilities were taking advantage of the situation to bash their unregulated competitors. But to a savvy entrepreneur, this was the opportunity we had been working on for a decade. Besicorp took advantage of this turnabout to make a major fortune. It took over a decade to realize the rewards, and how we did it is a story unto itself.

Back in the mid-1980s, Besicorp entered the power project development business with virtually no capital. Participating in this industry required professional talent as well as an image of competence and substance. The company's strategy evolved over time as I learned what the market needed. With next to nothing to invest out of Besicorp's own capital, our goal was to make money in any way we could from the projects we initiated.

We began by getting our feet wet with small projects such as co-generation facilities in hospitals, financing them with bank loans and limited partnerships. The typical capital budget for these early plants was in the area of one to three million dollars, and I contributed my personal funds to some of these ventures to enable Besicorp to launch its power business. The risks were great and I was never compensated for taking them; I shudder to think of how much our success depended on a great variety of complex factors coming into play and working together.

Our company's expertise began to form in the niche of early-stage development and financing of such power projects. We were able to establish long-term relationships that overcame our small size and eventually created some winning alliances. Over time, Besicorp developed a portfolio consisting of approximately one-half interest in almost one billion dollars worth of power plant assets. We financed these projects with 100% debt and invested no equity of our own, while holding on to virtually all of the ownership. We even recovered our initial investment from the banks at the closing of project financing and sometimes earned development fees as well. I must say, we were very good at that business.

We jumped into big-league power plant development and against all odds were able to build a successful business. The challenges we faced were huge compared to the business we were used to. Nothing in our prior experience prepared us for the complexities of creating major projects from inception and working in the world of high finance.

These major projects were financed entirely with "limited-recourse" loans. With this type of financing, the lenders depended solely on the success of the project for repayment of their loans. We raised more than $600 million for Besicorp's successful New York State projects and invested no equity capital at all. They were sound enough in all respects to attract all of the necessary financing from lenders and finance companies, and we and our partners retained almost 100% of the equity ownership. It was truly amazing.

It was hardly all fun and games. Developing each project consumed at least several years. Besicorp inevitably placed a few million dollars at risk, taking into account the cash we fronted as well as our time and internal costs. We survived by rolling the small amount of money we had from project to project. Each time I continued to roll over my personal guarantees. We raised our capital for the development of the projects from vendors of equipment and services such as Siemens and General Electric. Many of these companies loaned development financing as a lever to obtain contracts for business, whether as a supplier of a turbine or as a construction or engineering firm.

We also negotiated risk-sharing arrangements with the large law firms and investment banks that worked on our deals. They undertook to support our projects in exchange for the right to supply legal or investment banking services in the major project financing. We refined the creation of third-party-risk capital to an art form.

Despite all the third-party capital we were able to generate, we still took significant risk ourselves in the creation of these projects. Had even one project failed, we would have lost our shirts and could easily have lost the entire business. The projects we worked on were high-risk ventures during the development stage. The risk diminished considerably as certain milestones were achieved. The first major milestone that transitions a major power project out of venture capital mode is a construction loan closing.

Bringing off a construction loan closing is like dancing on the head of a pin. The slightest instability in a deal can derail it. Structuring the dozens of business relationships and hundreds of contracts necessary to put a construction loan closing together is a major undertaking, to say the least. It is the culmination of the development effort and requires excellent management and lots of legal horsepower.

Our closings generally took place at the law firm of Kelley, Drye, & Warren. Ten conference tables would be laid end to end, stacked high with documents ready for execution. All the conference rooms at the firm would be taken up by our last-minute negotiations; otherwise they served as holding rooms where the parties involved waited to execute documents. Sometimes dozens of lawyers would be in a room, arguing over obscure points in the contracts and financing documents. They would manufacture risk scenarios, such as "asbestos bombs," and get into heated arguments that raged into the middle of the night about whether the documents covered the point, and which party should shoulder the risk. The legal bills at closings could run as high as $10 million.

Closing these deals would take weeks. People camped under tables and slept on the floor (or a couch if they were fortunate). The tensions and pressures were enormous. Dealing with the greedy, last-minute money grabs required steely eyes and harder nerves, and sometimes we had to capitulate to unreasonable demands just to get the deal done.

∼

One of the most significant relationships we established in the course of building our project development and financing business was with a giant Italian company called Ansaldo SpA.

Ansaldo was one of the many companies seeking to bid on the construction of our projects. These contracts were worth between $50 and $80 million for each of the six projects we completed. To differentiate themselves and get a leg up in the bidding contest, Ansaldo let it be known that they were willing to offer high-risk financial support for project development in exchange for being awarded the contracts to build our projects. Deep pocket sponsorship was always attractive to a small company like Besicorp, so we jumped on the opportunity.

Ansaldo was part of a $60-billion Italian government-owned conglomerate and was one of the largest power construction and engineering companies in the world. By around 1988 they hadn't yet done significant business in North America, and they were keen to penetrate this lucrative market. This was why they were ready to buy their way in by offering their clients financing.

Stefano Moretti was President of Ansaldo North America, Inc., a venture capital subsidiary of Ansaldo for the United States. He was the lead negotiator for Ansaldo, and I took the lead for our team. He and I reached a general agreement to develop a long-term relationship, and we turned our business deal over to our lawyers to try and craft a contract.

After several months of frustrating effort, the lawyers succeeded only in creating totally unworkable documents. I was horrified. There were contract clauses that were two pages of single-spaced type, with multiple nested conditions within conditions. In order to interpret what the contract meant one had to refer to several other clauses elsewhere in the contract. I couldn't follow it, nor would I want to, and I could only imagine what the Italians felt about it.

I grabbed the bull by the horns and pushed the lawyers aside, determined to get the deal done. I wrote Moretti and his Italian bosses and presented the key elements of the agreement. If they agreed with my points, I said I would draft the agreement myself, working directly with Moretti. Ansaldo responded immediately and affirmatively, so I went to work. Within a couple of weeks, I had crafted a workable document that met the needs of both parties. Moretti and I considered the agreement to be quite an accomplishment. Although the lawyers ultimately got their fingers on the document and added a bunch of legalese, the agreement retained much of the simple elegance of our hands-on work and served us well.

Ansaldo's funding was extremely flexible. The terms were the best of any I had ever seen between a small company and a major entity, and we were able to draw funds for a wide range of early-stage expenses with minimal paperwork.

Over the course of the relationship, Ansaldo funded the early-stage development of six major projects and was awarded five engineering, procurement and construction (EPC) contracts worth $500 million in business. Ansaldo had the potential to make at least $50 million in profit on those jobs and establish for itself a major foothold in the American power market. They got everything they bargained for. It was up to them to make a go of it to establish their beachhead in North America.

∼

I loved going into New York to meet with Moretti. A Northern Italian meal was always part of the ritual. Espresso was always on tap at their offices. Along with great furniture and snazzy clothes, the Italians know how to live!

It seemed natural to try and build on that relationship and try to get Ansaldo to sponsor Besicorp in other ventures. To pursue that goal, in the spring of 1991 my project partner Hal Kamine and I went to Italy with Stefano Moretti to tour Ansaldo's facilities. We met some of the Ansaldo top brass in Rome and Genoa. There we broke bread and discussed business with the old men of the company in halting English. We toured Ansaldo's turbine manufacturing plants and visited their high-tech Research & Development operations that were competitive with the best in the world. Ansaldo worked in esoteric areas such as magneto hydro-dynamics (super high-technology magnetics) and cryogenics (technology for super cooling). I even met with Ansaldo's alternative energy specialists and had our first discussions about getting into the photovoltaic (direct conversion of solar energy into electricity) business. This was a business that Besicorp was soon to enter. The future seemed bright indeed.

Later in 1991, Hal Kamine and I hosted a major event to show off the first Ansaldo-built power plant in North America for Ansaldo's top brass from Italy. After the plant tour, the entire entourage of thirty people went by bus to the Saratoga Race Track and ate a fabulous Northern Italian lunch, complete with Italian wine, of course. I sat next to Mr. Lucia Clavarola, the Chief Executive Officer of Ansaldo. I had the honor and privilege of offering the toast to our visitors. I was the golden boy to Ansaldo and this was the golden age of the relationship that formed the backbone of our business.

Those were exciting times. But Ansaldo would end up playing a much bigger role in my life than I ever bargained for, and it was not at all positive.

5

TARGETED BY STOCK SPECULATORS

Besicorp's strategy had always been to build valuable interests in environmentally sound power projects. Unlike major companies, we did not invest large amounts of our own capital. Instead, as I have noted, we took early-stage risk with a relatively small amount of money and, through a process of bootstrap development, tried to bring our projects to fruition. Our goal was to retain as much ownership as possible while pulling as much cash as possible out of the project as it achieved financing.

Even when suitable contracts are arranged, power plants need to be permitted, designed, financed, and then constructed, and then they have to operate profitably before there is cash value for the owner. That process can take three to five years of high-risk effort, and even then the value of Besicorp's retained interest is still further dependent upon profitable project operations and many other external factors.

The creation of wealth and enduring value in a business based upon imagination and entrepreneurship requires patience and stamina, qualities that are sometimes incompatible with the impatient demands of stock speculators. In the quarterly earnings-oriented business environment of today's stock market, enterprises that invest for the future and report "losses" as a result of commitment to long-term projects are at a distinct disadvantage. Occasionally, savvy investors can discover these diamonds-in-the-rough, and as long as the expectation is sufficiently long-term, an investment in such a company can yield an excellent return. For the hundreds of people who put their money into our low-priced stock in the late 1980s and early 1990s, Besicorp turned out to be one of those gems.

Stock watchers noted Besicorp's presence in the emerging "independent power" industry. It actually wasn't much of a gamble to conjecture that our little company would be able to establish some sort of success even in an industry of giants; we were dealing with fairly large IPP projects and the potential was clearly there. Investors who had made money in the market on other independent power producers were looking for the next big independent power stock play. Besicorp was identified as an up-and-comer by a few savvy investors, and as the CEO I naturally encouraged their interest. By all logic, new shareholder demand should increase the stock price, and that was in everyone's interest. But many of these beneficiaries didn't celebrate our success; instead we became the object of increasingly invasive demands by shareholders looking for short-term gratification.

We were established as a minor player in the independent power business by the late 1980s and were involved in several early-stage development projects. We had built some solid relationships with engineering oriented partners and our efforts had earned us potentially valuable contracts with several utilities in upper New York State. But we still had a long way to go before our shareholders could realize substantial value. Even so, some of the speculators who "discovered" Besicorp stock fantasized about the company's enormous value. They hyped themselves up by projecting astronomical stock prices, ignoring the long gestation period as well as the risks necessary to develop these power projects and bring them to maturity.

Some of these speculators began to pressure the company to achieve immediate earnings in order to increase the stock price. They didn't appreciate the difficult and arduous process of creating shareholder value. Besicorp was competing in an industry of giant industrial corporations and major utilities without ever having significant equity capital invested in the company. From 1984 through the end of 1992, we had a negative net worth, a very erratic cash flow, and were technically insolvent. As a result, the company was completely dependent upon my personal guarantee for its survival. The company had survived only by borrowing, floating cash from project to project, and rolling over limited funds while watching every penny.

Determining the strategy for building shareholder wealth is the responsibility of the board of directors in a stock corporation. A majority vote of the shareholders determines who sits on the board, and it is the business judgment of those board members that determines company policy. The board and management must listen to shareholder concerns, but that is the beginning and end of the discussion. Shareholders who disagree in good faith are free to sell their shares or come to annual meetings and complain. I have absolutely no problem with legitimate dissent, but I have a problem with shareholders who cross the line and go beyond reasonable behavior. This is how the assault on Besicorp began.

Vee Hockmeyer was a shareholder who had attended several annual meetings in the late 1980s. He was initially friendly and positive, but his demeanor changed when Besicorp's stock didn't take off as he'd hoped, and he began to become increasingly vocal in his criticisms of the company's management. He was demanding that the company sell off its potentially lucrative power contracts to produce short-term earnings in order to increase the stock price, and he was expressing these demands before the company had anything of value to sell.

I explained our strategy over and over again to Hockmeyer and some other like-minded shareholders, both in private telephone calls and at annual shareholder meetings. Besicorp's SEC reports thoroughly discussed the company's strategy and explained the long time-frame involved in creating shareholder value. Selling off our irreplaceable contracts for short-term earnings would have been a foolish waste of opportunity. Developing projects was Besicorp's business, and deciding whether and when to sell was the responsibility of management.

A stockbroker himself, Hockmeyer cultivated relationships with Besicorp's Chief Financial Officer and the Shareholder Relations Manager. He even talked us into giving him a copy of the company's shareholder list, and we believed his pitch that he would call the shareholders to promote their purchase of additional Besicorp stock, a mission he said that would be good for the company and for him as a stockbroker.

Along with James Lichtenberg, another early Besicorp supporter, Hockmeyer's complaints became increasingly strident, and the two began to form a pressure group with other investors, alarming them with false information about Besicorp and its management. Over time, they actively added willing participants to their group, getting their friends to invest in the company, and eventually began an aggressive campaign against us. On the one hand, they were denouncing Besicorp's management, telling the world how they were being cheated, and, on the other hand they were telling their friends how valuable the company we built was and encouraging them to buy more stock. From my point of view, their hypocrisy was infuriating, to say the least.

Everyone is free to buy and sell stock in a public company. But it is a perversion of the process when a company is put under siege by small shareholders who hold themselves up as self-appointed representatives of the "public." Despite the constant pressure, I made the decision not to let these people bully our company, and to stay the course on our strategy. They did not know the dynamics of the business; they neither appreciated the long gestation period nor the steep and increasing value curve for a power plant to be brought into profitable operation. I assumed that they were simply ignorant. They were also mean and nasty. But I had no idea how far they would go to achieve their end.

The first battle was joined at the Securities and Exchange Commission. As an undercapitalized company involved in complicated business transactions, Besicorp's SEC reports were always themselves complicated. In reporting details, we strictly followed the reporting methodology dictated by SEC requirements and observed Generally Accepted Accounting Principles (GAAP). The "materiality" standard is a major issue facing any company in dealing with financial reporting, especially a small company like Besicorp that is involved in large projects. Items that may not even be worthy of a footnote to the financial statements of a major company can be quite "material" to a small company. Besicorp relied on outside attorneys and auditors to give opinions and sign our financial statements, and the issues of materiality made our disclosures agonizingly difficult for our attorneys and auditors as well. As small players in an industry of giants, we worked on potentially valuable contracts that could each be worth tens of millions of dollars, but if we failed, they were worth a big zero. As a result, our financial reports and disclosures were voluminous, giving investors far greater detail than a large company would be required to provide if they were working on the same projects.

Beginning in the late 1980s and continuing into the early 1990s, the SEC sent Besicorp highly detailed comment letters on every periodic filing we made, challenging Besicorp's disclosures regarding the power projects. The SEC comment letters were sometimes as long as fourteen single-spaced typewritten pages. Each time a new comment letter was received, we had to begin again the arduous process of dissecting every word in our SEC filings and comparing them with the SEC's comments. The company's lawyers and outside accountants were involved at great expense, and our accounting department was diverted from their work for weeks at a time, debilitating the business. Why was the SEC bearing down on us so hard? We couldn't figure it out.

Adding insult to injury, the SEC changed staff frequently, it seemed almost once a year, and each time we finished responding to comments by one SEC staff member, the Besicorp file would be assigned to a new staff person who would start the process all over again. They would sometimes make us revert to prior descriptions and management discussions, ignoring the work of their own predecessor.

The relentless SEC scrutiny became increasingly intolerable. Besicorp was spending hundreds of thousands of dollars a year on SEC reporting, and regardless of what we did, the SEC kept coming at us. We finally sent a Freedom of Information request to try and determine what was behind the SEC pressure. In response, the SEC sent us a pile of complaint letters with the senders' names and addresses redacted. The agency wanted to protect the identity of whistleblowers, but one of the authors was clearly identifiable. Over time we had received nasty letters directly from James Lichtenberg, containing outlandish accusations, with particularly noxious attacks on me, and the very same accusations, in the very same words, appeared in the letters to the SEC. They alleged that we were concealing assets in order to steal them from the shareholders.

Lichtenberg was an early Besicorp enthusiast who happened to live not too far from our corporate headquarters. When he first bought his shares, he had been very supportive. After Besicorp's 1988 shareholder meeting, he was quoted in the local paper extolling the company's virtues and paying me a compliment. "Mike Zinn really stepped up to the plate," he said. "I'm not looking to make one or two hundred thousand; I'm looking to make half a million on Besicorp." It turned out that Lichtenberg would eventually make over $1.5 million on his Besicorp stock, on an investment of only $100,000 in the public market.

We endured a number of additional years of SEC scrutiny. By the mid-1990s, they concluded that our reporting was proper; everything about the business was being properly disclosed in a timely manner, and the accounting treatment of our partnership interests was entirely correct. The SEC eventually backed off, but over the years our adversaries would continue to use this technique of complaining to regulatory authorities about Besicorp's operations.

6

CLASH OF WILLS

Throughout the balance of this book, I will be referring to the pressure group that formed among predatory stock traders with the intended purpose of forcing Besicorp into liquidation. I use the word "predators," "profiteers," "provocateurs," "raiders," and "pirates," for there seems to be no single word to adequately describe the particular people responsible for the assault conducted against Besicorp and against me as the CEO and majority shareholder. No offense is intended to those who generally buy and sell corporate stocks and make an honest buck.

The raiders described here purchased Besicorp stock in the market thinking the stock was going to make a run-up, and that they would then sell into an expanding market. When that didn't happen in the short-term, they began to pressure the company to force the stock to run up. When that didn't work, they began a campaign to force the company to liquidate the projects we were nurturing for the long-term, expecting that would get the stock to run up. When that didn't work, they began a campaign to get the company's CEO and majority shareholder (yours truly) investigated, indicted, incarcerated, and removed from the company, expecting that this would finally cause the stock to run up. If this scenario sounds implausible, please read on.

Stock predators are like termites, for it's impossible to detect the damage they're doing until it's done. With luck, you can save the building, but if you allow the damage to continue without taking action, the building can be undermined so badly that it may collapse. Those who play the game view themselves as entrepreneurs, but what they do is prey on other people's hard-won accomplishments and productivity.

This kind of activity begins with buying shares in a publicly traded corporation, and the game is played on the pretext of increasing its shareholder value. It is true that some companies are run by rip-off artists, and in certain such situations litigation is the only way to stop genuine abuse by a company's management. But I have seen the other side of the coin. In the 1980s, when Besicorp had less then nothing, it had pledged its meager assets as collateral for my personal financial guarantees. For many years, I'd had the opportunity to foreclose on the company and purchase its assets in liquidation. If I had done it, I would not have been litigated against, investigated, indicted, convicted, and incarcerated. Instead, I put myself at risk in order to preserve the company as a publicly traded entity.

One of the techniques used by corporate raiders and their contingency-fee attorneys is to sue a targeted company, charging various improprieties. That's no surprise in this lawsuit-crazy society, but my experience of over a decade has convinced me that for every legitimate shareholder suit filed by justifiably aggrieved investors, dozens of lawsuits are filed against honest companies by predatory parties that engage in this kind of litigation and corporate harassment as a routine business.

These suits are designed to beleaguer a company's management, burden it with a fortune in legal fees and the threat of more to come, and force a handsome settlement of the claims out of court. Most companies faced with such pressure have little choice but to pay off the litigants and their attorneys. These payoffs are known in the trade as "greenmail." Occasionally, a company's management and board ends up liquidating the entire company, putting its people out of work and collapsing under the campaign.

As I am the majority shareholder of Besicorp, the clandestine campaign to force the company into liquidation took the form of a personal and vindictive assault on me. I had no alternative but to fight, but I did so with a heavy heart.

In the late 1980s and early 1990s, my personal financial support continued to be the company's lifeline, and I was devoting my energies to developing Besicorp's long-term strength. Now the dissident faction among our public shareholders began to push us to sell assets so we could report earnings, to cut management salaries (we were still taking relatively small salaries then), and spend money promoting Besicorp's stock. It seemed absurd to spend desperately needed cash on stock promotion and divert the attention of our top management from the business at hand. In the early years of the business, I had actually tried stock promotion and had learned the difference between achieving stock price based upon intrinsic value, and stock price promotion based upon hype. The speculators who were now pressuring us had no compunction about trying to force the company to promote its stock so that they could sell it at a higher price to new investors. Under that scenario, I knew the stock would inevitably collapse, and the speculators would bail out, leaving management to pick up the pieces.

As the controversy between us deepened, they began to make public accusations that I was deliberately suppressing the value of Besicorp stock by employing accounting tricks designed to report losses. It had already become apparent that these were not just interested shareholders concerned about the company's well being. Their motives went far beyond disagreeing with the company's management over company policies.

One of their recurring complaints was that I continued to reject spending money on stock promotion. As I was putting myself on the line financially for the company and still not willing to spare money on promotions, I told the complainers to be patient, as we were being, to join us over the long run of the company's development. I said to them, "If you think Besicorp stock is so cheap, buy more and tell your friends, but don't pressure the company to spend precious money promoting stock so you can sell out at a short-term profit."

I call the style of stock manipulation that the dissidents were advocating "The Greater Fool Theory." The technique is to buy a stock that has potential for promotion while it's cheap. After you and your friends own it, get your clients to buy it. Then pressure the company to promote the stock. With a variety of tactics, such pressure can generally succeed in forcing the stock price up even if a high price is unsustainable based on actual performance. The trick is to sell out at the right time, take a huge profit, and pass the losses on to the next "fool." I rejected that business philosophy for Besicorp. I intended Besicorp to be a business for long-term owners, not short-term traders.

As I've noted, I have had the good fortune of owning stock in Besicorp since back in the early 1980s, when the stock rode a tidal wave in a bull market. I made a great deal of money selling some of my holdings as the wave was cresting, but I used that gain partly to support the company (and its employees and public shareholders) during the long years that it had no capital. My own experience turned out to be highly profitable, but I consider it in an altogether different universe from the actions of those who now targeted the company exclusively for their predatory gain in an assault that would risk its very survival.

～

While our management was busy building the business, the speculators were nipping at our heels, but I was still considering the situation as an everyday part of the market, the long-term price one pays for the short-term benefit of taking a company public. But soon the clash of wills began to become increasingly burdensome as the raiders escalated the rhetoric and opened new fronts in their attempts to pressure Besicorp. I was still providing the seemingly endless financial guarantees that ensured the company's survival. I was on the hook for millions of dollars, and while I didn't expect a pat on the back, I was hoping that our shareholders would stay the course with us. I didn't want the company to go into Chapter 11, so withdrawing my guarantees was never a serious option, but it was increasingly painful to maintain them. In reality Besicorp's financial condition was so weak that with the corporate guarantees in place my bank wouldn't even refinance my home mortgage. I felt increasingly aggrieved at the baseless accusations being leveled at me in what was now becoming an escalating war of words.

～

By 1991, I had been personally supporting Besicorp's bank debt for years on end and regularly made payroll out of my own checkbook when the company ran out of money. As some of the public shareholders who were benefiting by my personal risk continued their campaign against management, I decided that my financial support for Besicorp should not continue to go uncompensated.

Ever since our independent directors had resigned in the mid-1980s, Besicorp had a board of three that consisted only of members of senior management. We had to wear two hats. While we were running the day-to-day business, we were also dealing with major corporate issues as a board of directors. This was not unusual for a privately owned company, but most publicly traded corporations included at least some non-employee board members. It certainly would have been preferable to have independent board members, but we did what we had to do to survive. It was a chicken and egg scenario: we couldn't readily attract responsible outside board members until the company was successful, and we needed to make tough decisions in order to become successful. The lack of independent board members turned out to be a lightning rod for predatory litigation, exposing us to charges of impropriety.

It was in this environment that I made a formal demand on the Besicorp board for the company to issue one million shares of Besicorp stock to me in consideration of my ongoing financial support. The stock was selling at well under $1.00 per share at that time, less than a million dollars in total value. It was clear to everyone involved in the company that an arms-length investor would charge many times that amount for similar financial guarantees, assuming such a guarantor could even be found.

The two other board members deliberated and then negotiated me down to 700,000 shares. I didn't feel that I should have to negotiate, and I was a little ticked off, but I accepted their deal. The dissident shareholders might continue their attacks, but at least I wasn't giving the company life for their benefit without being compensated. Through that stock award, I boosted my ownership from 33% to 47%. This infuriated my critics.

∼

Adding fuel to the fire, by early 1992, Besicorp was on the threshold of a financial turn-around as a result of some of the projects we were successfully developing. Before the positive results were a certainty, our board decided that an incentive stock plan was an appropriate and necessary inducement for management to stay and finish the job of building a successful company. Most growth companies compensate their executives with stock options, but we had been so busy dealing with the survival of the business that we were neglectful of the need to secure long-term commitments from our most important people.

To insure that Besicorp receive such commitments, the stock awards were granted with certain restrictions on ownership rights which lapsed in steps over five years of continuous employment with the company. We adopted a plan that granted a total of 500,000 additional shares, spread among ten members of the senior management. Although I received some of those shares, my percentage of the company actually went down because of that grant, though I supported the grant as being good for the company.

This second stock award further infuriated the complaining shareholders. Those who were accumulating Besicorp stock in the public market gave management no credit for building the value of the business, just as they gave me no credit for saving the company from bankruptcy. They complained about our salaries and they complained about our stock compensation, but most of all they complained about the stock I had now received for my financial guarantees. They redoubled their campaign against the management of the company, with particularly venomous attacks on me. I just couldn't figure out what was driving them; Besicorp was a company built out of virtually nothing, and it was my leadership that had made it happen.

∾

Some companies find themselves unsuited to be in the public stock marketplace. The cost of public reporting may be considered too burdensome, or there may be an incompatibility between financial reporting requirements and public perception, or, as I had learned, a perceived conflict between management's long-term strategic plan and the short-term expectations of investors and stock traders. None of Besicorp's power projects was operational yet; the company had no earnings and was suffering negative cash flow. With the constant services of lawyers and accountants, being public was costing $500,000 per year, not including the ongoing drain on management's time and spirit. By 1992, I had endured several years of what was still relatively petty harassment, and I didn't want to put up with it any more. I decided to investigate taking Besicorp "private" again—purchasing back the publicly owned shares from their present holders.

I asked Larry Fisher, Besicorp's outside counsel, to tell us what was involved in taking a company private. Larry advised that full disclosure must be made concerning all aspects of the business and the "going private" transaction, and also advised that we retain an experienced, competent investment banker who could evaluate the business and provide a "fairness opinion" concerning the pricing of the buyout. We retained the services of Loeb Partners, a respected old-line Wall Street firm and began exploratory discussions.

If we went through with a going private transaction, a tender offer—an offer sent to shareholders via documents filed with the SEC—would be made for all of Besicorp's outstanding common stock, which would then be followed by a merger with a new private company. The price of the tender would be based upon an appraisal and confirmed by a fairness opinion. Each shareholder would be given specific instructions on how to take advantage of "dissenter's rights." By statute, if any shareholder objected to the price, he or she would have legal recourse, and all dissenting shareholders could act as a group to have an independent appraisal of the value of the shares. The Court would determine the final price if the parties could not settle on one through this process. This direction seemed attractive under the circumstances and certainly it was preferable to being at war with these shareholders indefinitely.

It was understood that an offer could not be priced until an appraisal and fairness opinion was completed, but that essential work was never even started. We established a reference price for planning purposes of $1.75 per share—more than double the stock price in the public market place, and far greater than the company's negative book value.

I was working very hard, totally focused on my work, but I was about to undertake an effort which would ultimately give my critics the leverage they needed to do great harm.

7

SWIMMING WITH SHARKS — THE 1992 HINCHEY CAMPAIGN

By the middle of 1992, I was feeling increasingly confident in Besicorp's future. The company didn't have much cash, but it had considerable forward business momentum and an excellent management team. I had been delegating more of the day-to-day management responsibilities, and thinking about longer-term projects. When the opportunity presented itself, it seemed natural to me to dabble in politics.

I'd be the first to admit that it was partly to gratify my ego that I got involved with Maurice Hinchey's congressional campaign. But I also expected that my involvement would help Besicorp by providing access to congressional offices (assuming Hinchey was elected). I also assumed that Hinchey, a Democratic New York State Assemblyman, would continue to be an environmentalist while he was in Congress, something that was a rare commodity. If he hadn't been an environmentalist in the first place, I never would have gotten involved. I was a lifelong Democrat, as were my parents. Wanting to protest over what I saw as anti-Semitic remarks made by the Reverend Jesse Jackson, I had changed my registration to Republican a few years earlier, but I still sympathized with Democratic party ideals, especially in the area of environmental policies.

In June 1992 I read in the newspaper that Hinchey had declared himself a candidate for the 26th Congressional District seat being vacated by Democrat Matthew McHugh of Ithaca. I wrote him a note offering to help, and he responded quickly. I remember the day that I took his call in my car. He told me that Matt McHugh was prepared to pass him the torch, but that he faced a serious financing problem. Within less than two months, he would be facing a primary election battle against a highly qualified and experienced opponent.

Maurice Hinchey's promotional materials touted that he had worked his way through college as a toll collector on the New York State Thruway and presented him as the defender of the "working man." With my working class roots, I related well to Hinchey's blue-collar message.

Before that day, I don't think I had talked to Hinchey ten times in my life. But he told me that he held me in high regard and wanted me involved in his campaign.

I was unsure where Maurice was taking the conversation, when he asked me to be the campaign's finance chairman. Surprised, I responded, "Maurice, I'm a registered Republican, and I've never done anything like that before."

"Michael, I've followed your career and I know what you can do," he said. "I really want you to do this, and I really need the help."

I hesitated again at what seemed like a daunting and time-consuming responsibility. Maurice said he needed my business and organizational skills at the helm of the campaign, that although his people were loyal and served him well in his State office, they lacked the capacity to mount a successful campaign financing effort. I said, "I guess I'm honored! All I can do is put my all into it." And I did just that.

As far as I was concerned, I was just another constituent, but to Maurice Hinchey, I was a unique asset. When the shit hit the fan, I was described in the media as Hinchey's "confidante." A better word would have been Hinchey's chump.

Flattered and excited, I fully expected to get a pat on the head when I got home and excitedly told Valerie about Hinchey's request. But my enthusiasm met a wall of opposition. With great foresight, Valerie saw what lay ahead. I was mesmerized by the image of being on the inside, helping to shape a political campaign and walking in the halls of power. But Valerie, who never hesitates to speak her mind, said, "You will be operating where you have no knowledge or experience. Besides, politicians are slime and you're just going to be used." She was sure that I would become a target for attack because of my prominence in our small community, and reminded me that I already had enough people sniping at me. When she saw that it was impossible to dissuade me, she said, "Just keep me as far from this as possible. I want no part of it." God, I should have listened.

My first order of business was to plan and organize the campaign. I called a mobilization meeting to gather the key participants. Maurice had told me that the campaign had no office space, so I offered the use of a conference room in Besicorp's office building. The conference room was quite lovely, with a custom-made stone-based conference table and a beautiful set of gray leather chairs. I remember how proud I was to put our facility on display.

Federal law clearly prohibits direct corporate support to a congressional campaign. But I was a complete political novice. All during the 1992 campaign, we met in that room week after week. In my ignorance, I never gave a single thought about officially charging the campaign for space, coffee, or the bag of bagels with cream cheese that we provided for the meetings. Several years later, when I was being criminally prosecuted for my involvement in the campaign, this financially inconsequential but illegal, in-kind corporate campaign support led off each of the prosecutor's diatribes against me. No action was ever taken against Hinchey or his entourage. Ostensibly, these professionals had no idea that it was illegal to run their campaign out of my office.

Sad to say, my internal Besicorp staff (including our in-house attorney) knew absolutely nothing about how to protect the company in a political campaign, and the Hinchey people were taking what they could get for as long as they could get it. During my prosecution, Hinchey would tell the media that his people hardly ever came to Besicorp's offices. They disclaimed any knowledge of the illegality or impropriety of their own actions. The military uses the term "plausible deniability" to mask their clandestine incursions into illegality; Hinchey's story was a case of "implausible deniability." I would be left holding the bag.

~

The 26th congressional district is a dumbbell-shaped aggregation with no major population center and no mass transportation system to link its sprawling reaches. Conducting a campaign in the district is challenging and difficult. Despite a significant Republican majority, it has had a Democratic representative in Congress since 1974, when the Watergate scandal swept Democrat Matt McHugh into office. Geographically and culturally diverse, the district spans from Ithaca, a Finger Lakes town in western New York and the home of Cornell University, to Beacon, an old factory town on the east side of the Hudson River. The district includes the cities of Newburgh, Kingston, New Paltz, Monticello, Binghamton, and much of the Catskill Mountains. It takes over four hours to drive from one end to the other, and there are no media markets that cover the entire district.

In 1992, Hinchey's base of operations was in Ulster County, which contained the city of Kingston as its population center and the nearby hamlet of Woodstock, the cultural outpost of the liberal left. Hinchey had long since locked up his New York State Assembly seat, and his Republican and Conservative opponents ran under-funded campaigns; as a result, his opponents were mostly political unknowns seeking name recognition.

As an Assemblyman, Maurice Hinchey was unbeatable. He had committed liberal and feminist support (not to mention the NRA) and was also considered by many to be the Hudson Valley's leading environmentalist. To win re-election, he had only to put his name on the ballot, and for that, he didn't need money. But to run for Congress required vastly increased financial support.

In the Democratic primary, Hinchey's sole challenger for the nomination for Congress was a formidable and experienced politician. Juanita Crabb was three-time mayor of Binghamton, New York, the district's largest population center, located near its western end, while Hinchey's home base was in the eastern end. Crabb had a strong Democratic organization, and, simply by virtue of being a woman, could cut into Hinchey's female constituency. Maurice had a fight on his hands, and with no money in the bank and no organization in place, he had to put it together, and fast, if he wanted to win the primary and get geared up for what was to be a hotly contested general election.

Soon after I agreed to chair the finance operation, Maurice sat down in my office and told me about his organization and its limitations. David Lenefsky was his personal attorney and would serve as campaign counsel. Allison Lee was a member of Maurice's Kingston-based Assembly staff, with whom he worked very closely. His wife Eileen and his brother and sister were to help out, and several members of the assembly staff would participate. Connie Goffredi was Eileen Hinchey's friend and was going to serve as campaign manager until a more experienced person could be recruited. Maurice said he had approached Eleanor Brown, the local district manager for incumbent Congressman Matt McHugh, and she had agreed to become actively involved. For reasons that I would understand only years later, Brown would be the de facto campaign manager, although Connie Goffredi would remain the "official" campaign manager.

Campaigning for Congress is expensive. Mailers, parties, events, big-name visitors, media and fund-raising consultants all cost lots of money. It's not only direct expenses that eat up a campaign's cash—fund-raising expenses themselves seem to be, by far, the largest single expense for a campaign. An incumbent with a reservoir of supporters and special-interest money may not have a problem, but this was Hinchey's first run for Congress. Because a political organization can expend a large percentage of funds on fund-raising costs alone, there's not much room in the budget for actually getting the message out. For example, a dinner that raises $20,000 might have cost that much or more for space and catering, advertising, and the free tickets given to politicians and staff, none of whom pay. These events also contribute to "budget creep," the dynamic that lifts campaign costs up to the seven-figure level.

It quickly became apparent that a large and unwieldy finance committee wouldn't get the job done, so Dave Lenefsky, Eleanor Brown, Eileen Hinchey, and I formed a small and efficient "executive" finance committee to run the finances of the campaign.

We organized a "steering committee" to coordinate the work of politicians and volunteer workers. Connie Goffredi was appointed Campaign Manager. Among her responsibilities was setting up a storefront operation and generating campaign literature. The steering committee was the place for supporters who wanted to be helpful but contributed little money to the campaign.

The finance committee held planning sessions and met frequently to get status reports and share information. I had no prior relationship with any of these people, but they seemed nice, and so I trusted them. I was getting an education in the inner workings of a political campaign, and I figured that I was also forging valuable relationships for my business.

The finance committee was responsible for budgets and expenditures as well as fund-raising. It was quite difficult to keep this group focused and coordinated, but everyone tried hard; most of the people involved recognized the limitations of time and money and made an effort to cooperate. It was clear that both Maurice Hinchey and David Lenefsky wanted me to take a leadership role.

I am a fanatic about written communications and I arranged for detailed minutes to be kept of every meeting. Eleanor Brown tried to dissuade me from keeping written records, but I insisted. There were cliques among the Hinchey staffers and I was determined to impose management disciplines on the campaign financing process to prevent ego problems from impeding our effectiveness. I was also concerned that, with various parties soliciting the same potential donors and with multiple mailings and follow-up phone calls being conducted, written minutes and plans would provide better coordination.

~

Dave Lenefsky was Maurice's personal attorney and best friend, and, at one of the first finance committee meetings, Maurice stood up and announced that Lenefsky would be the campaign counsel and would answer all legal questions about any aspect of the campaign. David and I got along well, and he became my confidante and legal advisor in matters relating to the campaign. He had the business experience to appreciate my skills as well as my access to people with money, and as a result, he tried to keep me motivated and address my legal concerns.

Lenefsky was a sharp New York City-based political operator and trial lawyer, and he had a second home near Woodstock. He had dark silver-streaked hair and wore wire-framed glasses, but despite his harsh features, his angular face exuded warmth. He was deeply involved in Democratic politics and was a former a Commissioner of the New York City Department of Corrections and a Director of the Brooklyn Navy Yard. His wife Barbara was a political operator for New York City Mayor Ed Koch.

Jim Dougherty had served as treasurer of Hinchey's numerous New York State Assembly campaigns. He was able to handle the workload for those low-key, low-budget local campaigns, but a high-pressure, big-dollar congressional campaign was too much for him and he was unable to keep up with all the necessary deposits, reports, and FEC filings, which had to be made on a timely basis. Jim was well intentioned, but he was a solo practitioner in the insurance business and he operated out of a home office with no secretarial or clerical help. His failure to keep up with the workload as treasurer was an Achilles heel for the '92 campaign that Lenefsky looked to me to fix.

It quickly became apparent that Connie Goffredi, who had been appointed the "official" campaign manager, was not able to do the job. A close friend of Eileen Hinchey with some political experience, she continued handling the "front office" function and the volunteer effort, but Eleanor Brown took over the work of dealing with political action committee fund-raising, large-donor solicitations, events, endorsements, and general finances.

Eileen Hinchey and I, the least experienced in politics, shared an amused disdain for the Washington wannabees who surrounded the campaign and were so transparently ambitious. When the various members of Hinchey's staff were backbiting and engaging in struggle for position, Eileen tried to temper the hostilities. She was savvy and intelligent and deserved respect she didn't always get, but Eleanor Brown and Allison Lee maneuvered her to the periphery. I experienced the same blatantly manipulative tactics, which annoyed the hell out of me, but as an outsider I decided not to engage in infighting. I was just there to help Maurice. I shrugged my shoulders and commiserated with Eileen.

As the campaign organization occasionally degenerated into chaos, Eileen Hinchey and I were on the outside looking in. We regularly asked each other, "Why are we doing this?" God only knows why I didn't walk away, but I told myself I had made a commitment to Maurice Hinchey.

∿

Soon after Eleanor Brown began to run the campaign, she made it clear to everyone that she was not to be referred to by the title of "campaign manager" or given any other official title. She worked full-time for months on the election of Maurice Hinchey to Congress, operating out of the local congressional office where she was the regional manager for incumbent Matt McHugh. I spoke to her almost daily, almost as frequently as I did with David Lenefsky.

Eleanor Brown remains an enigma to me. She didn't want to receive fax documents at her congressional office or have any meetings there. Later I would understand that she apparently was drawing payroll from the federal government at the time she was running the Hinchey campaign. I didn't give it a second thought at the time, but that was probably the reasoning behind her paranoia about minutes being circulated with her name on the list of attendees, and why she didn't want any titles used when referring to her involvement. She behaved as if what she was doing was improper, if not illegal.

Although I chaired the campaign finance committee for Hinchey, I was not in Eleanor Brown's inner circle, and she kept me at arm's length. She and I had a definite personality clash, and she displayed contempt for the business world and anyone who was a part of it. She openly displayed a haughty attitude towards me, and from time to time Dave Lenefsky had to soothe my ruffled feathers.

Nevertheless, Eleanor Brown was more than willing to use Besicorp's office, resources, people, money, phones, and accountants while she was looking down her nose at me. Her ambition to get to Washington with Hinchey was so strong that she was willing to use me and then look the other way when I was unintentionally breaking the law! She pushed me—hard—to raise and donate funds to the election effort, but she made no effort to hide her distaste for me or her suspicions of my motives.

Late one afternoon in early August 1992, after a lengthy finance committee meeting in Besicorp's conference room, I approached Eleanor Brown for urgent advice. The last of the meeting attendees had just left the room, and Eleanor and I were getting our papers together. I told her I was going to be raising money from companies I did business with, that I'd be approaching people I knew at a large Italian company that had funded many Besicorp projects, and I thought I could generate some contributions quickly. I was also soliciting contributions from executives within Besicorp, I said, and some of them received bonuses from the company. I needed advice as to how to handle all this.

Eleanor responded immediately. It sounded important, she said, and she needed to talk to Dave Lenefsky and have him discuss it with me. She looked flushed, but I didn't pay that any mind. She left, and I assumed I had set in motion the process to get the proper advice that I urgently needed in an area that I thought was sensitive.

Within a day, Dave Lenefsky came to my office. I repeated to him exactly what I had said to Eleanor, and he thought for a few moments, and gave me the following information: that individuals could be solicited, but that only American citizens could donate. The fact that I did business with a donor's corporation wasn't relevant, he said, as long as there was no direct link between my business dealings and any individual contributions. Soliciting people I did business with wasn't improper and in fact was essential if Maurice was going to get the money to win the primary.

I asked Dave about raising donations from Besicorp's employees, and he gave me what I took to be explicit guidelines. Of course, since he was a lawyer, I understood his direction as legal advice. He said all donations must be voluntary, and that no coercion was allowed. All donors must be donating their own money. When I asked him about raising donations from the Besicorp people who regularly got bonus money he said it was okay to do so as long as they were going to get the money anyway. "And don't swap checks," He said.

Based on this advice, I made bonus funds available to certain Besicorp executives who were contributing to the campaign, but as far as I was concerned, each of the donors understood that it was his or her money they were donating, fully earned and accrued and entirely legal.

By the end of August, the campaign was in high gear, But Jim Dougherty was falling further and further behind in his responsibilities as campaign treasurer. I often couldn't get vital financial information until weeks after it was required; the people raising money needed to know who was contributing, and the funds had to hit the bank daily, not when Jim got around to making bank deposits. Money was moving out of the account too fast to rely on him.

To try and alleviate the crisis, Jim asked Martin Enowitz for help in maintaining the campaign's records. Enowitz was Besicorp's chief financial officer, and already involved in the campaign. He agreed and recruited a Besicorp accounting employee to keep the contribution deposit ledger. Jim brought over a bank deposit endorsement stamp for the campaign account; it took only minutes to open envelopes, stamp checks for deposit, and keep the ledger up to date. Unbeknownst to me, this "in-kind" corporate support was illegal as well.

When Enowitz told me what he was doing, I thought it was a good idea. I wanted to make sure the reports to the Federal Election Commission were made correctly and on time. Talk about missing the mark! I had to plead guilty to the felony of aiding and abetting a false Federal Election Commission report. As unpaid campaign bills mounted and Maurice pressed me to bring in money, Brown and Lenefsky expressed constant anxiety to me about needing more contributions. The funds I raised were invaluable to the campaign. Those contributions from Besicorp employees came without fund-raising costs and arrived at critical times; the logistic support we gave was extremely valuable as well, enabling the campaign to function without an organization in place.

In hindsight I have learned why corporate support of a political campaign is illegal. Corporations have the infrastructure to get a campaign up and running quickly. I allowed myself to be used, and for that I apologize to Hinchey's opponents, for he would have won neither the primary nor the general election without the resources he so subtly yet effectively obtained from my people and me.

Unfortunately for me, under the "supervision" of Maurice Hinchey and his key people, Besicorp was trapped and I got screwed. I was lulled into complacency and was ultimately held responsible for acts that I had no idea could be construed as crimes. There's no doubt in my mind that Hinchey and his people should have been prosecuted instead of me. But by the time the government prosecutors stepped in, I was a particularly juicy target.

Hinchey won the primary by a hair and went on to win an extremely close general election. I was proud of myself, knowing that I had had a profound impact on the outcome of the election. I was content to stay out of the limelight, satisfied that Hinchey and his top people were aware of my contribution to his successful congressional run. A deceptive calm set in.

8

THE PREDATORS MAKE THEIR MOVE

The behind-the-scenes activities of the raiders were continuing. We were about to run into a buzz-saw of adversarial litigation at a level I had no idea existed in the modern world.

As I've noted, in the early '90s, Besicorp was a public company without independent board members; the board consisted of Steve Eisenberg (Besicorp's Executive Vice President), Martin Enowitz, (the Chief Financial Officer), and me. We were all busy working on the business and blissfully unaware of how the lack of independent directors on our board increased our exposure to attack by predators. I knew that the presence of independent board members would provide a stamp of legitimacy to corporate decisions that is generally accepted by the courts, but I still assumed that as long as the business was successful and everyone made money, there would be nothing to complain about.

The process of exploring taking Besicorp private had come to a dead halt with a single event in the summer of 1992.

Besicorp had been working on developing an 80-megawatt gas-fired, clean power plant project in South Corning, New York, within the service territory of New York State Electric and Gas Corporation ("NYSEG"). The project would cost about $120 million to build, and we had a fifty percent interest in its thirty-year contract to sell power to NYSEG at what we considered to be favorable rates. NYSEG wasn't at all thrilled about the prospect of independent power plants ("IPPs") setting up shop in their territory, and we were not the only one with such a contract. So NYSEG developed a solicitation to buy out IPP contracts, which they sent to all IPPs operating in their central New York State service territory. We immediately recognized a rare opportunity.

What NYSEG didn't know was that our project was actually in serious trouble. Although we were moving ahead with development, there were still many barriers to be crossed, and we hadn't yet arranged financing. If we didn't reach certain milestones on time, the contract with NYSEG was subject to cancellation, and we knew how vulnerable the project was.

We had recently closed financing for three other power projects, however, and NYSEG took us very seriously. We submitted our offer at $50 million, and then began a process of negotiation that culminated in a $34 million cash buyout of our contract. Besicorp's net was $14 million, a giant sum that allowed us to stabilize the company for the first time in our history.

The negotiation with NYSEG was bizarre and unpredictable. They assumed that if they didn't move quickly, we would have a plant under construction in a matter of a year and it would then cost them more than $100 million to buy us out. At the same time, they knew that they were only buying a piece of paper. The negotiation proceeded in fits and starts. We weren't sure if NYSEG would close until the very day that they signed the papers.

The closing took place in December 1992, and we made an announcement to the public immediately, as soon as counsel advised that it was appropriate. Besicorp stock had been languishing, which was extremely frustrating. Shareholders were continually beating the drum for our heads, complaining about the stock price, and now, suddenly, it seemed, Besicorp is going to net $14 Million!

That single transaction brought in more cash than Besicorp's total market value. We called our attorneys and our investment banker and asked their advice about the wisdom of including in a press release an announcement of the possibility of Besicorp going private. All of our advisors concurred that if the statement was sufficiently tentative, such a release could not hurt: it would either attract attention to the company, or nothing at all would happen. Since the complaining stockholders were agitating for increased promotion, it didn't seem like much of a risk, but a defining moment in my clash with the dissident shareholders was about to take place.

Besicorp sent out a press release that announced the Corning termination transaction and disclosed that Besicorp would receive significant cash payments, with further financial information to be released as soon as it was available. The press release also noted:

> The Board of Directors has approved going forward with deliberations regarding a proposal by a shareholder group, including members of the Board and management, to merge Besicorp Group and a company to be organized by the shareholder group....Consideration of the proposal, which was presented to the Board of Directors in September, had been delayed to enable the Board to assess whether the Corning Cogeneration Facility termination agreement would have a material effect on the proposal.

> The Board engaged Loeb Partners Corporation, an investment banking firm, to render an opinion on the fairness of the proposed transaction, from a financial point of view, to the unaffiliated shareholders of Besicorp. It is expected that the Board of Directors will meet in early January to review the proposed transaction.

> The merger would be subject to certain conditions, including receipt of shareholder approval.

> This press release does not constitute an offer to sell, or the solicitation of an offer to buy, the debentures. The offering of the debentures in connection with the merger would be made only by means of a prospectus. If approved by the Board, it is anticipated that the merger would be presented for shareholder approval in April, 1993.

The press release also discussed a proposed price of $1.75 per share in 11% subordinated debentures. Mentioning that price in the release was a horrible mistake. That pricing had been bench marked almost one year before and was clearly made obsolete by the Corning transaction and the general progress of the company.

By issuing that release, I gave a group of professional corporate raiders the pretext for filing a lawsuit. No subsequent explanation or factual testimony would ever stop them from chanting, in every possible legal and non-legal forum, how I tried to "steal" Besicorp from the shareholders. Nothing could have been further from the truth.

It is vitally important that the record be clear on this point. Besicorp fully disclosed the Corning transaction and its financial impact on the company in both press releases and SEC filings. The parties seeking my removal from the company repeatedly lied about that fact in court filings and elsewhere, in virtually every forum they could address.

All the press release did was announce that the board was going to consider a going-private transaction. As a matter of law the price was subject to appraisal, and a fairness opinion by a qualified investment banker would be required. Each shareholder would receive a proxy mailing (which was not prepared and would be reviewed and approved by the SEC). Each shareholder was entitled to "dissenter's rights," which would be clearly articulated, and then to review by a Court if they thought the price was unfair. The reality was that nothing at all happened. No contracts were drafted and no agreements were reached.

On the heels of our ill-conceived press release, we were hit with the first in a series of "derivative" shareholder suits. A derivative suit is a legal action brought by an individual shareholder, ostensibly on behalf of the corporation. Shareholder derivative suits are a specialty in the legal profession and they are one of the most potent tools employed by the corporate raider. Unfortunately, our announcement, which was intended to draw attention from investors, drew the wrong kind of attention. From then on, we were targeted for payment of greenmail.

The plaintiff in this first suit was Alan Russell Kahn of Forest Hills, New York. Kahn has been a nightmare to those who have had the misfortune to become his target. He is a professional raider and agent provocateur in the world of predatory stock traders and is highly skilled at what he does. His business is to engage in hostile assaults on corporate targets and to orchestrate campaigns against the management of those corporations. He gets away with it mostly because he covers his tracks so well. It was Alan Kahn who organized the clandestine campaign to force me out of Besicorp.

Kahn has trumpeted for years-on-end that he prevented me from stealing the business from the shareholders. He touts himself as a defender of the public shareholder, but he has made a lucrative business out of his sanctimonious corporate assaults. A partner in a New York Stock Exchange member investment firm, he was no innocent with his life savings in mismanaged corporations, turning to the courts for protection. On the contrary: I have evidence that Kahn has been a plaintiff in dozens of cases against various corporations, and God only knows how many other businesses he has attacked from behind the scenes, pulling the strings while another person acts as the plaintiff.

～

Alan Kahn's attorneys in the suit launched against Besicorp were Bernard Persky and Curtis Trinko, who, we would find, were speculators in the "business" of using lawsuits to extract money from corporate targets. They bring these lawsuits on a contingency-fee basis and even if they obtain any judgment at all, they are entitled as a matter of law to an award of legal fees. If a case is settled before trial, as it normally is, they get their fees paid as a condition of settlement.

Law firms that engage in predatory litigation spread the risks over a spectrum of targets. They correctly predict that most companies don't want aggressive attorneys digging around in the corporate records, which is why so many of their targets end up paying "greenmail" to the raiders and their attorneys.

Kahn's initial suit against Besicorp alleged that management was planning to steal the company by going private at too low a price. We immediately announced the cessation of deliberations by the board concerning the prospective going-private transaction and made a motion to dismiss the suit. Kahn was forced to withdraw.

Despite the incontrovertible fact that the going-private transaction never passed the concept stage, Kahn and his cohorts have never relented from their repetitive libels based on that embryonic effort. The alleged attempt to "steal the company" from the public has been the rallying cry of the raiders for years, even though their facts were fabricated.

After Kahn withdrew that first lawsuit, it was only a few short weeks before he surfaced again. This time he and his attorneys filed a lawsuit designed to be a much broader legal assault. And this time Kahn had a front man willing to step into his shoes.

Following up on press about the Kahn lawsuit, our longtime dissident shareholder James Lichtenberg contacted Kahn's attorneys and offered himself to Kahn as the plaintiff for the second suit. Persky and Trinko continued as the contingency-fee attorneys for the legal action, and this time they came at us loaded for bear. Jim Lichtenberg was going to learn at the feet of the master.

9

How They Work

Besicorp is controlled by a single shareholder (yours truly). This fact alone makes Besicorp unusual among publicly traded companies and inspired the effort on the part of the raiders to target me personally as part of their campaign to force the company into liquidation.

The raiders organized a secret stock acquisition group. In the initial stages, a select few accumulated substantial blocks of cheap stock, quietly filling their portfolios with Besicorp shares before they made a serious move on the company. Around 1990, Besicorp stock could be purchased for less than one dollar per share. In terms of the big-bucks stock speculator world of Alan Kahn and his friends, a large percentage of the company was purchased for chump change.

The raiders then gradually expanded their alliance to include a group of well-heeled and sophisticated lawyers, investment bankers, and stockbrokers. In the safety of anonymity, an informal and very dangerous syndicate was formed.

The participants played a no-lose game, with multiple strategies available to make their fortune. Even if they lost in court, they expected to obtain a higher stock price by attracting investor attention to the company and possibly putting the company under so much pressure that liquidation or merger would become the only way out. On the other hand, even if they settled, they would get cash and money for the lawyers. They spread the financial risk of being in this business by waging similar attacks on a spectrum of companies.

After they had acquired enough Besicorp stock at prices of around $1.00 per share, the actual pressure campaign began. This was when they complained that the stock should be higher and accused management of deliberately suppressing its price.

Their next step was to add "retail" clients to their group. The stockbrokers and "investment bankers" in their group slowly brought their friends and clients into Besicorp stock, being careful never to buy enough to run up the stock. Over time, they created a large pressure group, all the while denouncing our company management to the new buyers, asserting that Besicorp was a company of hidden value and that management was deliberately suppressing the stock price; that Besicorp's management was a den of thieves, stealing stock and plundering the company; and that Besicorp's management was hiding earnings and trying to steal the company.

Part of this strategy was to implement a campaign of phony complaints to various arms of the U.S. government. The people who wrote the letters were rewarded by the opportunity to piggyback on the stock manipulation. The campaign of complaints was designed to instigate a federal investigation. Broad and baseless allegations of criminal conduct were made, designed to stimulate the FBI, the IRS, the SEC, or any other interested agency, into penetrating Besicorp with a prosecutorial fishing expedition. According to federal securities laws, any group acting in a coordinated fashion to change corporate policy or implement a change in management has to file a disclosure under Rule 13D when more than five percent of a company's stock is involved. The group, acting in concert, represented well over 15% of Besicorp stock. But they went further than organizing an illegal stock acquisition and pressure group. They recruited allies from within and around Besicorp in a campaign to undermine Besicorp's ability to stay in business.

10

The Lichtenberg Lawsuit

The Lichtenberg lawsuit was a penetrating shotgun blast designed to create a beachhead into Besicorp. The suit was composed of broad allegations of wrongdoing against the board of Besicorp, including waste of corporate assets, self-dealing between the company and me, and allegations that large amounts of stock had been issued to management for what the plaintiff characterized as "little or no consideration."

Such a "derivative" shareholder suit is designed to accomplish, first and foremost, a finding by the court that the Board of Directors of the company is not willing, able, or capable of representing the interests of the public shareholders. If the plaintiffs are able to so persuade the court, the judge appoints them the "representative" of the shareholders, prosecuting wrongdoing on behalf of the corporation. Not only would they take control of one of the most important core litigations possible in a corporation's existence, but they also might be entitled to an award of legal fees. The statute awarding legal fees to such plaintiff attorneys is meat and potatoes for the corporate ambulance chasers.

This lawsuit was designed to squeeze money out of the company and force me to give up my own stock holdings. Over time, when we wouldn't settle and pay these people off, the lawsuit became just one element in a broader scheme to implement a forced change in control of Besicorp.

My decision to take a hard line in response to that suit was intended to send a message: "Don't come around here again." I bit off a lot, but at that point I was filled with courage. In retrospect, I was a bit of a zealot. There is a good reason why most people settle with aggressors like these: they are willing to do horrible damage if they don't get paid off. But, I was supremely confident in our ability to prevail in court and not willing to be pushed around.

Nineteen-ninety-two had been a pivotal year. Besicorp had turned the corner with the closing of the Corning transaction. The "going private" deliberation had been announced. And the war of nerves with dissident shareholders had continued to heat up. The Hinchey campaign had come and gone. After that experience, I decided never to get involved again in a political campaign. But the damage had already been done.

~

As 1993 marched on, the Lichtenberg suit percolated along in its early stages, and nothing much was happening. I was hoping that I could make 1993 as good a year as 1992, so I reluctantly instructed Jim McCabe, Besicorp's attorney, to set up a meeting in an attempt to settle the case. I was aware of the hardball nature of contingency-fee litigation, but I entered the settlement process intent on not paying them a single dime.

Lichtenberg, Persky, and Trinko came to my office. Also in attendance were Jim McCabe, Eisenberg, and Enowitz, Besicorp's management/directors and my co-defendants in the suit. I began by presenting a short history of the company. Then I explained how essential my personal support had been for the company's survival. I showed them charts I had prepared which overlaid the dismal financial position of Besicorp with the amounts of personal financial support I had provided. I explained that the stock compensation I received was fair and reasonable and that they would never win the litigation.

My bottom line was straightforward. "You picked the wrong target. I don't expect an apology for all of your baseless allegations. I just expect you to realize that you targeted the wrong company, pick up your chips, and go away. I will never give you any concessions nor pay you any money. I will not entertain any settlement that could be interpreted as an admission of wrongdoing."

I was obstinate on this point. I am still convinced that I was 100% correct in my assessment of the facts, and it is even clearer in hindsight what these people were after.

Years later, I would have to go into a Federal court and "admit" criminal wrongdoing in a plea bargain I made to end a federal onslaught. I'm sick to my stomach knowing that those people not only instigated the investigation, but also did everything possible to make sure I was sent to prison. I can honestly say that it would have been prudent to have settled with them then, even if I had had to pay them serious money. But back then I was not in a compromising mood. I still had much to learn about fighting a litigation war with professional corporate raiders.

$\approx$

Another year passed, and it was obvious that settlement was not in the cards. Jim McCabe continued to encourage me to keep an open mind about it, and the attorneys had gone back and forth with proposed settlement structures, all of which I considered to contain not only onerous terms, but far too much money for the plaintiff's attorneys. The settlement talks were going nowhere, and it looked to me like we were going to trial.

Jim then informed me of provisions in the New York State Business Corporation Law that would enable the company to take control of the lawsuit out of the hands of Kahn and Lichtenberg. As a "derivative" plaintiff, Lichtenberg claimed to be acting for the company. But if we could appoint new, independent directors to the board and empower them to conduct a thorough, arms-length investigation of the allegations in the lawsuit, we might take away Lichtenberg's position as self-appointed representative of the public shareholder. I was confident in the outcome of any such investigation. Implementing it would be something else.

$\approx$

Besicorp's financial condition during the '80s and early '90s had made it impossible to attract independent, nonmanagement directors to the board, but after the Corning buy-out, Besicorp was solvent, and the prospects of putting an expanded board together were greatly improved. Adding independent board members had numerous advantages. Approval of Besicorp's transactions by independent board members, especially in sensitive areas such as executive compensation, stock grants, and related party transactions, would insulate the company from litigation risk. As I've already noted, it was the absence of independent directors on the board that emboldened the predatory attorneys to approach this litigation with such confidence in the first place.

Under the law, prior to initiating a suit, aggrieved shareholders are supposed to make a formal demand for relief on a company's board asking them to address their grievance. The board has the responsibility to determine what course of action to pursue. If such a demand is made, and the board makes a good-faith effort to address the concerns, even if their conclusions are different from what the shareholders might want, control of the matter is inherently transferred to the board.

Kahn and Lichtenberg claimed in their lawsuits that they were excused from making such a demand on Besicorp's board, asserting that a demand would have been futile since all three Besicorp directors were "interested" in the alleged abusive transactions on which the complaint was based. Indeed, we were vulnerable on this point; it was true that all three directors at the time were full-time employees of Besicorp, and all of us had received stock and compensation levels that the plaintiffs charged were egregious.

I decided to throw down the gauntlet. It was important to me to be personally vindicated of these charges, and I was determined to send a message to any predatory attorney who might see Besicorp as a potential target in the future.

I began a process that resulted in three new members joining Besicorp's board. Even the process of recruiting directors had to withstand hostile scrutiny, so I paid careful attention to the independence issue. I didn't consider it essential to have "blue-chip" board members such as might be found on a New York Stock Exchange company's board. Besicorp was a small company and I wanted people who lived or worked locally. I needed people who had the willingness to accept a certain amount of personal risk; they would be joining the board in the middle of shareholder litigation, and the incumbent directors were being personally sued. The company did not maintain directors and officers liability insurance and the new board members would have to rely on Besicorp's future ability to indemnify and defend them if they were personally sued for their work on the board. With these adversaries, that was entirely likely.

Harold Harris, Gerald Habib, and Richard Rosen became the new members of the Besicorp board. Prior to accepting them, I had them screened by the American Stock Exchange. I reviewed and rejected a number of other candidates for having some recent business affiliation with Besicorp or close personal relationship with one of the present directors. I knew all three to be solid, mature, and experienced, and with their substantial business experience, I believed they would strongly contribute to the board. They didn't know each other before they joined the Besicorp board, and I was certain that any reasonable party would find them to be truly independent not only of me, but of each other.

Prior to each of the new members joining the board, I gave them a copy of the Lichtenberg complaint and discussed with them the possibility of forming a Special Litigation Committee (SLC) to deal with the allegations. They certainly had a right to know what they were getting into, but I made it absolutely clear that their work on the committee would be confidential, unfettered by the other directors or me. I also made it clear that if they found any wrongdoing, they were free to call it as they saw it. It goes without saying that I told them I expected to be exonerated by their investigation, but I made it clear that I would rely entirely on their judgment and would be bound by their decision.

The board voted to form a SLC consisting of only the three newly appointed independent directors. Their mandate was to investigate the allegations in the Lichtenberg lawsuit and make a decision how Besicorp should proceed. The SLC was granted the full authority to act for the company in determining what to do about the allegations in the Lichtenberg suit.

Lichtenberg and his attorneys then charged that the entire SLC was tainted because the other directors and I appointed the new directors to the board. According to that impossible standard for director independence, only directors that we didn't know could be considered independent. Ultimately, the court soundly rejected that absurdity.

The SLC began by interviewing several attorneys to act as "independent counsel." They ended up retaining the most expensive law firm that they interviewed. Tom Beirne, was formerly a branch chief for the Criminal Enforcement Division of the Securities and Exchange Commission. He was experienced both in the prosecution of criminal fraud by corporate management and in the defense of management against shareholder litigation. He guided the SLC in their conduct of a thorough and comprehensive investigation of the Lichtenberg complaint.

As soon as the committee was up and running, Besicorp's attorney, Jim McCabe, made a motion to stay the lawsuit pending the results of the committee's investigation. Lichtenberg's attorneys squealed like stuck pigs, but under New York State law, setting up a Special Litigation Committee made up of independent Board members was an established practice in corporate governance. New York State Supreme Court Judge Vincent Bradley gave us our stay, and the SLC went to work.

During the following 14 months, the SLC spent several hundred thousand dollars conducting their investigation. They reviewed thousands of documents and interviewed all of the defendant directors with the assistance of their attorney. They retained consultant advisors in the field of accounting, real estate appraisal, investment banking, and executive compensation. At the end of an arduous process, on March 28, 1995 the SLC issued a report fully exonerating all of the directors in a stinging rebuke to Kahn, Lichtenberg, and their attorneys. The SLC recommended that pursuit of the case was not in the best interests of the corporation and authorized Besicorp to make a motion to dismiss the Lichtenberg lawsuit. This motion to dismiss was responded to by the plaintiffs with even further attacks and unsubstantiated diatribes, which were now supplemented by personal attacks on the independent directors and their SLC.

~

As of 1993, Judge Bradley had apparently never before presided over a shareholder suit. In dealing with the initial pleadings, he seemed at times to be visibly baffled, conducting matters as if this was some sort of injury claim, and that we should just go in a room and hash out an amount of money the company should pay and settle the case. As the months passed, however, Judge Bradley would learn a great deal about shareholder suits.

Several years after Lichtenberg first sued Besicorp, a series of articles appeared in Barron's financial weekly alleging improper financial transactions at Wellcare Management, a small health maintenance organization. As a result, Wellcare's stock fell off a cliff. Within a month, seven competing shareholder suits were filed, with each law firm seeking to be declared the "representative" of the injured public shareholders. At the first possibility of any misfortune, they had pounced on the company, hoping for a quick kill, but ready, willing, and able to grind their prey down in order to get a payday. As luck would have it, Wellcare was the only other public stock company in the county where Judge Bradley sat on the bench, so he was able to observe Wellcare's troubles unfold as he was getting up to speed on the Lichtenberg case. I had the strong impression that he didn't like bloodsucking attorneys preying on a business.

Early on in the case, we were called to a settlement conference with Judge Bradley. Jim McCabe admonished me not to tick the judge off. I went in well prepared. The principals and attorneys gathered in the judge's chambers for the opening meeting, and Judge Bradley laid out the ground rules. He would conduct private sessions with each party to try to get settlement talks rolling. The plaintiff would go first, and then it would be our turn.

I was seated on Judge Bradley's right, and Jim McCabe was on his left. Jim framed the issues of the case. At one point, Judge Bradley turned to me to ask a question, and rather than stop at a simple answer, I carefully began an explanation of the case. I presented Judge Bradley with the financial history of Besicorp, along with charts and tables showing my financial guarantees. Jim McCabe was squirming in his chair, but Judge Bradley did not shut me down; he engaged me with questions and was keenly interested in what I had to say. I was able to present the evidence that I would offer at trial, along with the arguments I would make if I were trying the case myself. I felt that I had really communicated with the Judge and accomplished what in litigation is very difficult to achieve: a presentation of the case without all the procedural obfuscation.

Under New York State law and applicable legal precedent, the report of a Special Litigation Committee is supposed to be given great deference by the court. Judicial review is supposed to be limited to two areas of inquiry. First, the court reviews the independence of the directors and their disinterestedness in regard to the issues under investigation. Second, the court reviews the sufficiency of the committee's methods and the scope of their inquiry. If those two items pass muster, the judge is supposed to defer to the SLC's conclusions and recommendations and not second-guess the "business judgment" of the board members.

Now, Lichtenberg's attorneys shifted their attention from the underlying allegations they were making against Besicorp to challenge the independence of the directors. Try as they might, they were unable to hit a home run on this point.

Over the years that the litigation dragged on, Lichtenberg and his attorneys made a very significant error. Lichtenberg wanted to do everything possible to be in my face, so each year he submitted a resolution for inclusion in the voting proxy that Besicorp was obligated to include in our annual report to the shareholders. His resolution asked, "Should Besicorp's Board of Directors be required to be made up of a majority of independent non-management directors?" The submission described his proposal and stated his criteria for independence, which were straightforward and quite customary: that independent directors should not have done business with the company for at least three years and should not be in any conflicting relationship with the company or its directors.

Lichtenberg assumed correctly that I would vote against this resolution, and he intended that my vote would be a bludgeon to hammer me with. But this was not what happened.

I opposed Lichtenberg's resolution on principle. At the time the SLC report was received by Judge Bradley, the company in fact already had a majority of independent directors. My vote against Lichtenberg's resolution was not based upon my opposition to having a majority of independent directors; it was against being required to do so. And I had good authority for my convictions. Neither the American Stock Exchange nor the SEC required that companies elect a majority of independent board members.

Throughout the tortuous history of the Lichtenberg litigation, he repeatedly accused me of being against having independent directors, hoping that by sheer repetition it would become accepted as the truth. But Judge Bradley was too astute to be hoodwinked by such a transparent tactic. The mantra was just one more part of the diatribe that Lichtenberg and Kahn used in their continuing effort to build an alliance with other shareholders to force me out of the company.

It was clear that Judge Bradley saw these people for what they were. At one hearing concerning discovery matters, I was delighted when he observed to the Lichtenberg attorneys, "I don't want to diminish your case. I'm sure it has lots of merit. But the more I learn about cases like this, the more I come to the conclusion that I don't like what you people do for a living." It filled me with hope, for I thought it meant that Judge Bradley saw what predatory litigation was doing to a local company. But we still had to jump through many more hoops before the litigation wound its way into the drama that followed.

Following the issuance of the SLC report exonerating management on March 28, 1995, Besicorp renewed its motion to dismiss the case. Lichtenberg renewed his motion for discovery, which had been stayed for over a year while the SLC did its work. One day early in 1995, we were all assembled in Judge Bradley's court to argue discovery motions. ("Discovery" is the invasive process by which attorneys gain access to their adversary's internal documents.) Lichtenberg's attorneys said they wanted to pursue allegations that our company had been involved in irregularities in political fund-raising for the 1992 Hinchey congressional campaign. I couldn't believe what they were saying. I wondered whether they had gotten this idea from a man named Richard Altman, a recently discharged Besicorp employee. Altman had made a donation to the 1992 campaign and was let go shortly thereafter, taking a big grudge along with him. (More about him later.)

In rejecting their discovery request, Judge Bradley told them to take these allegations to the district attorney. Unfortunately, they followed his advice, and then some. They went straight to the FBI. But it would be a long time before I knew what would happen next. Although applicable case law limited discovery to issues related to the independence, process, and procedures followed by the SLC, Judge Bradley had allowed the attorneys for the plaintiff much broader latitude in discovery than we felt was warranted. He did rebuff them concerning the Hinchey campaign, but they were granted the right to take depositions of all Besicorp's directors and the SLC's independent counsel, as well as the right to obtain huge volumes of documents from the company.

Jim McCabe recommended that we file an appeal of Judge Bradley's discovery order, but my instinct was not to defy Judge Bradley. I felt the judge wanted to create a factual record before making a final decision in this case. I was confident that, if we gave Lichtenberg discovery in accordance with the judge's order, the facts of the case would not change. But if we appealed, and Judge Bradley was reversed, he could then find that there were doubts about the independence of the directors or the sufficiency of their investigation in order to get the information he wanted before dismissing the case. We would then have to go to trial. A ruling from Judge Bradley setting up a trial would be hard to reverse, as the appellate court rarely reverses the decision of a trial judge on factual questions.

11

THE **2000** POUND GORILLA

As 1995 and 1996 unfolded, Besicorp began reaping the rewards of our long years of work. The firestorm involving the dissident shareholders was still smoldering, but my contact with them was limited to sporadic court hearings and the annual shareholders meeting. Though I had to listen to Kahn's diatribes there, I was blissfully unaware of what was taking place behind the scenes. All the while, the government was investigating the allegations made by Kahn and his allies.

The raiders knew that the government investigators had no reason to care that they were pursuing leads originated by hostile parties. The motivation of possible witnesses didn't matter either. Tragically, so many people plea-bargain today that the veracity of government witnesses is rarely tested. Many of the government's best sources are poison-pen disclosures from people whose opinions and information at the very least ought to be placed in context before being believed—ex-lovers, angry ex-employees, and disgruntled former business partners. In the absence of other evidence, informers provide the grist for the government's mill, and Kahn and his cohorts knew exactly which buttons to push to instigate a massive investigation that would unleash all the powers of the criminal justice system against me.

The government's frontal assault began in early May 1996. The doorbell woke me up at 7 A.M. on a Friday morning and I was surprised to see two middle-aged men in dark suits at the front door. Still wearing pajamas and a bathrobe, I opened the door and was greeted by the flashing of government badges, one identifying an agent from the FBI and the other from the Criminal Investigation Division for the Internal Revenue Service. I asked them to step inside and wait while I went to dress.

Once I returned they said that they wanted to ask me a few questions about fund-raising for the 1992 congressional campaign of Maurice Hinchey. I tensed up and responded carefully. "You should know that allegations regarding that subject were made by parties involved in adversarial litigation against me." Valerie had come out of the bedroom and joined me. "I hope you understand that I can't talk to you without an attorney present," I said. They asked Valerie if she was taking the same position and she said she was. They said it would "go easier on me" if I cooperated. Perhaps they were right.

They then produced papers which they said were subpoenas issued by a Grand Jury, announced that I was under investigation, presented me with the papers, and left. Puzzled, Valerie and I had no idea what had just happened.

The first call I made was to Dave Lenefsky, as I was still under the impression that he had been my legal adviser during the 1992 Hinchey campaign. He groaned when I told him what had happened. I also told him that I was about to fly off with some friends in my small airplane for the day to play golf. Unaware of the weight that had just descended on me, I was planning to keep my schedule and deal with the subpoenas on Monday. Dave suggested strongly that I not go; he had friends who had been in the same situation, he said, and I should not believe that life would feel normal for very long.

I asked him what to do next, and he said he would get back to me. He also told me to get another lawyer.

I would learn later that day that at the very moment that the agents appeared at my door, other teams of federal agents were conducting identical early morning visits to numerous past and present Besicorp employees. Federal agents are not required to advise witnesses that they are under investigation. If the person talks before a subpoena is handed over, the government has circumvented that person's right to be represented by counsel. Clearly the element of surprise was intended to prevent potential witnesses from talking to one another or from reaching lawyers before the moment when, groggy and half-asleep, they were questioned. Most of the people questioned that morning talked freely. As the agents had expected, they were not thinking about consulting attorneys or worrying about being under investigation.

I took David's advice and canceled my day of golf. Instead, I spent the day on the phone, trying to find out what had happened. As information poured in, I became increasingly upset.

One of the things I found out was that David Lenefsky did not consider himself to be my attorney—not then, and not during the 1992 campaign, when he had been continuously giving me legal advice about it. He'd attended most of the meetings, consulted with me almost daily, and was watching the cash flow like a hawk. But now I found out that he was only Maurice Hinchey's attorney, from start to finish. The problem with that implausible story was that he had never bothered to tell me until that moment, four years later.

The subpoenas served by the government opened up a fishing expedition to find "crimes." We learned that the scope of the subpoenas was immense, encompassing the production of documents and financial records generated over seven years of Besicorp's business. In addition, all my personal investments and financial records were being subpoenaed.

The sheer burden of document production took its toll on our personnel and was soon depleting the resources of Besicorp. Our expenses mounted at an alarming rate, partly due to document reproduction costs and partly because of the astronomical bills we were receiving from our lawyers. In just a few short months, a lead weight began to hang around the neck of the business.

From the scope of the investigation, it was apparent that the government was probing every allegation made by Kahn and Lichtenberg. The investigators bore down on Besicorp as if it were a criminal enterprise. Each and every aspect of the company's business was sifted through with a fine-toothed comb. Each document had to be consecutively numbered, with one copy for defense counsel and another copy for retention by the company. By the time we were finished, Besicorp had produced more than eighty file cabinet drawers full of documents for the government investigators. Our document production costs alone were in excess of $200,000.

It had always been my policy not to throw documents away or shred sensitive information. I'd always assumed that good records are necessary in the event of some kind of civil litigation; the prospect of those records being used as evidence against me in a criminal prosecution never crossed my mind.

The government spent hundreds of thousands of dollars of investigation time putting Besicorp into a state of siege. With that immense effort, all they generated was a trumped-up criminal charge that I had improperly raised funds for Maurice Hinchey. Nevertheless, armed with the tools to parlay any minor deviation into a multiple felony indictment, they were not about to let go of me; I found out that the criminal justice bureaucracy needs to justify its investments, both financially and emotionally.

Besicorp hired Douglas Lobel as its defense counsel. He was a former federal prosecutor who was based in the Washington D.C. office of Kelley, Drye, & Warren, Besicorp's corporate law firm. Doug dealt with responding to the subpoenas, but after a short time, it became apparent that I was going to be targeted as an individual. Bill Brodsky was recommended to me as a criminal defense attorney with a good track record in defending white-collar cases. Bill was in his fifties and also a former U.S. prosecutor. We met, and I felt reasonably comfortable that he could do the job.

My first instinct was to sit down with the Assistant United States Attorney leading the investigation and simply tell everything I knew. I was certain that the truth would exonerate me, and that if I had made any mistakes, it would be apparent that I had done so without any criminal intent. But as former prosecutors, both Bill and Doug told me horror stories about what went on in a government prosecution, and they were extremely cautious about letting me go in and tell the story. Experience had shown them that talking to the government is often disastrous. They went on to inform me about something that I found hard to believe: that the government uses perjury and obstruction of justice charges as weapons to force their targets to their knees; that information innocently provided can result in a terrible widening of the scope of the investigation. I have since learned that some prosecutors also regard unwillingness to "cooperate" as a signal of guilt and a reason to step up their attacks.

The legal team's defense strategy was to try and prevent the government from getting any information that they couldn't glean from documents or hostile witnesses. I was in a box. Looking back, how I wish I could have brought it all to a conclusion right up front. So much money was spent and so much life wasted, but I didn't have the knowledge or the background to override the judgment of experienced criminal attorneys.

～

As we examined the demands in the subpoenas, we tried to figure out what the government was after. I explained to my attorneys all about Besicorp's shareholder litigation. Bill Brodsky insisted that where the charges originated was irrelevant, that once in gear, a government investigation steamrolls ahead. The possibility that business enemies were feeding the government false information was of limited significance, he believed. But it turned out to be quite significant indeed.

It soon became apparent to me that Kahn and Lichtenberg had formed an alliance with some people who had left the company under not very pleasant circumstances. I was aware of at least two such people, one of whom, it turned out, held a personal grudge against me, and another who stood to make a fortune if he could succeed in ousting me from Besicorp. My attorneys prevented me from telling my side of the story to the government; I had no alternative but to follow their advice.

The government was just after a conviction—any conviction, they asserted. If I said nothing, at least I couldn't be indicted for perjury. This seemed preposterous to me, but having lived through this experience, I believe that the government might well have twisted any statement I made into a perjury indictment. But I still have to ask, "If you can't honestly explain what happened, how can the government investigators understand what really occurred?" I couldn't believe what I was hearing. My attorneys were telling me that the government's purpose was not to get the truth, but to get a conviction. That they were right, I would learn the hard way.

As the Grand Jury continued its secret deliberations, even months after the subpoenas had arrived we had no idea of who said what to the government. One of the elements of our defense strategy was to limit the government's access to information by entering into joint defense agreements with as many witnesses as possible. To accomplish that level of cooperation, we offered to provide legal counsel for the people who had received Grand Jury subpoenas. I was warned not to discuss the case with anyone who was even a potential witness, lest I be charged with obstruction of justice. Although I was permitted to deal with my employees in the ordinary course of business, even though some of them might become witnesses, I followed that warning to the letter. It dawned on me that some of my employees might even end up as witnesses for the prosecution—willingly or not.

The offer of legal representation was made to most of the present and former Besicorp employees who had been subpoenaed, and several of them took advantage of the offer. John Riecke was retained through a referral from a Kelley, Drye, & Warren attorney I didn't know.

A few months later, the counsel team decided that independent defense counsel needed to be provided for Steve Eisenberg and Michael Daley as well. As corporate officers of Besicorp, they couldn't use John Riecke, who was already representing several lower-level present and former Besicorp employees, so yet another attorney was required. The new attorney was engaged, this time by referral from Bill Brodsky. We now had four law firms working on the case, running up the bills and making a coordinated defense that much more difficult.

Regardless of who paid the bills, each attorney had ultimate responsibility solely to his clients. All our attorneys hoped to garner at this point was some useful information about what had been presented by the prosecutors to the Grand Jury, as well as cooperation in my defense. Besicorp had an obligation to indemnify its directors and officers against the costs of any legal proceedings arising out of, or relating to, their involvement in the company, and a moral obligation to do the same for employees. For the most part, the defense attorneys shared information, so at least we knew some of what was being said in Grand Jury testimony.

Legal bills began to mount geometrically as the number of attorneys and witnesses increased and the investigation continued. My attorney, Bill Brodsky, began to drop hints about plea-bargaining, but knowing that I did not intentionally break the law, I could not plead guilty to some negotiated "crime." All I wanted to do was end the misery, but there didn't seem to be an exit available.

By early in 1997, the preparation of our defense was in full swing, even though no indictment had been handed down and we didn't even know what it was that we were going to be charged with. But the die was cast. It was clear that the government was not going to go away. An immediate task was to figure out who the government's witnesses were likely to be, and what they were likely to say.

12

INFILTRATION

It was apparent from the broad scope of the subpoenas that the government was not just investigating a particular crime they suspected had taken place. They had subpoenaed hundreds of thousands of documents as well as many present and former Besicorp employees for Grand Jury appearances. Dozens of witnesses had been interviewed.

This was clearly a fishing expedition with the goal of finding a crime. Although we were certain that, at the very least, the 1992 Hinchey campaign would be part of whatever charges were brought, we were completely in the dark about what others might be.

I searched my memory to come up with a list of every person whom I thought might be willing to become a witness against me. Despite the fact that I had tried to conduct myself reasonably over the years with our employees and in the business in general, from time to time hard decisions had had to be made, hard positions had to be taken, and hard feelings were sometimes the unfortunate result. There was no doubt in my mind that I had accumulated some enemies over the years, even though I had never before even thought about my life in those terms. Now, with the prodding of my attorneys, I had to think not only about what they might say, truthful or not, but how to discredit them in the event that we had to go to trial.

Martin Enowitz, Besicorp's former chief financial officer who had also served on the board, was certainly on the list of possible hostile parties. Enowitz had already left Besicorp under a cloud, and he and Besicorp were locked in litigation over a large block of stock and a potentially fraudulent disability claim. Debra Berenda also came to mind, a person who was in a particularly sensitive position in the accounting department of Besicorp, and who, for reasons that I was never able to fathom, had taken a particular dislike to me.

Within days of the arrival of the agents and their subpoenas, the federal investigation had become a major news story in the regional media. The coverage was far more detailed and negative than any of us could have imagined, especially at this early stage in the process. The media saw it as a major opportunity to build a scandal. The Times Herald Record, a large regional newspaper known in the area for mud-slinging, hit me particularly hard; it ran a tabloid-style front page with the headline "DIRTY MONEY" in large, bold-faced type, and included portraits of Hinchey and me facing one another, more than half a page tall.

Many of the other local and regional media, including television and radio stations, followed the tone set by the Record. We were instantly transformed from a small, successful company into a den of iniquity, and I was transformed from an alternative energy entrepreneur into a villainous financier.

In the days following the receipt of the government's subpoenas, Besicorp held several emergency board meetings, and our accounting staff began the arduous process of gathering data and documents to provide to our attorneys, who would then number the documents and provide them to the government. Day after day, The Record reported what it presented as the "inside" scoop about what was going on at Besicorp. Clearly, one of our own people was the source. Although it seemed that everyone was upset each time the company was hit with a new media blast, her co-workers began to take notice that Debra Berenda seemed entirely unfazed.

My top management team and I went through the list I had assembled of employees who might possibly be the source of the reports. I met with other individuals in the company whose loyalty and dedication was unquestionable. It was only in talking to them that I learned that Berenda disliked me personally and that she had been hate-mongering in the office for quite some time.

Two employees informed me that Berenda had stated that she was taking documents out of the office and intended to use them to ruin me. One was told by Berenda that she was meeting with "shareholders" and that she was concerned that she had been seen in New York City after having gone there to meet with them. Both had thought she was joking, and they blew off her comments as just hot air. They also said that Josh Margolin, the Times Herald Record reporter who was our most vitriolic critic, was a regular patron at a bar where Berenda worked evenings.

Within Besicorp's accounting department, Berenda seems to have been far from silent about her resentments, but the people she worked with hadn't understood the implications of what she was saying. "Debbie, if you're so unhappy here, why don't you just find another job?" a colleague asked her. But she stayed where she was, and when the opportunity presented itself, she offered herself to the federal government.

My loyal employees came to me crying, too late, "We knew she was rotten, but we didn't know what she was doing." I consoled them. Clearly, they hadn't a clue.

~

I ordered Berenda's immediate dismissal. Suddenly, there were no more "inside" reports about what was going on inside Besicorp. We had also stopped the flow of confidential documents to Kahn and Lichtenberg, but it was far too late; Berenda apparently had been cooperating with Lichtenberg for years, taking company documents and feeding him confidential information to use in his assault on the company.

This explained why during depositions in the Lichtenberg shareholder lawsuit, Besicorp's attorney, Jim McCabe, was repeatedly presented with confidential company documents that had not been produced by Besicorp. It was clear that documents were being stolen from the company, but I wasn't able to put my finger on who was the thief. I'd also wondered how Lichtenberg and Kahn were able to make contact with ex-employees immediately after they left our company. Now it became clear; Berenda had been giving them the names and addresses of our employees, informing them whenever people left, flagging significant accounting transactions, feeding them confidential records, and providing details of stock options, bonuses, and donations. Kahn and Lichtenberg had used her as a mole to infiltrate the company.

~

I could see that I might be facing a government prosecution based upon the testimony of hostile individuals supported by Kahn and Lichtenberg and their allies. I knew now that I had to develop the capability to discredit Berenda and anyone else who became a government witness. If I was indicted, I would only win at trial if I had a credible defense and the government's witnesses were suspect. My attorneys had been educating me on the poor odds of fighting out a criminal case with the government, including the depressing fact that most Americans who sit on juries still believe in the veracity of the American government and refuse to believe that it would use tainted witnesses or perjured testimony. For the first time, I understood that I might be fighting a losing battle.

~

It was now a given that Berenda would be a government witness in the investigation against me. All I could hope for was that our attorneys would be able to neutralize her as a witness; to do so, we had to be able to prove that she was biased against me and lacked credibility.

Berenda had joined Besicorp in November 1987, while we were still based in Ellenville. Besicorp was a "counter-culture" company, where all types of people found it easy to fit in, but she had never seemed comfortable working with us.

She began as a bookkeeper and worked her way up the accounting ladder. As she did, we steadily increased her salary and even paid for her college education. Nothing pleases me more than to see my employees do well and advance. In the mid-eighties, at about the time Besicorp made the move to Kingston and began to do big-league business, apparently something changed. Whenever she and I talked, she would turn beet red. It became something of a joke, but in hindsight I can say that something strange must have been going on in her mind.

∾

I'll never know for certain why Berenda was so hostile, but I have an idea of where it might have begun. My wife Valerie served as Besicorp's Human Resource Manager for more than ten years. In this position, Valerie supported those in the company who had health or personal problems, empathized with their grief or pain, and helped them restructure their lives while they continued to be productive members of the Besicorp "family." She shared her personal knowledge of nutrition and health: Besicorp had a smoke-free building a decade before it was fashionable or mandated, and we constructed our corporate headquarters out of low-toxicity building materials. Valerie also asked our employees not to wear scented colognes, perfumes, or hair sprays.

Most of our employees were solidly in favor of our "clean work environment" policy, but Berenda was clearly offended—I had no idea how much so, and I never paid it much mind. Was this what had first alienated her from the company to such a degree that she would voluntarily team up with Alan Kahn and James Lichtenberg?

Knowing the probable psychology behind Berenda's disaffection was not the same, however, as knowing how to discredit her. In a trial, I would be severely constrained by what was permissible under the rules my attorneys described to me. I was clearly vulnerable to an obstruction of justice charge, which had to be avoided at all costs; everything relating to my defense needed to be done by attorneys. I had an idea, however, about how to discredit her as a witness.

It turned out that after Berenda was fired from Besicorp, she went to her part-time employer at the local restaurant where she worked evenings as a bartender and asked the owner to let her work "off the books" so she could collect unemployment insurance while she was working for cash. The restaurant refused, so she quit and took a job at another local restaurant, where she was able to work for cash and simultaneously collect unemployment. I learned this almost a year after she had been fired from Besicorp.

∾

With great care, under the supervision of Besicorp's outside defense counsel, Steve Nachimson, Besicorp's inside counsel, hired a private investigator to look into Berenda's unemployment situation. He began to frequent the restaurant where she was then working, and he gradually managed to strike up a friendship with her. Wearing a wire and recording his conversations with her, over time he goaded her into admitting that she had been working at this job for almost a year, just about since she had left her job at Besicorp. He obtained the evidence we needed to use at trial; we could now prove that Berenda had committed fraud in collecting unemployment.

At the very end of his work, the investigator tipped his hand, and somehow Berenda figured out that he was not just another Joe. What happened next confirmed our worst fears. A team of FBI agents descended on the private investigator and hammered him with questions. He refused to answer, but as they were leaving, they served him with a subpoena, and at the same time, Besicorp received another subpoena asking for everything we had concerning the investigator and Berenda. The government's actions confirmed my intuition. Not only had Berenda been taking corporate documents, to which she had no right, for Kahn and Lichtenberg, but she was in all likelihood a government informant.

Besicorp's attorneys went right to Elliot Jacobson, the Assistant U.S. Attorney in charge of the investigation. They informed him that Besicorp was investigating Berenda for entirely legitimate reasons that were unrelated to the criminal case, which was entirely true, but they refused to tell the government what it was that they were investigating. The prosecutor was angry, but there was nothing he could do. The company had a right to hire its own investigators in the conduct of its business, especially if an attorney conducted such an investigation. That the company obtained information that would help it at trial was a benefit that our attorneys were totally comfortable was legal and appropriate.

Every dollar paid out under unemployment insurance in New York State is collected back in premiums from the employer, and Besicorp still had to deal with Berenda's unemployment fraud, a matter that was financially significant even if it paled in comparison to what she had been doing with the raiders and then the government. Besicorp's inside counsel sent the evidence of her off-the-books employment to the NYS Labor Department, and in due course, the department retroactively denied Berenda's unemployment insurance payments.

The government investigators were surely licking their chops over the possibility of bringing an obstruction of justice charge against me. Thankfully, that went nowhere. Our attorneys had smoked out the government in the course of Besicorp's "investigation" into Berenda's off-the-books employment, but there's no doubt that, in the conspiratorial mindset of the government, those events confirmed that I was a "bad guy." How dare I hire my own investigator! Only the government gets to plant crooks and spies in peoples' lives and businesses. After all, anything goes so long as they get the "bad guys."

13

THE CASE FOR THE DEFENSE

In retrospect, I understand that I committed a series of innocent acts that were imprudent because they enabled adversaries to make allegations that drew the attention of the government.

The big lesson here is the vital importance of appearances in avoiding such allegations of impropriety. I had no idea how a hardball prosecutor could turn allegations into an indictment. And with 90% of cases today settled by plea bargain, prosecutors are bolder than ever today in using tainted and self-motivated witnesses, and about buying testimony with sweetheart deals. Beware: when they want you, they will get you.

In the criminal justice process, the subject matter of an investigation can be withheld from the person or persons under investigation. All we could do was guess, and the tension was unbearable. As the new subpoenas arrived, and as the new witnesses were called before the Grand Jury, our lawyers began to assemble a framework to try and anticipate what, beyond the 1992 Hinchey campaign, the government was investigating. I was confident that there was absolutely no wrongdoing in my life, but I was not yet aware of how that made absolutely no difference during the investigation process.

Based on this limited understanding, I began putting together a "Bible" for the case. This was to be the working reference document for the lawyers. It would contain the financial records of each Besicorp employee who'd contributed to the Hinchey campaign, and my own narrative description of everything I could think of relating to the investigation, the allegations we imagined might be made, and my preliminary defenses. This was a massive effort, but it was quite clear to me that I was in for the fight of my life.

I was learning about a criminal justice system to which I had never before given as much as a thought. I learned that going to trial meant risking a long period of incarceration as opposed to what would ostensibly be a relative slap on the wrist if I capitulated to some sort of negotiated plea-bargain deal. I understood that the government would probably allege that I had illegally reimbursed contributors to the '92 Hinchey campaign.

Bill Brodsky told me that pleading guilty to a minor charge in exchange for a lower penalty was the safest thing to do almost any time the government conducted an investigation, but I still couldn't stand the idea of pleading guilty to a crime when I knew damned well that I hadn't intentionally broken the law at all. My lawyers were adamant that if I went to trial and were convicted of anything, even a peripheral charge, most judges would slam me with a stiff sentence—especially if they felt that I should have pleaded guilty. It was crucial, therefore, that my defense be iron-clad. I had to break the case down—and it was getting more and more complex—piece by piece, and I had to be able to answer every charge. This meant anticipating the testimony of every witness, in particular, every present and former employee who had made contributions to the '92 Hinchey campaign.

∼

The first witness I would present was Steve Levine, who had served as my most senior executive and inside counsel at Besicorp between November 1986 and March 1994. Steve was one of my closest associates at the time of the campaign, and he'd played an important part in it. Steve would be a cornerstone of my defense.

Besicorp's attorneys, accountants, and executive staff were charged with ensuring compliance with all laws and regulations. This was especially necessary in a publicly reporting company such as Besicorp; we were so thoroughly audited and responsible for making full disclosure of all material events and activities that we operated with a heightened sense of awareness of the importance of legal compliance. We had a skilled team, and I relied on them to make sure that our business activities were legal and compliant. I dealt with the Hinchey campaign no differently than I dealt with other matters, relying on the advice and input of those I trusted. Steve Levine was not only head of the company's power development group, he was the only attorney on Besicorp's staff at that time. I routinely went to him for consultation and support on legal matters that didn't seem to require the advice of outside counsel.

Steve had been among the throngs of people who came to visit our backwoods company workshop after the appearance of the 1979 Popular Science article that helped launch Besicorp. For Woodstock generation members like him (and me), solar energy in the 1970s was a spiritual mission. An attorney by profession, he was no longer practicing law at the time he entered the solar business, but in the mid-1980s he made a niche for himself in energy law and plunged back into the practice. He was a natural fit in our effort to become a power developer.

Besicorp landed our first major contract for a cogeneration plant in 1986, and Steve worked as my right-hand man for several years as we built a team of qualified people. He was flexible, casual, and exhibited a refreshing lack of greed. He was handsomely rewarded, but he never made remuneration his primary focus. Unfortunately, his wife was not happy living in New York State, and when they had their second baby in 1991, he informed me that they had to return to Boston because she wanted to live near her mother and sisters. His departure was a great loss for the company.

When I decided to get involved in the 1992 Hinchey campaign, one of the first people I turned to was Steve, who was gradually phasing out his association with the company at the time. He embraced the idea of working on the campaign and threw himself into it with enthusiasm. He believed that Hinchey was a leading environmental politician and would be good for our business.

Steve participated in many of the campaign planning meetings that took place within the confines of Besicorp's office, and I assumed at the time that his attendance gave a blessing to the effort. He was an attorney whose integrity I trusted, and I assumed that he would keep us out of trouble. In retrospect I realize that he didn't know what he was doing any more than I did, but one of the key elements of my defense would be my good faith and lack of criminal intent.

Early in the campaign, I'd received the Federal Election Commission campaign finance regulations. Foolishly, I'd scanned them only in a superficial manner and immediately passed them on to

Steve as my internal checkpoint. I didn't realize their significance, nor did I realize that violations of them could have criminal implications. I had a complete lack of understanding of what regulatory crime was.

I was planning to raise money from executive employees of Besicorp. Steve and I had specific discussions about the advice that I had been given by David Lenefsky. As I've noted, I relied on Lenefsky to guide me through the process and was greatly reassured when Steve concurred with his advice.

Steve recited to me his own version of the regulations: that each donor must donate voluntarily, and each donor must donate his or her own funds. You can ask for a contribution, but you can't pressure or imply a threat or the lack of future benefit for not participating. It was clear to both Steve and me that we were in compliance with that fundamental point with respect to each of the donors within Besicorp. Even though Steve was not experienced in campaigns, he was smart. He had the campaign financing regulations in hand and knew the company's compensation practices.

He and I discussed how we should deal with the regulations in Besicorp's bonus-oriented environment. Periodic bonuses were the rule, not the exception. At Besicorp, individual performance, company results, and the passage of time were all factors in determining whether a bonus was granted. An additional complicating factor in the company was the number of compensation arrangements that were in use. Most management employees had a set base salary and a defined bonus range with a guaranteed minimum bonus. In some instances, a bonus earned over the year was paid out in small periodic installments over the course of the next year.

Steve was so convinced that what we did was entirely legitimate that he drew a $3,000 bonus himself and made a $2,000 contribution to the campaign. At the time, he had earned a lot of money in accrued bonus compensation that was yet unpaid, and he and I discussed the fact that he was getting his own money as a bonus and that he was giving his own money to a candidate he supported.

It was in this context that we concluded that what we were doing was legal. It was absolutely clear in my mind that there was no way a bonus could be misinterpreted as pressure to make a contribution to the campaign or as a reimbursement, because bonuses were a matter of course before the campaign began. This didn't change once the campaign was in full swing, and our modus operandi continued on long into the future. What I didn't know was that a circumstantial criminal case could be constructed from innocent acts naively executed.

~

Steve Levine's advice during the campaign of 1992 was central to my belief, still held to this day, that I was acting correctly in dealing with employees' campaign contributions. I still believe in his sense of right and wrong and his integrity, but we were both looking at the issue through the wrong end of a telescope. We were more concerned with how things really were than with how they might be made to look by a hostile federal prosecutor.

When the FBI and IRS made their 7:00 AM visit to Steve at his home in Massachusetts in early May 1996, he notified the company promptly, and Besicorp provided him with John Riecke as his legal counsel. Riecke advised Steve not to testify without a grant of immunity, which was never given to him. So the Grand Jury that eventually indicted me never got to hear from Steve a true explanation of what had actually happened. All they saw was the contribution check and the bonus check, dated at about the same time. This was the circumstantial evidence of "swapping checks" the government needed.

Steve had reason to be petrified that he too would be targeted by the government. If he were criminally implicated, he could be disbarred, if not worse, and he was supporting a family with two babies. I was learning that putting on a criminal defense was nothing like a TV movie. Although my consultations with Steve (supported by the record of his compensation) would form part of my defense (I would claim that I acted in good faith with "advice of counsel"), those discussions did not meet the strict legal standard for that defense. Steve's advice was not in writing. My defense relied upon Steve agreeing to testify and not taking the Fifth Amendment at trial. In the surreal world I had entered, we were unable talk to Steve except through his lawyer, who gave us no assurances. Steve could have ended up taking the Fifth and not testifying in the trial at all, even if that contributed to my conviction.

∽

Another Besicorp executive who had made a contribution to the Hinchey campaign was someone I knew would be hostile to my defense. Richard Altman had been a Besicorp vice president who worked as a project developer and reported to Steve Levine. When I let it be known around the company that I was getting involved in the campaign, he had been one of the first to express his support.

Altman had been fired by the company shortly after the '92 campaign. He, too, had received a bonus in close proximity to the date of his campaign contribution. As far as the prosecution was concerned, this amounted to circumstantial evidence of reimbursement, and there was no doubt that he would be one of the prosecutor's key witnesses against me. The real story is as follows.

Richard Altman had been asking for some of his accrued bonus money for months. Steve Eisenberg had held back Altman's bonus since the beginning of 1992 due to poor job performance, and, by the fall of 1992, Altman had received $20,000 less than his prior year's bonus earnings. He wanted some of that money (some of which he was in fact owed), regardless of the campaign, and had been increasingly agitated over the situation.

The Hinchey campaign was his opportunity to turn up additional heat for some of his bonus money. He made a $1,000 contribution to the campaign and then became increasingly vocal about getting some of his bonus money, not just with me but also with Levine and Eisenberg. About ten days later, I authorized Besicorp to gave him $1,500, which all of us understood was paid against his earned bonus. Eisenberg and I told him we would settle up with him at the end of the year. Far from my pressing Altman to contribute, he used his contribution to pressure the company into paying him some of his bonus money, which we all felt he didn't yet deserve to draw.

Prior to giving Altman bonus money, I went to Steve Levine to discuss Altman's situation. Altman went to Steve Levine for advice as well. Steve was totally familiar with the facts and circumstances, and, with David Lenefsky's advice in mind, told both of us that it would be legal for Altman to get some of his accrued bonus money to reimburse his cash flow needs, even though he had made the campaign contribution. Steve concluded that Altman's contribution was voluntary and that it was his money, not Besicorp's, that was being donated.

Altman was very bright and often a good performer, but he was erratic and suffered from mood swings. He would go for weeks at a time in a deep funk, acting withdrawn and displaying temperamental behavior. By the fall of 1992, Steve and I had reached the conclusion that Altman had to leave Besicorp. We dragged it out for a long time, hoping his work would stabilize, as we liked Richard and didn't want to hurt him.

But by the end of November, we just couldn't continue the situation, and we terminated his employment. I consulted with Steve Eisenberg, Besicorp's executive vice president, and we determined that Altman was owed $20,000 in earned but unpaid bonus, less $1,500 he had received (the supposedly illegal reimbursement), less one month he didn't work during the 1992 calendar year. We gave him $17,500, but Altman was far from satisfied. He wanted much more and thought he had been cheated.

It's amazing how different perceptions can be. Altman earned $120,000 in his peak year with Besicorp; only three years before, he'd started out with a base salary of $40,000. But he left Besicorp angry over money.

Altman was called before the Grand Jury in the early stages of the investigation. His attorney, John Riecke (paid by Besicorp), waited in the hallway outside the Grand Jury room. Besicorp's attorney, Doug Lobel, waited in the hallway too, hoping that after his Grand Jury appearance, Altman would be in the mood to talk.

Lobel found out that Altman's testimony was in accord with my description of the events, except for one little twist that Altman added. Even knowing what was at stake for me, he told the Grand Jury that he believed he was being reimbursed for a campaign contribution. He even acknowledged to the Grand Jury that he had consulted with Steve Levine and satisfied himself that what he was doing was legal. That little bit of hypocrisy gave the prosecutor enough to run with. Altman's hostility wasn't based solely on getting fired or not getting enough bonus money. There was more to the story.

Immediately after Altman was fired, James Lichtenberg had contacted him, soliciting his support to join the stock speculators and oust me from the company. He already had Debra Berenda feeding him the names of Besicorp employees as soon as they left the company. Altman offered his cooperation, and it wasn't long before Lichtenberg's attorneys appeared in court in Lichtenberg's suit against Besicorp's directors, making allegations that we realized could have only come from Altman. That really ticked me off, for I knew how well Altman had been treated financially, and all of us running the company knew that he had brought about his own termination.

By the time Altman left Besicorp, he had also accumulated about $50,000 under the company's long-term deferred compensation plan, which was to have been paid out over time from projects he worked on. Altman was violating written confidentiality agreements that were linked to his deferred compensation when he began collaborating with Lichtenberg. I had called Altman at his home and confronted him on this issue. He acknowledged that he had, in fact, been talking with Lichtenberg, and on that basis I refused to pay him any more money.

A few months later, about a year after Altman left Besicorp, one of our projects needed his testimony in litigation. A partner mediated and Besicorp paid him off in exchange for his testimony, but apparently his hostility was only further inflamed.

I learned from this unfortunate chapter that the company technically had "facilitated" Altman's contribution, and thereby inadvertently violated campaign finance laws. That means Altman's expectation of reimbursement through receipt of his own bonus money made it more likely that he would donate. My defense in light of the situation was that I sought and obtained advice of counsel and I acted in good faith. I didn't know I was breaking the law at the time. That should have been enough to take my case to trial and lead to an acquittal, but Altman's hostile testimony was one reason that I ultimately came to believe that I had to plea-bargain and settle with the government.

～

A third witness was sure to be Joyce DePietro. In 1992, Joyce was then my executive assistant (she's gone on to become a corporate vice president). She was a central figure in the government's theory of the case, but the government was dead wrong, and they trampled on Joyce to try and get her to lie under oath.

Joyce had a successful New York City career as a market research executive when she and her husband made the risky leap from New York City to live in the country. Joyce and I found each other in 1991, and she immersed herself in the business starting at $30,000 per year, a fraction of her prior earnings. She knew it would be just a matter of time till she moved up. When the opportunity came to work with me in the Hinchey campaign, she jumped into the project. Neither of us gave a second thought to whether her assistance was "official" Besicorp work. Joyce routinely worked fifty-hour weeks and took work home, so her limited involvement was considered to be insignificant. And neither of us considered what this would look like to a federal prosecutor looking for an indictment.

Joyce was there to make my life easier so that I could produce more for Besicorp. That was her job. She attended most of the Hinchey campaign finance committee meetings, where she took notes and followed up important action items. Joyce was the communications backbone for the initial financing effort. As I've noted, most of the other committee members seemed to have very little business skill. They seemed incapable of pulling off the monumental task of getting a congressional campaign off the ground. This is why Maurice Hinchey wanted me for the wretched task in the first place, and why I made such a mistake mixing business and politics.

Attacking Joyce became central to the government's case. Forcing the "executive secretary" to testify is a standard government technique to acquire evidence against people in powerful positions.

Who better knows all that goes on behind the scenes? And who is more vulnerable to intimidation and can be pressured more easily into testifying against "the boss"?

Unfortunately for Joyce, the prosecutor's view of the case differed substantially from the truth. When she refused to "flip," to become a government witness as her own attorney urged her to do, the prosecutor became enraged and began a campaign of brutal harassment against her.

But Joyce never compromised her integrity. Rather than give false testimony to the Grand Jury that would incriminate me, she risked being indicted herself. During the period that she was repeatedly brought in front of the Grand Jury and threatened with a perjury indictment, she had a three-year old toddler and was in the late stages of a second pregnancy; after two prior Grand Jury appearances, the prosecutor recalled her to the stand when she was eight months pregnant. A few weeks later, immediately after she gave birth, he pressured her to plea-bargain by threatening her with an indictment for perjury.

Joyce's husband Guy was a former corrections officer and was well aware of the coercive tactics that went on in the criminal justice system. He supported Joyce right down the line. How easy it would have been for them to capitulate to the pressure to give testimony against me!

The true story was this. Joyce had joined Besicorp in August 1991, and at her first anniversary review, I had the option of giving her a bonus, a raise, or both. I decided to give her a bonus and had a check made out for $3,000. When we met, Joyce pointed out her value to the company and her exceedingly low base salary. I agreed with her, and in preference to a bonus, she negotiated a hefty raise of $10,000. I never even offered the $3,000 check to her. But the government obtained the never-canceled check in the subpoena process and tried to parley it into evidence of my guilt. Five years later, Joyce was shown the check before the Grand Jury and was asked to explain what it was. In a halfhearted attempt at humor, she exclaimed to the Grand Jurors, "Why wasn't I given the money?"

Painstakingly, she reconstructed the facts. Her first bonus was on December 3, 1992, the same day numerous Besicorp employees received a year-end bonus. According to the government's theory, I reimbursed her for her campaign contribution, either through her raise, or through a bonus three months later, which the prosecutor maintained must have been promised to her at the time of her contribution.

It didn't matter that a raise is forever, or that the following year, Joyce received another $10,000 raise. And then another. And then another, until her salary reached $80,000 per year.

Joyce had donated to the Hinchey campaign from her personal funds for reasons of her own. That is why her testimony was unshakable. She had made her campaign contribution from her own savings and by borrowing from her father. He had maintained a ledger of his loans to Joyce and to his other children, showing balance, debits, credits, and monthly interest. Just two weeks after Joyce made her $2,000 campaign contribution, she had received a $2,000 loan from him. But such facts were only barriers to be demolished by the prosecutor's office.

The Grand Jury hearings ground on, dividing former friends and making life a living nightmare for those who were called to testify. The fourth Besicorp employee who had made a contribution to the Hinchey campaign was Michael Daley, Besicorp's vice president of Finance and Administration. He handled Besicorp's SEC reporting and regulatory requirements. I pushed Mike hard at times, but he had developed professionally and had steadily expanded his responsibility over the years. Prior to Mike's joining Besicorp, our SEC reporting had been a major difficulty. It was Mike's efforts that finally put to rest the long period during which Besicorp was under the gun of the SEC.

Mike was a family man with four beautiful kids, and he had left New York City to raise his family in upstate New York. His growing family and the ensuing decline in his income had rendered him under water financially at the time he joined the company. Although his income grew and he was granted valuable stock options, he had a hard time accumulating any savings and remained in difficult financial circumstances well into the '90s. The reason I mention such intrusively personal information will become clear.

As vice president and Corporate Secretary, Mike had signed the company's 1992 corporate tax returns. Sadly, this made him another potential victim in the cat-and-mouse game the government was playing in order to get at me. In his capacity as the corporate officer in charge of financial reporting, he simply reported what he was told by other executives with respect to an enormous number of transactions within the company. But the fact that he was not the source of that information didn't stop the government from putting pressure on him.

Mike Daley had unequivocally donated his own money to the Hinchey campaign and was not reimbursed, but the government charged that I did reimburse him, which, in the eyes of the prosecutor, made him a co-conspirator. He was very close to being put in a position where, to save himself, he would have had to testify against me. But to do that he would have had to lie. Lying wasn't in Mike's spirit, but I now understand that sometimes it's the only way to escape the US government's juggernaut toward indicting anyone who fails to "cooperate."

Mike's attorney managed to keep him from testifying before the Grand Jury by demanding that he be granted full immunity from government prosecution in exchange for his testimony. After the prosecutor's frustrating experience of giving Joyce full immunity and then not getting the testimony with which he had been expecting to incriminate me, he assumed he would get the same story from Mike Daley, so he was not about to grant him immunity. Mike lived this horrible period in total fear, knowing that the truth didn't matter.

Because Mike Daley was a senior officer of Besicorp, which was also under investigation as a company, he was one of the few people involved in the case whom I could talk to without fear of being charged with obstruction of justice. During the preparation of our potential defense, Mike and I discussed the expectation that the government would allege that I coerced Besicorp executives to donate to the Hinchey campaign. When I told him that the prosecutor probably would allege that I "forced" him to donate and then reimbursed him, he replied emphatically, "If you had agreed to take on the campaign finance assignment for Moppert (Hinchey's Republican opponent), I would never have contributed. I wouldn't support a Republican. That's just the way it was."

Here is more of the way it was: In August 1992, Mike Daley donated $1,000 to the Hinchey for Congress campaign. Several weeks prior to that date, he had written me a letter in which he described his personal financial difficulties in excruciating detail. Through the subpoena, the prosecutor got hold of that letter from Mike's personnel file. He intended to use it to "prove" that Mike was reimbursed for his campaign contribution, regardless of his testimony.

Mike had received a bonus of $4,600 in response to his letter, from which he took home more than $3,000 after taxes. After he wrote his campaign contribution check, I went to his office and asked him why he would donate only $1,000 to the campaign when he could legally donate $2,000. His answer was immediate and unequivocal. "That is all I can afford." I shrugged my shoulders, thanked him, and left. That was the last time I asked Mike to contribute.

If Mike Daley got a bonus of $4,600 but donated only $1,000 because he felt that was all he could afford (and it was his money), where was the illegal reimbursement? And if Mike was a willing co-conspirator in a criminal scheme, why didn't I just increase his bonus to hide another $1,000, which would have brought him up to the legal limit of $2,000, or another $2,000 for the primary campaign, for that matter? The answer is that there was no conspiracy and no illegal reimbursement.

The records also show that Mike received regular and periodic bonuses over many years. The prosecutor had all this information when he brought this case to the Grand Jury. Yet I was to be indicted for reimbursing Mike Daley, among others. Assuming that I would eventually be forced to plead guilty to reduced charges, the prosecutor didn't hesitate to include such accusations in the case he was building against me.

~

Several other Besicorp executives also donated to the campaign; all received what I considered to be entirely legal bonuses. As I've noted, I was aware that it was illegal to solicit donations to the campaign and offer a bonus as a reimbursement, but that is never what we did: all the bonus funds Besicorp paid were genuinely part of the recipient's bonus. And if I had taken my defense to trial, every recipient would have testified accordingly—except for those few who viewed this as their opportunity to avenge old grievances.

All of these facts were presented to my attorneys as we prepared to battle the government charges. I was convinced that I could handle going to trial and was still willing to take the risks.

14

Contributions from my Family

As Hinchey's finance chairman, I donated generously to the campaign myself, and my family proudly supported my efforts. When I was eventually indicted for illegally contributing $27,000 to the Hinchey campaign, the contributions from the Besicorp employees I've described represented roughly half of this allegedly "illegal" money. The remaining half of the illegal contributions the government charged, had come from my mother and father, my brother and sister-in-law, and Valerie and me. The government hypothesized that Besicorp had reimbursed me for the money my family contributed. This was patently false. As Besicorp's CEO, I not only made a sufficient income to have easily covered their contributions if I had so chosen, but I was entitled to ask the board to adjust my pay whenever I felt it appropriate. By what conceivable logic would I take an illegal reimbursement?

When Hinchey had asked me to join his campaign, my mother and father were very proud. They had worked their way up as first-generation Americans, and, to them, I was being profoundly honored by this request. Not only had I "made it" in business, but now I was being asked to fulfill an important role in the political world.

In the summer of '92, I asked my parents to contribute to the campaign, and they did so enthusiastically. My mom wrote a check for $2,000 for the primary, and then another $2,000 for the general election, contributions that were within the legal limits. She also gave my brother money, and he and his wife made a contribution. None of us had the slightest idea that such acts could be construed as illegal.

In the eventual indictment, the government charged that I reimbursed my family for their donations; the "smoking gun" payments, it would charge, were two checks for $4,000 each that I had written to my parents in September and October of 1992. In focusing on these, the government conveniently ignored all the other checks I gave my parents over the years, including two $4,000 checks in the same months the year before.

Since I routinely gave my parents monetary gifts, it didn't occur to me that I could be accused of reimbursing my own family. I grew up in a family culture that emphasized caring and sharing. My parents were generous with other family members, helping aunts and cousins with money I had given them. If I had gone to trial, I would have been able to prove that I gave my parents about $30,000 in each year between 1990 and 1995. Every month, I usually gave them either cash or checks in amounts between $2,000 and $5,000. Not only did I support my family generously with these gifts, but my parents and my brother had made several hundred thousand dollars on Besicorp stock. If I had asked them, I know they would have donated to any worthy cause I suggested without hesitation. And why shouldn't they?

My father passed away in September 1995, after a series of strokes, and Mom passed away in March of 1997. The night before she died, she was sitting in the living room watching television with me. The local TV station was covering the Hinchey fund-raising scandal that day, and without realizing what I was doing, I switched the TV channel to the local news. As I saw the beginning of what was going to come on, I quickly switched to another channel. Mom turned to me and asked, "What are you trying to hide?" I didn't answer. I could never put anything over on my mom. Until the last day of her life, Mom's mind was sharp, her wit endearing. She made friends easily and was well liked. She would have made a great witness in my defense.

My attorney, Bill Brodsky, told me that if we took my defense to trial, the government would in all likelihood oppose the introduction into evidence of all the checks and gifts that I customarily gave my parents. The prosecutor would argue that any other money I gave my parents was irrelevant, and that the charge was that certain specific checks were direct reimbursement for my parents'

campaign contribution. The judge might grant the government's request, he advised. I couldn't imagine that any fair-minded judge would deny me my ability to establish that these payments were part of the pattern of my relationship with my parents, and hardly could be interpreted as part of a conspiracy to corrupt an election campaign.

But I've come to learn that it is no longer enough to simply avoid deliberately committing a crime if a motivated prosecutor decides to push the limits of reality to cobble up a case. The key to avoiding prosecution is to stay so far away from any transaction that could be intentionally misconstrued as crossing the line that nobody could get you, no matter how they lied. But it would be virtually impossible to conduct business under these absurd constraints. And to conduct one's life under such circumstances conjures up the kind of hellish existence most of us are familiar with only from reading about what life is like in a police state.

15

THE TROJAN HORSE

A s I was building the case for my acquittal on charges that I could still only guess at, the government was building its case for my prosecution.

Preparation of the defense "Bible" could take me only so far. I could tell my attorneys what had happened. I could describe what I knew about potential witnesses against me and their biases and motivations. But I couldn't control what a person intent on seeing me destroyed might say under oath. Who would believe that the United States government would jump at the chance to use a corrupted witness?

Besicorp and Martin Enowitz, our former chief financial officer and formerly a member of the board of directors, had been locked in a tough legal battle over valuable stock rights. In the course of that case, he had made veiled threats that he had the power to cause the company major harm. I ignored those threats, certain that I had never intentionally broken the law. I thought I had nothing to fear, but I was wrong, and now it was apparently too late. The scope of the government's investigation was continuing to emerge, and my worst nightmares were beginning to be confirmed.

Enowitz served as Besicorp's chief financial officer from January 1992 until August 1994. I'd thought I knew him well when I decided to bring him on as CFO. In another display of my wife's powerful intuition—intuition that I often ignored—Valerie had implored me not to hire him. She felt that Enowitz was only in it for the money, and had no real personal devotion to Besicorp. Like an innocent, I thought that a CFO should be totally focused on money. I just didn't get her point.

I didn't question Enowitz's basic character, but it turned out that he was a Trojan Horse. His decision to turn government witness in retaliation over the civil litigation dispute pushed me into a dreadful abyss where the risks of going to trial became so great that I did what I had sworn never to do: I made a deal with the prosecutor, a deal that ultimately sent me to prison.

~

Enowitz and I first met in 1981, when Besicorp was a newly public company and the solar energy business was considered a hot investment. He called me up out of the blue and invited me to address a meeting of the Metropolitan Solar Energy Society in New York City. I gladly accepted, and I was thrilled that the audience was so highly receptive to my vision of the future, one where the world had practical solar energy-based alternatives and people were educated, aware, and committed to a sustainable future. Many of those who heard my presentation had dreamed about the dawn of the solar-energy era and regarded me as a pioneer who was helping to create it. Enowitz saw something in me that I now wish he hadn't noticed.

He was an accountant by training and after he had spent several years working in public auditing, he had moved on to become a staff accountant for a major manufacturer. Of greater relevance was that he'd spent several years developing and marketing a newsletter for investors in solar energy stocks. It had several hundred subscribers at the time I met him, and he had used it to launch a financial consulting business.

Enowitz was a financial matchmaker. Early in our relationship, I occasionally caught glimpses of disputes he had with clients over fees. I found his adversarial dealings with them amusing, but considered it none of my business; my antenna for detecting danger was far from refined, and I never contemplated that he would turn his talons on me.

Aside from Valerie, others, too, had warned against hiring him. Two of these advisers called him a "bloodsucker," a person who gets a cut on other people's deals without making a contribution. I disagreed, because I thought that having someone who was tough, adversarial, and looking to make money would be good for Besicorp, so I went ahead and hired him. I was trying to overcome my own naiveté in business, and I felt that the company needed to be toughened up.

In 1982, Enowitz and I entered into our first agreement, establishing him as a "finder" of business deals. He was always trying to broker business relationships, and he sent me lots of junk, but he generated one golden lead. Enowitz introduced me to Harold Kamine, and Kamine and Besicorp went on to develop numerous major projects together. Hal had heard of Enowitz's newsletter and called him up, seeking a financial partner for new energy projects. Enowitz made the introduction by telephone, and Hal and I went on to create a long-term business partnership. Enowitz received a handsome finder's fee and substantial residuals from several projects, including bonus amounts that were far in excess of the contract requirements.

Martin Enowitz was burdened with congenital clubbed feet, but he was physically normal in all other major respects. He wore specially manufactured shoes, and, much to his credit he was determined not to let his deformity dominate his life. He even had custom-made sneakers and sometimes played tennis.

Enowitz often remarked to me that his job at Besicorp greatly enhanced his life. His last job in Manhattan had required the daily use of mass transit as well as a lot of walking. During his tenure at Besicorp, he drove to work and stayed at a nearby hotel on occasion, making his commute from home quite tolerable. Enowitz's disability was always part of his equation, but he assured everyone that it was entirely manageable.

I spent a lot of time during the course of the federal investigation not only thinking about what Enowitz might be saying to the prosecutors and what he might testify, but reflecting on our soured relationship. I realized that he was enacting what was tantamount to a mortal threat to my existence: trying to get me incarcerated. I had once considered Enowitz a real friend, and now there was no doubt that he was in the process of engineering my destruction.

In my capacity as CEO of Besicorp, I must admit that I had often dealt with Enowitz firmly, as I do with all management employees. I demanded performance on the job, and I wouldn't tolerate mediocrity. But I felt that I was always fair and never unduly harsh. That was my perspective, however. Obviously, Enowitz had looked at our relationship and had reached an entirely different conclusion.

On the seventeenth day of August 1994, Martin Enowitz had walked into my office and handed me his letter of resignation. The letter stated that the reason for it was total and permanent disability.

For almost a year prior to his resignation, Enowitz had been performing poorly as chief financial officer. He wasn't cut out for a position where quick-paced decisions were required, and he'd been allowing the areas of the business under his supervision to languish. We were restructuring his job and had exchanged a number of constructive proposals. In his new position, he could do what he did best and act as "business development" manager, fulfill cash management "treasury" functions, and remain on the board of directors.

I thought we were making progress and I was pretty positive about his ability to fulfill his new role. We had both acknowledged that the restructured position would involve a salary reduction as well as a reduction in his long-term stock award. Despite these ongoing negotiations, I had no intention of firing Enowitz, and he knew it. Our relationship appeared to be cordial and friendly until the end.

I've described how in 1992 the Besicorp board created a stock incentive plan that was designed to secure long-term commitments from senior management. Enowitz received 100,000 shares of stock under that plan. To encourage a long-term commitment from the recipient, the stock was to "vest" (become the unrestricted property of the recipient) in installments on the third, fourth, and fifth anniversary dates of the award. This program was designed to give the executive a generous incentive to stay the course for the long haul. If employment terminated for any reason prior to those dates, the stock would be forfeited. There were only two exceptions to this waiting period: death or permanent total disability. These exceptions were intended to protect the recipient's family. If the employee died or became permanently disabled, the restrictions would lapse, and all the stock would become the property of the executive or his estate.

Contained within Enowitz's resignation letter was a statement that he was totally disabled and therefore would be keeping his 100,000 shares of restricted stock. The statement was at least highly suspect, and though in due course, Besicorp requested proof from him that he was in fact totally disabled, satisfactory proof was never provided. I was now in the horrible position of potentially having to initiate legal action against a man who had served on Besicorp's board and been a close associate for years. But it was clear that if Enowitz's disability claim was not bona fide, I had to defend Besicorp's interest in recovering the stock. The decision to contest Enowitz's right to the stock was unanimous among Besicorp's entire management team. All of us suspected that his disability claim was phony, but we had no proof. Initially, he was entitled to the benefit of the doubt. But then what? After all those years of working together, he and I were now going to be at odds. I understand that he did indeed have physical problems, but there were no prior indications that he was totally disabled. And here the story gets quite bizarre.

Shortly after Enowitz's abrupt resignation, Besicorp had demanded proof that he was totally and permanently disabled. Eight months later, we received a one-paragraph letter from his doctor, completely devoid of detail and expressing only the vague conclusion that Enowitz was not capable of working. The lack of any reasonable effort on Enowitz's part to prove that he was disabled indicated that in all likelihood his disability claim was a sham. We felt compelled to file a legal action to force him to return the 100,000 shares or prove his disability in a court of law.

The case was assigned to State Supreme Court Justice Anthony Carpinello, and the judge held a series of conferences in an attempt to get the parties to settle. I attended each one, and put forth bona fide offers on behalf of Besicorp. Despite being certain now that

Enowitz had tried to rip Besicorp off, I wanted very much to put this dispute behind us. I recognized his long-term contributions to the company, but I still had a responsibility not to let him keep all of the stock based on a phony disability claim.

Enowitz did not attend a single settlement conference. Instead, he sent his attorney, Charles Gormally, with instructions not to compromise a single share.

I attended the last of these conferences with Besicorp's general counsel, Steve Nachimson, and outside trial counsel Rich Reed. The judge laid out the ground rules and each party shuttled in and out of his conference room. I started by offering to settle the litigation by giving Enowitz 25 percent of the contested stock, no questions asked. By the fourth round of discussions, I was up to 70 percent, but Enowitz's attorney had not compromised by a single share. Instead, Gormally made additional monetary demands on Enowitz's behalf that were not even part of the lawsuit.

I was exasperated. "How can we continue to negotiate against ourselves?" I asked the judge. "Enowitz is not negotiating in good faith. He wants over a hundred percent of what he's claiming in the lawsuit!" Judge Carpinello agreed. He said he would take one more crack at trying to get some movement, so out we went and in went Gormally.

I met with Judge Carpinello one last time. He turned directly to me and asked me point blank if I weren't concerned about what Enowitz could do to me, considering his former position. He had the impression, he said, that Enowitz had something on me, and that I might be concerned about having someone with his knowledge as an enemy.

I was flabbergasted and asked if the judge was saying that Enowitz had made a threat through his attorney. The judge replied that he thought it was more of a warning than a threat, but that I could do with it what I wanted. He was only the messenger, he said.

I became very angry and told the judge that I had been running a public reporting company for almost fifteen years. I had a large staff dedicated to legal compliance and reporting and I had run an entirely clean company. If Enowitz was making a threat, I rejected it entirely as a basis for negotiations. The judge just shrugged his shoulders and told me it was my decision.

I remained convinced that I was on solid ground because I had an absolutely clear conscience.

I had no idea how serious a threat had just been made. It was just several weeks later that the U.S. government agents descended in their early morning raids, and my nightmare began. Enowitz had offered testimony that Besicorp had reimbursed employees for contributions to the 1992 Hinchey campaign.

16

My Enemies Sign In

By the end of 1996 the federal investigation had entered a very difficult stage. There were long periods of silence in which we heard nothing from the government. The defense attorneys told stories of people who remained under investigation for long periods, living in a state of constant anxiety and sometimes never even being informed of the final status of their case; the investigation eventually just faded away, with years passing while they lived in limbo, not knowing whether an indictment would come down.

But I knew in my heart that their silence didn't mean that the prosecutors were abandoning the case. With the combination of stock raiders and aggrieved former employees, there were just too many people working together to get me removed from Besicorp. It was clear from all the information that had come to light during the initial stages of the investigation that the feds were unwittingly dancing to a tune played by the raiders. During quiet times, I would agonize over what I was facing.

In a strange twist of fate, Besicorp and Enowitz were still "allies" as co-defendants in the Lichtenberg suit. Lichtenberg was still pressing his case, seeking to reverse stock awards issued to various members of the Besicorp management team, and Enowitz held 100,000 of those shares—the same shares about which Besicorp was litigating against Enowitz. It would have been funny if it weren't so enraging, exhausting, and now, ominous.

Jim McCabe was still defense counsel in the Lichtenberg case as he had been since 1993 when it was initially filed. Enowitz had for some time been trying to bring Charles Gormally into the case, and incidentally trying to get Besicorp to pay the legal bills. Ironically, Enowitz charged that McCabe had a conflict of interest due to his representation of Besicorp, citing the fact that he and Besicorp were adversaries in other litigation! Besicorp rejected that position, and refused to pay Gormally to represent Enowitz. Gormally was not a "white-glove" legal practitioner, and my impression was that he practiced law with a baseball bat in one hand: he was the one who passed along the "threat" on behalf of Enowitz that preceded the government investigation.

Over the course of time, Jim McCabe did have various conversations with Gormally about the Lichtenberg case. During one of those talks, it came out that Enowitz had been conducting secret settlement discussions with Kahn and Lichtenberg. This was absolutely shocking. There was no way Enowitz could settle the Lichtenberg case with respect to his own stock without all of the defendants participating (Steve Eisenberg and I were both co-defendants), but after the feds showed up with their subpoenas, it became quite clear what had transpired.

There's no doubt in my mind, that during these secret negotiations, Enowitz had laid out how he could force me out of the company by offering testimony that could incriminate me. He attempted to create an unholy alliance, foolishly expecting to barter his perjured testimony for a "deal" to keep his stock. But he was in for a shock. I wasn't forced out of the company, and he never got his stock. But he did give Kahn and his associates the information they needed to get the government to come down on me, and he became the government's prime witness in my prosecution. Lest anyone doubt his motivation, the 100,000 shares of Besicorp stock being contested with respect to his phony disability claim were worth more than $2 million in 1997 when this horror was taking place.

Right in the middle of the investigation, a new front opened in the battle with predatory shareholders. Among the assets I'd acquired when I made the journey from working class kid to CEO of Besicorp was the local small-plane airport in Kingston, New York, and I had obtained almost two million dollars in federal grants for airport infrastructure improvements. Now the Federal Aviation Administration sent me notice that they had received a letter alleging criminal wrongdoing in connection with these federal grants. Specifically, the letter alleged that Besicorp and I were padding bills that were charged to the grant, and that either the FAA was getting ripped off or Besicorp was getting ripped off.

The letter was sent by one Paul Shaheen, who had been let go by the company in 1991. He was a junior attorney who worked in our legal department, and I fired him for both insubordination and poor performance. He never forgave me, and it became clear from their camaraderie at annual meetings that he and Lichtenberg were in cahoots. I don't believe that Shaheen alone could have come up with a plan to get the FAA to investigate my operation on the basis of a deliberately false allegation; I think the logistics of it had to come from the more sophisticated machinations of Kahn and Lichtenberg.

The FAA conducted a full audit of the grants and not surprisingly, unceremoniously issued an unqualified letter of exoneration. I have gone on to do more work with the FAA, and the airport has become a valuable community asset.

In the course of this investigation, it came to the attention of the FBI that the FAA had given me a copy of Shaheen's letter. I heard through the grapevine that some of the people at the FAA with whom I did business were grilled by federal agents over that. What a shame that the FBI would go to such lengths to protect the identity of a lying instigator.

I should add that Shaheen did not instigate this investigation solely because of a personal grudge for having been fired. He and his family had been actively accumulating Besicorp stock. He had apparently bought Lichtenberg's line about how they could get more money by forcing the company into liquidation, and he acted accordingly.

While grand juries may once have served to insulate citizens from the unadulterated power of the government, today all too many function as rubber stamps, considering the evidence presented to them by prosecuting attorneys and deciding to indict on the proposed charges. In his book After the Madness: A Judge's Own Prison Memoir, former New York Chief Judge Solomon Wachtler (who had endured the terrible ordeal of having been prosecuted in a sex scandal), writes, "A prosecutor can get an indictment on a ham sandwich."

Through the fall of 1996 and into the winter of 1997, we proceeded with preparing for our defense, still making only educated guesses as to the actual focus of the government investigation. We were concentrating on document discovery in the ongoing litigation and monitoring witness appearances at the grand jury.

Unlike trial juries, grand juries sit for relatively long periods, meeting once or twice a week and following cases with a prosecutor. If a particular case extends beyond the term of the grand jury that began hearing the evidence, either the term can be extended or, which is more likely, the prosecutor can bring the ongoing case to a new grand jury. That the new panel has heard none of the witnesses is considered of little consequence: all the prosecutor has to do is bring in a stack of deposition transcripts and plunk them down on the table. He can offer to let the grand jurors read the prior testimony (fat chance) while he summarizes his findings and the charges he is proposing.

Besicorp's attorneys had met with whatever witnesses were willing to talk with them after their appearances before the grand jury investigating our company. Having access to witnesses was one of the benefits of providing counsel for the people who had received subpoenas; Brodsky and Lobel were kept advised by the cooperative defense counsel as to when their clients were going to testify. Then one of them could wait in the hallway of the courthouse and interview the witnesses then and there as they emerged from their testimony, while their recollection was fresh. Most of the people said what I'd told the attorneys they would be likely to say. There were good things and there were bad things, but no new hostile witnesses emerged. Brodsky and Lobel were thus reasonably confident that we had a defensible case, even if it had weaknesses, primarily the circumstantial evidence of bonuses and contemporaneous donations, backed up by witnesses who were hostile. No doubt there were gaps in our knowledge of what the prosecution had been told as well as voluminous materials available to the government out of which to construct charges. Almost since the inception of the investigation, Bill Brodsky had been periodically urging me to offer to plea bargain to something. He made it clear that it was entirely my decision, but he said that experience had shown that the best deal could be cut if I went to the government prior to being indicted, even if I was offering to plead guilty without knowing what I was even going to be charged with. I considered that line of thinking to be almost insane, but I eventually discovered that most defense attorneys recommend this course to their clients.

At the time, however, I just couldn't accept what I felt was Brodsky's defeatist attitude. Knowing that I hadn't intentionally broken the law, I was very much opposed to pleading guilty to a crime. I just couldn't accept the idea of justice so harsh that I had no alternative but to plea-bargain.

Brodsky told me that if I did go to trial and I was convicted, I could be facing a far longer sentence than if I plea-bargained. He said I could get eighteen months, or even two years. Despite that gloomy prognostication, I told him that I would rather go to jail for longer and be able to say till the end of time that I was innocent. I just couldn't do it. This was an extremely emotional time.

Looking back now, I don't think it was false pride that kept me from plea bargaining at that early stage. Although there were clearly problems with my defense, Brodsky still was telling me that I had a defensible case. There was going to be circumstantial evidence presented, and there were definitely going to be witnesses who wanted me removed from the company and punished for the "crimes" the corporate raiders were alleging. Bill reminded me that jurors tend to believe the government and that the judge could get angry if my defense was based primarily on discrediting the government's witnesses. If I were convicted, this could hurt me badly in sentencing. But at that point, I still felt optimistic that I would be acquitted at trial and that we would present a positive defense.

17

ESCALATION

Early on in the investigation, I told Bill Brodsky that the government would closely scrutinize Besicorp's relationship with Ansaldo, the Italian company with which we'd developed so many projects. I knew that the big-bucks transactions typical of that relationship would draw the government's scrutiny and my anxiety was reinforced when Enowitz became a government witness.

It was soon clear that Enowitz had done more than offer up testimony that Besicorp had reimbursed its own employees for contributions to the '92 Hinchey campaign. From the questions that witnesses reported having been asked at their grand jury appearances, it was apparent that the government was probing whether Ansaldo had somehow funneled money into Besicorp. There was only one plausible explanation for this troubling turn of events. It appeared that in order to make sure that the government came down as hard as possible on me, Enowitz had conjured up an allegation that I took money from Ansaldo and funneled it into the Hinchey campaign. This allegation escalated the case to money laundering, foreign-influence peddling, and who knew what other realms of wrongdoing.

Considering the huge sums of money involved in the relationship, Besicorp's funding relationship with Ansaldo had been highly flexible and entrepreneurial. We did business with many institutions, from General Electric Capital Corp. to DeutschBank, as well as various major manufacturers and constructors of power equipment, but our relationship with Ansaldo was unique. While they employed one of the largest law firms in the world and documented all their funding with appropriate loan documents, they were much easier to do business with than any company of comparable size in our experience. I was to learn, however, that that flexibility had a downside.

As I've noted, much of Ansaldo's funding was high-risk capital used for early-stage development. Documentation of these transactions is inherently different from the method that would be used in documenting a bank loan; the specificity for the use of loan proceeds and the terms of payback were vague, as the object of the funding relationship was to create larger business opportunities. The consequence of this looseness would be that it allowed ample room for the government to run with manufactured allegations. This was troublingly apparent to me as I began to assemble the complete history of the Ansaldo relationship and add the material to my "Bible."

I briefed Bill Brodsky on the entire history with Ansaldo, and assured him that there was no impropriety involved in the Ansaldo relationship. Besicorp had documentation for each and every aspect of every transaction. But it was a fact that I had solicited contributions for the '92 Hinchey campaign from Ansaldo executives, and some of their people, indeed, had made contributions.

At the time of the '92 campaign, Ansaldo was funding significant amounts of ongoing development costs for several large Besicorp projects and was also smack in the middle of building two of our projects. The relationship was fast-paced and lucrative on all sides, involving hundreds of millions of dollars in business, and tens of millions of dollars in high-risk capital. It was an irony that the sums that turned out to be problematic were, in comparison, quite paltry.

In August '92 Ansaldo paid $30,000 to fund Besicorp's work on a new business venture and then funded another $10,000 the following October. This was right in the middle of the Hinchey campaign. Bill Brodsky was particularly concerned that we document precisely where those funds had been used, and we set about to build our file. Little did we know that Ansaldo was going to play a much larger role in the criminal case than any of us anticipated.

In his urgent mission to help me accurately reconstruct our relationship with Ansaldo and to prepare my defense, Bill called a friend who was a partner at the giant law firm of Skadden, Arps, Slate, Meagher & Flom, which was Ansaldo's law firm. His friend confirmed that indeed Ansaldo had been subpoenaed by the federal grand jury, and that the Skadden attorneys were still trying to get their arms around the situation. Bill set up a meeting with them so that I could report my version of the events. I brought the appropriate records to the meeting, and they listened to my story.

I went through the history of the relationship between Besicorp and Ansaldo and explained Besicorp's proposal from June 1992 involving the Photovoltaic ("PV") business. I explained how Ansaldo had funded that work, showed them documentation, and explained why, even though we were in a $500 million relationship, informality had been customary and appropriate. I explained that although I'd solicited the Ansaldo executives for Hinchey, knowing that they were probably not American citizens, I did it not to convince them to make an illegal contribution, but with a request that they pass information about Hinchey on to their many American employees. Beyond the fact that some people from Ansaldo had attended a fundraiser for Hinchey and donated a few thousand dollars, this was all I knew.

Several days after that meeting, Bill reported back to me that Ansaldo's attorneys had discussed the situation at length with their client and confirmed that their report of these events was the same as mine. Although the attorneys were still uncomfortable with the level of documentation for the PV venture, they gave us no cause for concern.

18

ANSALDO

Ansaldo's funding for Besicorp, as it turned out, was going to play an important role in the government's case. The series of payments Ansaldo made in connection with Besicorp's PV business drew the particular attention of the government's investigators. To make the story clear, some understanding of the PV venture is in order.

Photovoltaic (PV) technology converts solar radiation directly into electricity. Much of the PV business takes place in Third World countries, but telecommunications and infrastructure projects increasingly use PV technology for remote power supplies. It's a small industry with great growth potential, at the cutting edge of environmental technologies.

After Besicorp's acquisition of a small PV company (SunWize Energy Systems, Inc.) in 1991, I decided to take advantage of our strong relationship with Ansaldo, which had interests in many sectors including turbine manufacturing and infrastructure construction as well as banking and finance. Like several other major European companies, such as Siemens, Total, BP, and Royal Dutch Shell, Ansaldo had a small PV business. This was a perfect opportunity to expand our affiliation with a powerful international corporation.

Ansaldo's successful venture-capital support for Besicorp power plant projects was a feather in my cap. My close working relationship with Stefano Moretti, the President of Ansaldo North America Inc., made him quite receptive to expanding our business relationship. I had first broached the PV business with Moretti back in 1990, and by the beginning of '92, I decided that it was time to get the ball rolling. I pushed Moretti to introduce SunWize to Ansaldo. In May of 1992, Moretti received a positive response from Italy. He asked me to prepare a formal development proposal for the Italians.

By June 1992, Martin Enowitz and my assistant Joyce DePietro had prepared a detailed presentation. It contained a broad spectrum of market information and detailed a variety of business options for introducing Ansaldo's PV subsidiary to the American market. I brought the proposal to Moretti to hand carry directly to the responsible parties in Italy. At the end of July I received the call I was waiting for.

The people in Italy wanted us to bring them into the PV business in North America. I was elated. It was time to ask Ansaldo for seed money for the PV venture, just as they had been providing such funding for our larger power projects. I asked Moretti for $30,000 to cover our costs for the proposal and for initial market research. Moretti thought about that for a few days, and in our next phone call, asked me to fax him an invoice for the $30,000. He wired Besicorp the funds on August 8, 1992, and we were off and running in developing a PV venture with Ansaldo.

As soon as the funds arrived from Ansaldo, Enowitz pitched me for a bonus. I was very busy with the Hinchey campaign and other business responsibilities and I didn't want to deal with Enowitz, who always seemed to have his hand in my pocket. But he had led Besicorp's PV effort and had prepared the Ansaldo proposal, and it was customary that he would receive financial recognition when he brought in money. I authorized him to receive a bonus check for $5,000, but he felt that he should get more; I authorized another $2,500, but told him this was it until year-end.

All these events were unfolding during the same time period that I was running the finances for the Hinchey campaign, and Enowitz informed me that he was planning to use some of his bonus to donate to the campaign. Considering the guidelines I had been given by David Lenefsky, I didn't think it would be improper at all for him to use his own bonus money to make a campaign contribution. I found out too late that appearances are everything, and that reality can be turned on its head.

After getting the PV funding from Ansaldo, we began to beef up our technology staff for the project. In early September 1992, we interviewed David Kulik for a technical and marketing position. Kulik was then with Westinghouse and had a strong background in PV. At his interview, he was briefed about the Ansaldo relationship and what it meant for Besicorp by none other than Martin Enowitz; Kulik joined Besicorp in early November 1992, right after the election that sent Hinchey to Congress.

I stayed in regular contact with Moretti during the fall of 1992. Moretti advised me to send a team to Italy to move the PV project along. I told him I wanted Ansaldo to pick up the tab for the trip. When he asked me how much, I replied that $10,000 should cover the costs. That was petty cash in our $500 million relationship, and he readily agreed. Joyce DePietro faxed another invoice to Ansaldo for the $10,000, and Besicorp received another payment in the last week of October 1992. Unfortunately, the timing was awful, and this gave the government even more ammunition against Besicorp.

In November 1992 Enowitz and I were planning the trip to Italy when the Ansaldo PV people seemed to disappear. Calls weren't returned and faxes went unanswered. We found out only through an industry newsletter in December 1992 that Ansaldo's PV unit was involved in an internal reorganization. At long last, in March 1993, we received an apology letter from our Ansaldo counterparts in Italy, along with a request to accelerate the PV program.

Enowitz and Kulik made the long-delayed trip in May of '93. They spent five days in business and technical meetings and, over the course of the next two years, attempted to work out a deal to bring Ansaldo's PV business to the United States.

Unfortunately, Ansaldo's PV technology was not price competitive. Their prior PV business had all been Italian government-funded projects where price was not a factor, and they were not prepared to compete for private business.

Now, five years later, the U.S. government was investigating whether funds Besicorp had received from Ansaldo were part of a campaign finance fraud. Besicorp was served with a broad subpoena concerning every aspect of the Ansaldo relationship. In response to the subpoena, we delivered the file of documents to the government that related to the Ansaldo proposal (along with the 80 file cabinet drawers full of other documents). The information on the PV venture included all the correspondence and technical work we had generated and was several inches thick. In their zeal to bring criminal charges, the government chose to ignore the exculpatory information that was in their possession.

Had my case gone to trial, Dave Kulik would have testified that in September 1992 Enowitz had told him that Ansaldo had funded Besicorp's PV business, and also that he was hired specifically to work on that program. He also would have testified that when he arrived to work, Enowitz told him that Ansaldo had paid Besicorp in advance for a trip to Italy to develop the program. During the federal investigation, he sent a letter to Besicorp's board, detailing all of this important information. Dave's testimony would have exposed the government's "Alice in Wonderland" story—that is, if my defense had ever made it to a court of law.

19

Ansaldo's Political Contribution

In late July of '92, I was attending a routine meeting with Moretti where we were reviewing outstanding business. I went through the list—development funding; construction; long-term project financing; and the new solar PV technology business venture. Last on my list, I excitedly told Moretti about my foray into politics and my need to raise funds for Maurice Hinchey.

I explained to Moretti that Hinchey would be supportive of our industry in Congress. As our local representative in the New York State Assembly, he helped us in the past; through Hinchey's intervention, we'd been able to break through the state environmental bureaucracy and secure critical permits for one of our projects. Moretti was interested in hearing more.

I gave Moretti and Vincent Nardi, an Ansaldo executive who also was at the meeting, literature on Hinchey. I asked them whether they were American citizens, and when they answered in the negative, I asked them to pass the information along to their executives who were American citizens.

To be absolutely clear, I told Moretti and Nardi that foreign nationals could not donate. I never asked Moretti or Nardi to reimburse their employees for any contributions that might be made; on the contrary, in principle I felt that in light of our relationship, some of their executives could easily reach into their pockets and make a contribution that would support their employer's business objectives. This is no different from what takes place at many corporations, large and small, and is not illegal. I explained that whoever in Ansaldo wanted to be helpful could either donate directly by mail or that they could attend the next fund-raiser we held in New York City.

From time to time over the late summer and early fall of '92, I reminded Moretti about the Hinchey campaign. Lenefsky and Brown were pushing me hard for money, and I pestered some of the people whom I thought could get me some contributions. In due course, three Ansaldo managers attended a Hinchey for Congress fund-raiser in New York City, which had been specifically organized to raise money from the independent power industry. The three Ansaldo people donated $1,000 each. The fund-raiser was well attended, and we generated many thousands of dollars for the campaign. Hinchey was there and made a speech supportive of independent power. I was proud of the effort and thought this was the last I'd ever hear about it.

It must be stated again that my solicitation of funds from people I did business with was entirely legal. There is nothing illegal about pitching a prospective donor when a candidate is good for that person's business. The entire campaign finance system may be undemocratic in the long run and ethically offensive as well, but until it is changed, this will continue to be the way most campaigns raise money.

20

A Relationship Goes Sour

In describing Besicorp's power development business, I've noted the successes of the company's relationship with Ansaldo. They were deep-pocket backers for Besicorp; despite Besicorp's limited financial capability, we were able to get some major projects off the ground by using Ansaldo's money.

Unfortunately, good things don't always last. Over the period from 1988 to 1994, the Ansaldo relationship changed from a dream into a nightmare. Through incompetent execution, Ansaldo blew their opportunity to establish a construction and engineering business in the United States. All five major jobs Ansaldo constructed for us were very late, grossly over budget, and far out of compliance with contractual specifications.

On each project, Ansaldo continued a pattern of running the construction budget out of capital (spending millions of dollars from our reserves), losing huge amounts of their own money, and throwing the final negotiations to an army of engineers and attorneys. They repeatedly strong-armed millions of dollars in concessions from us to cover up their incompetent work.

One day at an informal lunch over a glass of Italian red wine, Stefano Moretti confided to me that Ansaldo's construction subsidiary was papering over their losses on our jobs by showing them as "start-up" costs for their business. Ansaldo management in Italy was being deceived while we were being screwed.

Things got so bad that we became quite desperate. Ansaldo was bleeding our projects, and in the development business, we didn't make money unless our projects performed up to specification and were built on or near budget. Hal Kamine and I consulted with our attorneys and decided that we had to go for broke before we went broke! It was time to take some risk in an attempt to correct the situation.

On March 16, 1994 I wrote a letter to Mr. Lucia Clavarola, Ansaldo's CEO in Italy. I told him that his people in America were losing tens of millions of dollars for Ansaldo while costing us a fortune. The letter fingered Ansaldo's senior construction executive, Vincent Nardi, by name. I signed the letter myself because Hal Kamine dealt with Ansaldo day-to-day; in signing it, I voluntarily became the sacrificial lamb.

Mr. Clavarola formally rejected my letter, a matter of protocol that was not unexpected, but Ansaldo subsequently made big changes in its project management team. Many more Italians arrived and construction greatly accelerated. Neither Stefano Moretti nor Vincent Nardi lost their jobs, but they probably lost face in the company. Unfortunately, the price was that the close relationship we had forged was forever damaged. I had burned bridges that could never be rebuilt.

21

Ansaldo Cuts a Deal

Forgive this gruesome imagery, but I have learned that a criminal case is like a metastasizing cancer; you never know where the next tumor is going to erupt. From the latter part of 1996 and through the early part of 1997, we experienced a relatively quiet period on the grand jury front. Then, as if out of nowhere, circumstances radically changed, and the momentum of the case turned against me.

From the time the subpoenas had arrived in May 1996, I never discussed the investigation with anyone at Ansaldo. I had no cause to, for I knew nothing wrong had been done. Even after Bill Brodsky learned from his friend at Skadden that Ansaldo had been subpoenaed, I still didn't talk to anyone at Ansaldo about the investigation. I was scrupulously following my attorney's advice on how to avoid a charge of obstruction of justice or witness tampering.

Then, on March 21, 1997 an article appeared in the New York Times reporting that Ansaldo North America, Inc. had pleaded guilty to making illegal campaign contributions to the 1992 Maurice Hinchey for Congress campaign. The article went on to report that Ansaldo had admitted that $40,000 in payments to Besicorp were disguised with phony invoices, and that Ansaldo reimbursed their own employees for $3,000 in campaign contributions using falsified expense accounts. The article further reported that Ansaldo stated they had made these payments and reimbursements at my behest. The government was quoted as noting that "the investigation is ongoing."

The pieces were falling into place. It appeared that Vincent Nardi had arranged to have Ansaldo's employees reimbursed for their contributions to the campaign by having them falsify expense vouchers and post their $1,000 donations as seminar fees. When the government investigated the allegations that had been made by Martin Enowitz, Ansaldo was caught red-handed in a campaign contribution fraud entirely of their own making.

This grotesque turn of events, in which Ansaldo pleaded guilty and gave testimony against me, didn't occur in a vacuum. The government was procuring testimony from wherever it could and tightening its web around me. It had snared Ansaldo, and once they were snared, they were offered an attractive deal for testimony against me.

Ansaldo was permitted to plead guilty to a single misdemeanor charge in a plea bargain agreement that didn't require a single person to appear in court. No individual was required to give sworn testimony to any facts in front of a judge. Their plea was entered by outside counsel in the name of Ansaldo North America, Inc., an inconsequential subsidiary that had no appreciable assets. After paying a fine, Ansaldo liquidated the subsidiary, and that was the end of the matter for them.

As opposed to what was to happen in my case, no individual was ever prosecuted, even though Ansaldo and their executives had committed deliberate crimes. Documents were intentionally falsified (which was not true in my case), and nondeductible political contributions were taken as deductible expense account charges. These offenses could have been prosecuted as felonies against the individual perpetrators, as well as against the parent company. But Ansaldo got off sweetly. All they were required to do was to turn on me, an easy decision in light of our deteriorated relationship.

Why would a company like Ansaldo take a plea at all if they really weren't guilty of the charges that were likely to be brought against them? What happened was easy for me to see. Ansaldo was caught in a flagrant document crime, and there was no defense to an obviously falsified expense account. All they could say to lighten their burden was "Michael Zinn told us to do it!"

And why, one might ask, would Ansaldo have sent three representatives to a fund-raiser with $3,000 in reimbursed campaign contributions if, as the government charged, we had organized an elaborate scheme by which Ansaldo funneled $40,000 into Besicorp to use for illegal campaign contributions? Why not just increase the amount to $43,000? Obviously because the scheme didn't exist, except as a figment of the imagination of an overzealous federal prosecutor. But I never got to ask that question in front of a jury.

I could picture it. The Skadden attorneys, suddenly confronted with damning evidence of Ansaldo's crimes, go to the government and say their client wants a deal. "What can you tell us about Michael Zinn," the government asks. "What would you like to know?" the lawyers, in effect, respond. These are the very same lawyers that originally confirmed my account of Besicorp's relationship with Ansaldo. I ran my mental movie of what must have happened next: A Skadden lawyer flies to Italy and meets with the Italian bosses. He explains what is at stake, saying something like this:

"If Ansaldo is convicted of a felony, the entire company, and all of your subsidiaries in the United States can be 'debarred' from doing business with the United States government. That can potentially cost your company hundreds of millions in business for several years. The people involved can also be prosecuted for felonies. But what a deal we've negotiated for you! Just a simple guilty plea to a single misdemeanor and an inconsequential fine, less than the legal fees would have been."

The old men look around the table at each other "Bene! Ottima idea. Procediamo così." Even now, I can't get it out of my mind.

22

UNCHARTED WATERS

E ven after the Ansaldo plea, I still insisted to my lawyers that we could discredit the government's case. I was sure we could prove that Ansaldo was lying to protect themselves. But how many other hostile witnesses would I have to discredit to get acquitted of all charges? We still didn't even know what charges I'd be indicted on.

It was now one year after the federal agents had first appeared at my door, and it was apparent that the government was attempting to build a major case against me. They had subpoenaed my personal accountant and had him appear for an "interview," grilling him under lights over the details in my personal tax returns. They scrutinized every transaction I had reported, including the exercise of stock options and the filing of forms with the government declaring valuations. They seemed determined to fish up as many things as possible to charge me with before they finally dropped the other shoe.

After his "interview," my accountant characterized the agents as "frothing at the mouth." They were so hot on getting me that they had lost all objectivity, it seemed. My accountant told them, that I routinely give him my financial records and tell him to prepare my tax returns. He then meets with Besicorp's auditors and the company's attorneys as required, and then determines what entries to make. He told them that I never tell him what to do, and that when he presents me with my completed tax return, I simply sign it and write a check. He even told them what I've often said to him: that I view paying taxes as a function of making money, and that I feel fortunate that I am able to make money and have to pay taxes. The IRS people who were doing the questioning at this point apparently just couldn't believe that I wasn't a tax cheat. They clearly were determined to get me on a tax charge anyway.

On March 24, 1997, Besicorp and I both received what is called a "target letter," an official declaration that we were the target of a grand jury investigation (as if we didn't know). One full year had passed since the agents first came to my door. An indictment was imminent.

Bill Brodsky was still encouraging me to plea-bargain. He returned to his refrain that I would get a better deal before the indictment. But I still said NO.

Sometime during the spring of 1997, when the federal investigation was in full swing, I'd had the occasion to meet alone with Maurice Hinchey's wife, Ilene. We had run into each other accidentally and resolved to meet for a cup of coffee just to share a conversation. She was always a sweetheart, and I bore her no ill will. I was sure her heart was bleeding for what I was going through.

We met in a nearby Pizza Hut and reminisced about the leeches that had surrounded Maurice, recalling how manipulative they were. We mused about our naiveté concerning the dangers of the political process. Over a cup of coffee, we did more than a little commiserating. I could see that she was in pain watching me go through such a horrible experience as a result of my good-natured help for her husband.

We didn't meet to discuss the case. Both of us knew there was nothing either of us could do but let it run its course. But during our conversation, we ended up discussing more than I'd expected, and I was floored by what Ilene told me.

Sometime in September of 1992, when the campaign was regularly meeting at Besicorp's conference room, she was in uptown Kingston, she said, and ran into Connie Goffredi, the campaign manager. Connie had said that the campaign had better rent some space, because it was illegal to run it out of Besicorp's office. They rented a storefront, though they'd never rented an office.

"Why didn't anybody tell me?" I asked Ilene. "How come they kept meeting in Besicorp's office, knowing it was illegal?" Ilene just shrugged. I asked her to tell Maurice about how his people were screwing me in the testimony we'd been learning about, and that maybe he could get them to come clean. But this was to be of no avail.

Ilene and I left each other knowing that more sadness was coming my way. She would never purposely hurt me, I knew. But that was not true of others in the Hinchey camp.

It wasn't until the Spring of 1993, months after Hinchey was in Washington, that Dave Lenefsky told me the campaign should have been paying for the use of Besicorp space and the refreshments we served there for the 1992 campaign. We casually discussed a rate so the payments could be made retrospectively and agreed upon charging $50.00 per meeting. Lenefsky told me that the payments needed to be made only from Election Day forward.

"What about prior to the election, during the campaign?" I asked. Lenefsky told me not to worry about it, that Maurice wasn't a congressman then. No mention was made about the value of secretarial or administrative support.

It's all so clear in hindsight. Lenefsky analyzed the retroactive obligation to pay for the use of Besicorp's conference room without bothering with the other in-kind support Besicorp provided; either he assumed that they could get away with it or he was grossly incompetent. At the very least, he failed to foresee a relentless investigation that would sift through my entire life with a finetooth comb. The use of Besicorp's space is only a micro-issue in the overall case, but it exemplifies the way they used Besicorp—and me. By pretending to be very concerned about legality, yet not informing me of what they knew the law to be, they lulled me into complacency. The result was that an isolated and innocent act would be prosecuted as part of an alleged pattern of intentional illegality.

23

In Judge Bradley's Courtroom

While the criminal case was being developed, the Lichtenberg lawsuit continued to wind on. After the Special Litigation Committee of the Besicorp board rendered its report recommending that the Lichtenberg case be dismissed, Jim McCabe renewed motions that were pending before Judge Bradley seeking to dismiss the case. Discovery proceedings were complete, and there was a huge factual record to satisfy Judge Bradley that the plaintiffs had not been denied any opportunity to present evidence that might sway his mind.

We had endured an enormous drain on our time and money in an effort to comply with Bradley's ordered discovery. More than 100,000 documents had been produced to Lichtenberg's attorneys, and twenty-one days had been spent on actual depositions. Finally, after a year, their discovery process was over. But by the time Besicorp was able to renew its motion to dismiss, the criminal investigation of the company was well under way.

In March 1997, we had occasion to appear in Judge Bradley's court to argue Besicorp's renewed motion to dismiss the Lichtenberg lawsuit. The regional media had been playing up the federal investigation as a major story, and we had no idea what impact it might have on Judge Bradley's attitude towards me. But I was hopeful that he would not be negatively influenced by the charges in the press; after all, it was in his very courtroom that Lichtenberg's lawyers had first raised the Hinchey campaign allegations.

~

In the quiet of Judge Bradley's courtroom, the three independent Besicorp directors stood close to me. They intended to show Judge Bradley that while the lawyers fought, they stood behind their SLC findings and behind me as well. No matter what scandalous accusations were being made or what stories were appearing in the newspapers, they were steadfast. Judge Bradley questioned the attorneys sharply during their oral arguments. Jim McCabe reviewed the findings and the law. He made much of Lichtenberg's own proxy submissions, where he'd proposed his own definition of the qualifications for independent directors; McCabe made the point that each Besicorp director more than met Lichtenberg's own qualifications for independence. When Lichtenberg's attorney, Bernard Persky, replied to McCabe, he tried to distance himself from Lichtenberg's damaging proxy submissions by claiming that Lichtenberg had prepared his submissions without the benefit of legal counsel, arguing that he should not be held responsible for them. Judge Bradley, incredulous, turned on Persky and asked, if he didn't want to be held to those statements, what about Mr. Lichtenberg? A moment later he said he was only kidding. But we knew he wasn't. We left the court that day to await Judge Bradley's decision. I was hopeful that he was as wise as his behavior seemed to indicate. My world was coming apart, and I needed something positive to happen at this point in my legally intensive existence.

24

DEATH AND DYING

My mom passed on March 28, 1997. Three days later, the evening after she was buried, a small crowd assembled at my house for Shiva services, the Jewish mourning period at the home of a bereaved person. I felt that the spirit of my mother had not yet departed, and that she was watching everything.

In dealing with the stress of keeping my family on an even keel and also with my mom's long decline and now her passing, the pressure had been getting to me. I finally decided to authorize Brodsky to meet with Assistant U.S. Attorney Elliot Jacobson to see if a reasonable deal could be cut. My bottom line was that if I entered a guilty plea, Jacobson had to agree not to seek my imprisonment.

Bill Brodsky and Doug Lobel met that very day with Jacobson. They phoned me on a conference call that began at around 6:45 p.m. to report bad news: Jacobson wanted me in jail. He would not agree to a misdemeanor plea. I caught my breath. Brodsky asked me if he could go forward and negotiate anyway to find out the best terms I could get in a plea bargain. I said that I would rather go to trial and declare my innocence, even if I had to go to jail at the end.

Bill admonished me again, and strongly, that the best time to negotiate a plea bargain is before the indictment comes down, otherwise, he said, I could be facing years in jail. After the indictment, the charges would be set in stone, and the information in the indictment would be part of the record. Now there was still at least some leeway. But I could not do it. I could not bring myself to look at the mistakes I'd made as criminal acts.

After I put down the phone, I fell into Valerie's arms, wailing and crying, and then into the arms of my brother and sister-in-law. We locked ourselves into the bedroom and we all cried together, hugging each other. I told them what I just heard from Brodsky and Lobel, and we hugged and cried some more. It was terrifying not to know what was ahead.

We were in such pain over our mother's death that we couldn't make sense out of what was happening, anyway. While we should have been praying and sharing the consolation of our friends and family, we were watching my life go down the tubes. Even after all this time, it all seemed incomprehensible.

The rabbi had arrived, and all of our friends were waiting for us. We finally emerged and sat in a circle, and the rabbi conducted a memorial service for my mother. I was trying to keep my mind on my grief and my mourning, but I wasn't fully present; I knew that my mom was watching and that she understood. She knew how much I loved her.

After my mourning period and some healing from my mother's passing, I gradually re-entered the business world and directed my attention towards preparing the defense.

I kept updating my "bible," the issue-by-issue, witness-by-witness account of the events of 1992. But the more I learned about the process of presenting information at trial, the more concerned I became about how difficult it would be to present this complicated story in a logical manner that could be understood in the way it had actually happened. Brodsky told me that much of the evidence and testimony I wanted to present might not be admissible. The prosecutor could present virtually anything he wanted, but our defense was far more limited by the rules of evidence, by hearsay, by the need to overcome challenges by the prosecution on relevance, and by the potential impatience of the judge; the judge, whose good will we relied upon, could easily become bored or exasperated with the degree to which our defense depended upon laying out background information. He could stop us in our tracks at any time, Brodsky explained.

He tried to assure me that by the end of the trial all the necessary information would somehow get in. But we would not be able to recall witnesses to present our case in a sequential manner. Each item of testimony that brought out a small shard of information had to be woven together in the closing arguments. We wouldn't even be able to gain access to the government's files until perhaps the day before trial! This was not at all encouraging, for I knew how complicated it was to tell the story of the events of 1992. Bill warned me again that if the judge thought we had a defense that lacked credibility, he would sentence me harshly.

We could try to "nullify" the jury—that is, try to convince them not to convict me in spite of the evidence. To accomplish this we would have to badly damage the credibility of prosecution witnesses, but attempting to do that would be perilous. We would have to attack the witnesses aggressively in order to demonstrate their personal hostility and show that they were motivated to see me convicted. But if, at the end of the day, the judge believed that I had tried to put one over on the jury and they convicted me anyway, he could penalize me severely in sentencing.

I told my attorneys that I would not lie. If that meant saying that I did something that was in hindsight illegal, I would at least be able to say, truthfully, that I didn't know it to be illegal at the time. I had sought and received what I believed to be informed legal advice from two attorneys, and I believed that the political professionals in the campaign were watching out to keep the process legal. Nevertheless the fantasy that I could face down the power of the U.S. government and be acquitted at trial was growing increasingly difficult to maintain.

25

INDICTED!

The indictment was handed down on May 15, 1997. It was as bad as we expected. It charged both Besicorp and me with five felony counts against the United States of America.

The prosecutor had had many options regarding how to charge my "crimes." A prosecutor can charge identical sets of facts as either misdemeanors or as felonies; there are even Class A, B, and C felonies, with C being the least serious. Assistant U.S. Attorney Elliot Jacobson charged my case very severely: five Class B felony counts of conspiracy.

The preamble named the parties involved—namely me, Besicorp, Ansaldo, and then Assemblyman Maurice Hinchey, recited a few words about the campaign finance statutes, and then mentioned the Federal Election Commission as the allegedly injured agency of the U.S. government. The indictment then listed all the ways that the law was allegedly broken: the supposedly "secret" payments from Ansaldo to Besicorp totaling $40,000; and the "scheme" by which I'd supposedly asked Ansaldo to reimburse their own employees another $3,000. Next came the list of every Hinchey campaign contribution made by anyone related to Besicorp or to me, followed by a recitation of the "bonus, advance, or raise" that the government alleged was paid as an illegal reimbursement.

The reason there were five felony counts was that the "conspiracy" charge generated a separate count for each of the monthly FEC filings Hinchey made during the campaign. The indictment concluded with the following statement:

> On or about the dates set forth below, in the Northern District of New York and elsewhere, Michael F. Zinn and Besicorp, the defendants, in a matter within a department and agency of the United States, to wit, the FEC, unlawfully, knowingly, and willfully did falsify, conceal,

and cover up by trick, scheme, and device material facts and make false, fictitious, and fraudulent statements and representations, and make and use false writings and documents knowing the same to contain false, fictitious, and fraudulent statements and entries, to wit, the defendants Michael F. Zinn and Besicorp aided and abetted the creation and submission to the FEC of false FEC Forms 3.

Election law and campaign finance violations are routinely disposed of in civil proceedings brought by the Federal Election Commission ("FEC"). In the course of research performed by my attorneys, we catalogued dozens of FEC enforcement actions where far more egregious cases were disposed of without any criminal action being brought at all. The FEC has the power to levy fines and obtain consent decrees. We had received a subpoena from the FEC, and our attorneys tried to get Jacobson to back off the criminal investigation and the let the FEC handle it, but Jacobson would have none of it. Fortunately, the FEC agreed to hold their investigation in abeyance pending resolution of the criminal case; otherwise, I would have been fighting with them at the same time I was fighting off a criminal charge.

The underlying crime of filing a false campaign finance report with the Federal Election Commission is a misdemeanor. But instead of being charged with the "crime" that supposedly occurred, I was charged with five felony crimes, conspiracy charges, that carried a statutory maximum twenty-five-year prison term. I was in danger of serving twenty-five years for having raised a total of $27,000 for a political campaign.

Our review and presentation of comparative sentences and dispositions from other election law prosecutions showed that virtually all of the cases were charged by the government as misdemeanors. Elliot Jacobson had cobbled up conspiracy charges so he could make my "crimes" into multiple felonies.

Despite the severity of the charges, Bill Brodsky was confident that the Federal judge would not want me to serve time. At this stage in the case, with the indictment still fresh, our main concern was winning at trial. Now I was discovering the combination of factors that made going to trial a very risky option.

First, in order to combat organized crime and drug dealing, the government has greatly strengthened the conspiracy statutes over the years. The underlying reasons make sense. It's a well-known fact that organized crime figures act through others to run crime syndicates. They set up their organizations to insulate themselves: you don't see "the Godfather" beating up a storekeeper for overdue protection money, but by using information gained through wiretaps and informers, the tough conspiracy statutes allow the government to prosecute "the Godfather" for orchestrating the crimes. The law, however, does not specify that organized crime and drug dealers should be the only targets for conspiracy prosecution, so the conspiracy charge has become a tool whereby prosecutors hungry for convictions can indict people in the hope of extracting "voluntary" plea-bargain convictions.

Second, in response to the desire not to appear "soft on crime," legislatures have created "sentencing guidelines" and "mandatory sentencing" for many crimes. If a person with no previous record of criminal behavior is convicted of a serious felony, the judge may not have the option of handing down an appropriately lenient sentence in the light of the defendant's ignorance of the law or otherwise impeccable character. Sentencing is thereby taken out of the hands of the judge and delivered over to the prosecutor in his selection of which level of crime to charge.

Third, because of overcrowded court schedules, judges themselves often favor plea-bargaining over going to trial, so defendants are further encouraged to plead guilty to reduced charges in an effort to accelerate the judicial process. Most people charged with a crime for the first time are astonished to learn this, as I was.

All these factors made the risk of going to trial intolerable and, in essence, combined to deny me the right to trial by jury. Because the charges were so out of proportion in relation to the actual offense, I faced the prospect of a long jail term on a derivative crime. That's why Bill Brodsky wanted me to plea-bargain, but despite all of the above, I was still not yet ready to surrender that precious right.

26

Staying in Control

A fter the indictment was handed down, retaining control of Besicorp became increasingly difficult. Even though it had been expected, the event triggered an avalanche of problems. There was never a question of my actual voting control of the company, but the board was nervous. I had to balance my own needs against the feelings and concerns of others, while making sure the company remained effective in business. For instance, in deference to the independent directors, I routinely went the extra mile to insure the independence of the critical deliberations of the independent board members. That approach began during the Special Litigation Committee's tenure in dealing with the Lichtenberg shareholder suit. Continuing that policy during the criminal case proved that the "cure" was worse then the "disease," because isolating me from the board produced negative consequences for both the business and the joint defense of the criminal case.

In an attempt to protect the company from more shareholder suits, Besicorp's outside counsel imposed artificial barriers between the board members and me. It was an admirable, if elusive, goal, but in this difficult time, those unnecessary barriers created damaging paralysis at the board.

I didn't realize at the time where it might lead. Because I needed to make the board members feel good, just to keep the board on an even keel, I made the grave error of confusing my confidence in each director's personal integrity with confidence in their collective wisdom and competence as a group. I never gave sufficient consideration to the corrosive, demoralizing effect of long-term litigation, the pressure employed by the predatory shareholders, and the long-pending criminal case.

∼

Until the indictment was handed down, I had been successful in keeping the company on a relatively even keel. Despite the debilitating investigation, my own confidence, determination, and positive spirit kept the people around me optimistic and effective. Many marveled at how well I was weathering the storm, but storms of even greater intensity still lay ahead. Even after the bombshell of the Ansaldo plea bargain, I maintained my innocence and was determined to go to trial and be vindicated.

After the indictment, we implemented the plans we had made for that eventuality. The first step was a meeting with corporate counsel to assess the legal position of the board and determine what actions should be taken with respect to my executive and board positions.

A board meeting was scheduled for April 17, 1997 at the offices of Kelley, Drye, & Warren (KDW). For a week after the indictment, and up to the day of that Board meeting, Alan Epstein, the KDW partner in charge of our representation, did not return my numerous phone calls. This made me angry and nervous and was a sign of the danger to come.

∽

On the day of the meeting, the board assembled at KDW. Bill Brodsky was in attendance as my personal attorney, and several other KDW attorneys were there as well, including Doug Lobel, who represented Besicorp in the criminal case.

The meeting began with Epstein's pronouncement of the ground rules. After an initial briefing, the board was to be advised by a senior attorney who had no prior connection with any Besicorp transactions or people, and all other KDW attorneys would be removed from the matter. That attorney was to give the board "independent" advice, free of influence. Alan Epstein had decided that his first priority was to eliminate all possible conflicts of interest within the law firm.

After listening to Epstein present the overview, Bill Brodsky and I were asked to leave the room. Doug Lobel briefed the remainder of the board on the status of the case, and then departed from the meeting, leaving the board alone with the new attorney, who in fact didn't know anything about the situation or anyone involved. He gave the board a technical picture of how to proceed with the deliberation process and then also left.

The board was therefore severed from every attorney with any background that could be useful to the company at this time of crisis. To make matters worse, the attorney that Epstein provided gave the board only superficial advice and then abandoned them to their own confusion.

❧

Hours passed while Bill Brodsky and I cooled our heels in an empty office. In mid-afternoon, we finally were called in to meet with the board members, whose meeting was still in session: Steve Eisenberg, my-right hand man, Besicorp's Executive Vice President; Harold Harris, my long-standing mentor; Gerald Habib, and Richard Rosen. They asked my opinion as to what should be done. The company needed strong, positive leadership to get through the next period, and I knew I was the only one who could keep it together and maintain the coordinated defense required to win the criminal case at trial. I told the board that I did not think it was necessary to do anything, that I was perfectly capable of continuing as CEO while we took the joint defense to trial. After all, both the company and I were indicted, and we jointly proclaimed our innocence.

I left the room again, and the board deliberated once more. We reconvened shortly thereafter, and the board members dropped their decision on me as gently as they could.

In light of the legal pressure they were under, they said they had decided that they had to do something to show that they were independent of me. They didn't want to hurt me, they said, but they needed to act in a way that looked like they were willing to. They asked me to step down from the board and to resign my executive officer positions. They recognized that they needed me to run the business, they said, so I could keep my base salary and stay involved in the major deals. I could keep my office and car, but I would have to stay in the background. They said that it was for my own good and for the good of the company. The board would now take a more active role in the business, they said, and Steve Eisenberg would be the new president.

After painful discussions with Bill Brodsky, I accepted the board's decision. He felt that I had to make some concession under the circumstances, so I reluctantly agreed. We documented the agreement in outline form and signed a piece of paper that seemed to codify it.

I made a serious mistake by going far beyond what I was legally required to do; in absenting myself entirely from the board's deliberations concerning the criminal case, I allowed the board to deteriorate into chaos. All this was orchestrated on "advice of counsel," just to be able to tell a judge in a lawsuit that had yet to be filed that I hadn't dominated the board. Several of the Kelley, Drye attorneys who had been dealing with Besicorp over a period of years later told me that the first priority should have been to hold the company together and minimize the damage from the criminal prosecution.

Over the next week, I watched as things deteriorated. I was amazed by how quickly the edges frayed. The board meetings and conference calls degenerated into bickering and became paralyzed. The board seemed unable to execute the simple act of writing and approving a press release about the change in management. They also wasted a phenomenal amount of time.

To cap it off, the board proclaimed that they would run Besicorp's legal defense by committee, even though I was the central defendant in the government's case against both the corporation and myself. An unprepared and ill-informed board was now in control of the company's legal case.

According to the instructions that Alan Epstein had given the board, I wasn't supposed to talk to the board members about the legal case, even though Besicorp and I were subject to a joint defense agreement. Within this weird architecture, I could not talk directly to Doug Lobel, Besicorp's defense counsel, even though he was co-counsel with Bill Brodsky for the joint defense, I was the main witness, and I had been talking to him regularly up to that point. I was supposed to communicate with Lobel only through Brodsky, my personal attorney.

With all these cumbersome constraints, I was supposed to develop and present a coordinated defense for both the company and for myself.

Compounding the corporate paralysis that the legal problems created at the board, all of the Kelly Drye attorneys were instructed not to discuss the case with the board or with me.

Steve Eisenberg, who had been my right hand man and had made lots of money working with me, began to edge me aside. He began letting me know that he was "uncomfortable" with my presence in the building. He told me that he had a hard time functioning as "president" with me lingering around, and that it would be better for everyone if I spent as much time away from the building as possible. "What about the agreement that I can keep my office?" I asked. "What about my secretarial support? What about my access to the people in Besicorp who are necessary for me to see so I can work on my defense?" Steve gave me the cold shoulder and acted as though he thought that he would be fulfilling the company's agreement if he didn't order my personal belongings to be put in boxes and left on the roadside. This was not what I had in mind, and I had no intention of going along.

After reviewing the document the board members signed concerning my resignation, Besicorp's outside counsel informed the board that the "agreement" was not binding because it was signed only by the individual directors and not by the corporation itself. They recommended that we sign a revised agreement, and I jumped on the opportunity to tell the board members that not only was I not bound by the current agreement, but I was not going to sign a revision.

During several phone calls and meetings, I made my position clear and firm. I was not going to lose more valuable time. In one intense encounter, I said, "I just wasted an entire week. If we have a trial in July, you have cost me one-twelfth of the available time to prepare for it. I will not accept this burden. You all have taken an already difficult situation and made it impossible. So I have made a decision to withdraw my offer of resignation. The deal is off."

Some of the board members felt that I was morally committed to go through with my resignation. But I just didn't care what they thought at that point. There was no way I was going to let them "experiment" with management by committee to see if they could handle it.

～

Now we were meeting or having telephone conferences almost every day, and it was getting ridiculous. This process had to be resolved. Steve Eisenberg and Gerry Habib collaborated on a position paper that they were going to present to the board. We convened a meeting and I resolved to hold my tongue and let the process unfold. I didn't want to precipitate resignations by any of the board members, which could be very destructive, and it would be a delicate balancing act.

Richard Rosen came to the board meeting armed with his own position paper supporting my decision not to resign and noting his observation of current paralysis and weak leadership. The board agreed that Richard should read his paper first; he did. Then Gerry Habib read the position paper he had drafted with Steve Eisenberg. My blood was starting to boil; the letter demanded my resignation and stated that I hadn't given the new structure "enough time." Steve and Gerry were presumptuous enough to have added signature lines for all of the directors (except me).

After hearing their position, I went around the table, asking each of them their intentions. "Steve, are you prepared to sign that letter now?" I asked. "Yes," he answered. "Gerry, are you prepared to sign that letter now?" "Yes," he answered. "And what about you, Harold?" I knew where Richard stood. Harold said, "I want to hear first what you have to say before I make up my mind." Harold was long on years, but longer on spunk. He still had an open mind. I turned to Mike Daley, the CFO, who was not a board member, but whose opinion the board valued. He answered in a diplomatic manner designed to keep peace with as many people as possible: "It could have worked the other way, but it's obvious now that it isn't going to work."

It was my turn, and I turned on my flame-thrower. "I have just experienced the worst week of my life. A year of being investigated followed by an indictment was nothing compared to the agony of dealing with this board's paralysis. There might be only eleven weeks left before trial, and you, Steve, you say you'll be president? And you say you can't do it unless I'm out of the building. Well, what hired president would tell the majority owner of a corporation to get out of the building? And you, board members, what about leadership for the company? This company needs to be led through its difficulty. You can't get Besicorp through this as a committee. I have more leadership capability with both hands tied behind my back, blindfolded, then all of you could muster together. If you want me out, you will have to fire me! But be prepared for litigation. If I am at war with everyone else, I will go to war with you too. Be prepared for the fight of your lives."

Gerry Habib was amazed. "Are you threatening us?" he asked.

I said, as calmly as possible, "Yes." Then I left the room for a much-needed break and to let the other board members deliberate.

On my return, the room had taken on a more subdued mood, and they asked me to sit down. The board asked me to continue in my role as CEO and President.

Over the next few weeks things slowly returned to a state of semi-normalcy in my dealings with the board. Counsel-imposed barriers to communication still hobbled us, and we lurched our way through spring and into summer. The board members now knew not to bring up the subject of resignation again, at least until we knew what the outcome of the criminal case was going to be.

27

VENUE DECISIONS

Once the indictment was handed down, all the anticipation and planning regarding the case went out the window. We were in a new realm. The top of the pressure cooker was screwed on tight, and the flame was turned up to a new level and could blow the top off at any time. Outwardly, I continued to maintain my personal calm. Dealing with my life required as much of an appearance of normalcy as possible.

I was still unwilling to accept that I could be convicted at trial, even though the odds had certainly shifted. I had spent months preparing my detailed "bible" of the defense. Each anticipated allegation, fact, and witness was now the subject of a detailed memorandum. But my personal determination was still very strong: I had been misled, I had acted without criminal intent, and I was sure I could demonstrate that to a jury. But It was getting more difficult to keep all the balls in the air at the same time.

Bill Brodsky tried to maintain a dialogue of a sort with Assistant U.S. Attorney Jacobson, trying to feel him out and soften him up, all to no avail. One day Bill reported to me that, out of the blue, Jacobson had called to tell him that he was planning to bring a supplemental indictment on tax charges, and by the way, would I consent to being indicted on tax charges in the Southern District of New York?

I was shocked! What did taxes have to do with this case? Bill explained that it seemed that the IRS had played a big role in the investigation, and they wanted a piece of the action. I recalled that one of the two agents that had come to my door was an IRS Criminal Enforcement Division agent. It seems that the political campaign contribution charge had an unintended but very serious consequence: a tax law violation. If, as alleged, people were given bonuses with which they made illegal campaign contributions, then according to the government's theory, Besicorp took an improper tax deduction for the bonus. But why would Jacobson need my consent to indict Besicorp or me on a tax-related criminal charge? It turned out that venue—the legal term for the proper jurisdiction where a case is to be brought and tried—all of a sudden became an important factor in our pre-trial strategy deliberations.

The government "lacked venue" to bring tax charges in the Southern District of New York (a federal judicial district). One of the federal courts for this district was in White Plains, a suburb of New York City. That was where Jacobson's office was located and where the grand jury hearing Jacobson's case was based. Besicorp was located in the Northern District of New York, and Besicorp paid its federal taxes into a tax district in Massachusetts. Although Besicorp was not in the Southern District, a sufficient part of the activities involved in the alleged campaign crimes had taken place in the Southern District for venue to not be an issue for the government. But that was not the case with respect to tax filings. In order to charge Besicorp or me with tax fraud, Jacobson would either have to take the entire case in front of a grand jury convened in the Northern District, or bring two separate cases.

Now a new period of anxiety began over how to deal with venue. This was all still based upon the assumption that I was going to plead NOT GUILTY and the case was going to trial. We had the option of playing "chicken" with Jacobson: If we simply refused to consent to venue for tax charges in the Southern District, he could proceed in the Southern District without tax charges at all. That would be a plus. If he went to Albany, where the Federal Court for the Northern District was located, and presented the entire case to a grand jury there, it would be an inconvenience to him; he would be away from his home turf and possibly would be forced to spend several weeks at trial without the immediate support of his staff and without the home-court advantage—that was also a plus. But offsetting these advantages were some very significant risks. If we went to trial in the Southern District on only the campaign finance violation indictment, Jacobson still could bring the tax charge to the Northern District of New York. He could bring this parallel action in the Northern District whether or not he lost at the first trial. In either case, we could face the prospect of having two trials. All of our surprise defenses and evidence would have been exposed in the first trial, significantly compromising our defense in the second one. If we were faced with this circumstance, we would make a motion to consolidate the two trials, which Jacobson would oppose. We might successfully force Jacobson into one trial in the Northern District, and then again, the judge might not grant our motion, and our gamble would have backfired. We would be stuck with two trials. Stranger things have happened in the legal system.

In making the venue decision, we also had to take into account the demographics of the judicial district. The jury pool would have very different characteristics and political perspectives in Albany as opposed to White Plains.

I wanted to be tried in the Northern District. Jacobson would lose his advantage, and I felt an Albany jury would be more sympathetic to me than a jury from White Plains, a town in the Westchester suburbs of New York City. I wanted the jury to understand me as an upstate New Yorker, a self-made entrepreneur who'd started in a garage and built a successful business that provided employment to the people of upstate New York. My defense would show how a slick suburban financial executive was trying to squeeze millions of dollars in stock out of Besicorp and was willing to destroy its CEO to get the money. A major Italian corporation had gotten their own officers off the hook by falsely implicating me, and I thought an upstate jury would be especially concerned that New York City corporate raiders had been orchestrating a campaign to bring the government down on me.

To assist in trial preparation, we hired Julie Blackman, a forensic psychologist jury consultant, and Bill Brodsky asked her to take a look at the venue issue. Her view was that the upstate New York jury pool would not necessarily be drawn from the area around Albany, the state capital, and that the case might not actually be tried there: it could be tried in Syracuse or in Binghamton, both upstate New York cities with populations far less educated than in the regions near the state capital.

Julie also advised me that I was misjudging how the jurors might see me. It was her opinion that by the time we got to plead our case, the prosecutor would have presented me as a fat-cat corporate CEO looking to buy a congressman. That was not how I pictured myself, but I had to reckon with the fact that despite my self-image, I was a wealthy, successful CEO of an AMEX company that had become involved in politics as a financier. Julie also said that if the trial were held in the Northern District of New York, we would undoubtedly draw rural jurors who might not necessarily relate to my New York City Jewish roots. I hadn't even thought about that!

I also had to decide whether being tried in the state capital was such a good idea. Hinchey had served in the New York State Assembly for seventeen years before going to Congress. He was well known and probably well regarded in Albany: a Democratic juror could be angry with me for hurting him, and a Republican juror might be angry because I helped a Democrat. Perhaps Albany wasn't such a good idea after all.

But the clincher was the issue of jury diversity. Julie explained that what we needed, as a fallback position, was a hung jury. That would come about only if the jury were comprised of disparate religious and ethnic groups with diverse educational backgrounds. Julie's research indicated that a White Plains jury would probably have more racial diversity, more religious diversity, and a higher level of education. We were much more likely to get a hung jury with the White Plains jurors than with jurors from Albany.

In hindsight, I should have followed my instincts to bring the case into upstate New York, but I didn't. At that point, I was still intending to go to trial. But as part of my eventual plea-bargain, I had to waive my right to object to venue so that a tax charge could be brought in White Plains. When jury demographics were no longer an issue, the choice of venue proved to be a terrible mistake. According to Bill Brodsky, I had drawn a tough judge. I still harbored the fantasy that I would rather go to jail for longer and be able to declare my innocence to the end rather than admit to "crimes" I contested had never even taken place. Six months in jail would be a disaster, I said to Brodsky, so who cared whether it was twelve or eighteen months? JAIL was JAIL!

The first time I encountered Judge Charles Brieant was at my arraignment, immediately after the indictment was handed down. He was an imposing figure—burly, bald, and bespectacled, with a handlebar mustache. In legal circles, he was reputed to have fashioned himself after Teddy Roosevelt, as a "rough rider" type—strong, controlling, and intolerant of any BS in his courtroom.

He sharpened his talons on our adversary, Elliot Jacobson, and it was encouraging to see that there was no love between them. Judge Brieant exclaimed from the bench, "What are you doing here with a case from 1992? That's five years ago." Jacobson's voice went up an octave, and he squirmed to answer. But Judge Brieant's slashing eventually turned on me. Perhaps if we had made a different decision on venue I would have had a more lenient judge, but there's no crying over spilled milk in this deadly serious game.

28

SUCCUMBING TO THE PRESSURE

The government had based its prosecution case on the testimony of Martin Enowitz, a man who stood to make millions from my incarceration. The government had bought Ansaldo's testimony with a sweetheart corporate plea-bargain, and had lined up every adversary they could find to testify against me. Even the most glaring bias on the part of the government's witnesses didn't matter to the prosecutor. Almost all defendants indicted by the US Government cave in and plea-bargain before trial , so the credibility of Jacobson's theories and witnesses would, in all likelihood, never be tested.

I was aware that I had certainly done something, but what it was I still could not quite understand, and I still felt that none of the acts would ever have risen to the level of a criminal prosecution if it weren't for the instigation of the people who wanted to remove me from Besicorp.

Julie Blackman's intelligence and compassion were powerful influences on me. She had read all my case notes, and we met with the attorneys for a full briefing on the case. I gave a narrative presentation of the defense strategy as I saw it. I laid out the bonus and compensation histories of the donors, the history of my financial support of my parents, and the whole story of the campaign, and I asked for her learned opinion.

Julie deliberated carefully. In a compassionate way, she told me that my defense was vulnerable simply on the basis of its complexity. No matter how we presented it, the hostile forces at work were not likely to be visible to a jury. Neither my generosity nor my aggressive personality in business were going to be understood or appreciated by a jury of ordinary people. And the level of my financial support for my parents was incredible, she said. That might be unbelievable to a jury as well, even with the evidence to back it up.

Julie recommended that I plea-bargain. She explained that jury nullification was a long-shot strategy. In order to "nullify" the jury, we had to convince them that, even if technically a law had been broken, I was innocent in spirit and a good person, and therefore should not be convicted of a crime.

Bill Brodsky told me, "Michael, a plea bargain is the best chance I have to keep you out of jail. But there are no guarantees. As a matter of policy the U.S. attorney in the Southern District will not agree to a non-jail disposition. The decision will be in the hands of the judge. But even if the judge, God forbid, wants you in jail, by plea-bargaining and avoiding a trial, at least you'll be facing the shortest possible sentence."

If I decided to plea-bargain, Besicorp would have to plead guilty as well. It was only my personal denial that would allow Besicorp to plead not guilty. As a target of investigation, the company was devoid of defenses if I decided to capitulate.

I recalled that Bill Brodsky had said on several occasions that it would be better to plea-bargain before the indictment was handed down, but I had refused. I myself had wanted to cooperate before the investigation had even gotten going and before the prosecutor had hardened his position. I had wanted to tell the prosecutor my side of the story before we spent a million dollars on a useless defense.

Brodksy had also argued that court agendas are so crowded that many judges are automatically prejudiced against any defendant who refuses to plea-bargain and insists on his or her right to trial-by-jury. A friend of his had once heard a senior judge remark about a defendant, "He was guilty of two crimes. One, he committed the offense, and two, he went to trial." Bill said, "Take a hint. Don't go to trial."

I trusted Julie deeply. I understood that the prosecutor was going to use my success against me. This U.S. Government that I had once revered and that is still held in high esteem by most of its poorly informed citizens, would spare nothing to portray me in the most negative light in order to secure the conviction they had worked so long and hard on now. The decision was still solely mine, however. In that horribly lonely moment, I bit the bullet. I told Bill Brodsky to get the best deal he could. I would plead guilty.

29

THE PLEA AGREEMENT

At that point, I had fought the government for sixteen months. I knew that Jacobson wanted me in jail. Keeping up my confidence was getting increasingly difficult, and only my stamina was propelling me forward. I had kept Besicorp moving and even maintained an outward semblance of normalcy in my life. Even with all that had been going on, I had still been able to occasionally fly my airplane, an activity which required considerable clarity and gave me a desperately needed diversion. But all that was over. Now I was exhausted and I consciously surrendered to the horrible necessity of pleading guilty to something I knew I didn't do in order to keep from sinking deeper into the abyss.

Bill began negotiating a plea-bargain agreement with the government. First, there would be the plea agreement itself, which set forth the contract terms of my "deal." Second, there would be the "allocution," or the admission of crimes.

The plea agreement had to address numerous technical issues, many of which were far beyond my experience. The indictment charged five felony counts of "conspiracy." The plea agreement reduced the number of felony counts to two, and changed their character in significant ways. As part of the deal, I would be required to allow the government to present a new statement of facts concerning the case. I had to agree not to contradict the government's statement, even if I knew it to be untrue and based on perjury. Bill Brodsky told me this was unimportant. He was wrong.

They changed the charges to one count of "Aiding and Abetting a False Statement" in connection with the reports submitted by the Hinchey campaign to the Federal Election Commission, and one tax-related count of "aiding and abetting a false corporate tax return" in connection with the Besicorp deductions for the bonuses. Brodsky told me that the change in charges didn't matter, because the sentencing guideline was comparable for both "conspiracy" and "aiding and abetting," and both were more severe than the tax charge in terms of sentencing risk.

The next step was preparing the plea "allocution," the written statement constituting an admission of guilt. I was prepared to plead guilty to having committed acts that violated the law, but I didn't want to plead to knowing that I was violating the law at the time those acts were committed. Bill said that I should be able to fall back on that statement at all points in the process, and beyond. We spent a lot of time fine-tuning the language in the plea allocution to get to the point where my statement would satisfy the minimum requirements for acceptance of responsibility and entry of a guilty plea and still meet my now limited goals. Brodsky said that ignorance of the law in performing an illegal act is not a defense, and that therefore acknowledging that the act itself was intentional should be a sufficient admission of responsibility to satisfy the requirements for a guilty plea.

Whatever mistakes I'd made, however harsh my treatment, whatever sentence I received, I needed to be able to say that I didn't know I was breaking the law when I committed the acts that were later charged as crimes. The implications were clear. I would carry the burden of a felony conviction, and I faced the additional risk of a prison sentence. But I could take some small solace in knowing that there is a difference between violating the law in a true criminal conspiracy and being trapped and squeezed to admit that aggressive but innocent acts were "crimes." I knew the difference then and I know the difference now. Yet I also understand that few people who haven't been through this experience would bother to draw the distinction.

Brodsky and I spent a lot of time preparing the allocution, but I had virtually no input into the terms of the plea agreement itself, which was negotiated lawyer to lawyer. Brodsky was trying to keep me out of prison, but only in retrospect did I learn that the die was apparently cast by the one-sided terms of the plea agreement: I was marched down the gangplank blindfolded, with my hands cuffed behind my back; the plea-bargain agreement virtually guaranteed that I would be pushed into the deep waters of the prison system.

I don't doubt that Bill Brodsky truly wanted to keep me out of jail, but his judgment was deeply flawed as to the effect of the concessions that were extracted from me in my "voluntary" plea-bargain agreement. The deal turned out to be worse than no deal at all.

If I had pleaded guilty to the indictment as it was originally handed down, there would have been no agreement with the government at all; I would go to the judge and enter a guilty plea without the consent of the prosecutor. The judge would have taken my plea, and I would have thrown myself on the mercy of the court. If I had done it this way, I would have been able to explain to the judge what happened, with the facts and figures to show that I did not commit the alleged offenses with criminal intent. My instinct was to go that way.

But Brodsky had warned me of the dangers of pleading guilty without an agreement with the government. The prosecutor could actually bring additional charges, even after I pleaded to the original indictment. The judge, he reminded me, would, in all likelihood be impatient with charges being added at that point, but even he couldn't stop the prosecutor from doing it. Jacobson could also have filed tax charges in the Northern District of New York, using my guilty plea in the Southern District as evidence to get a quick conviction. These were not at all pleasant scenarios, and they'd weighed heavily in my decision to allow Brodsky to negotiate the agreement.

I signed the plea-bargain agreement with a great sense of foreboding. One of the only "concessions" I had obtained from the government was an agreement not to bring any additional charges relating to my involvement in the Hinchey for Congress campaigns. This supposedly closed the investigation, at least with respect to me; I'm quite certain that if I had not plea-bargained, the government would have manufactured additional crimes.

The signing was in a far different realm from my past experiences with the settlement of commercial disputes. There I expected a feeling of camaraderie with my adversary for having gone through a war of litigation. But the plea agreement was not a settlement. There was no compassion in the prosecutor's heart. I had sought any light at the end of the tunnel, no matter how faint. I couldn't have known that the faint light was a freight train picking up speed.

One of the most damaging concessions in the plea-bargain agreement was my agreement not to contest the government's version of events. All along, I'd told Bill Brodsky that the allegation regarding Ansaldo's funneling of money into the Hinchey campaign through Besicorp was a fabrication. I had proof, documents, and the testimony of those involved, people whose testimony would directly contradict the government's case.

Brodsky had negotiated the plea agreement so that I would not be required to plead guilty to charges that incorporated the Ansaldo allegations. But in a perverted twist of the law, the government retained the right to use these very allegations against me for purposes of sentencing, just as if they were proven facts. Without understanding the implications of what I was signing, I agreed in writing that everything contained in the information statement in which the government alleged its charges, (even that which was based on perjured testimony), was relevant conduct for sentencing purposes. So for purposes of both probation review and sentencing, I might as well have pleaded guilty to every lie the government threw at me. At least if I had gone to trial or just pleaded guilty up front, my explanations could have gone before the judge.

Prior to the sentence being handed down by the judge, a defendant, even after pleading guilty, is supposedly permitted to submit a legal memorandum concerning both the facts and the law. As a result of the plea-bargain agreement, I was limited to only skirting the important issues that would influence the judge's thinking regarding my sentencing. Unable to deny what wasn't true, I was left to play a stupid game with facts and figures. The memorandum Brodsky submitted probably looked manipulative to the judge. At the same time, the prosecutor was able to fill his papers with lies and tell the judge that I was being evasive with my explanations. Jacobson went so far as to say that even if I hadn't used the Ansaldo money for campaign contributions (as I couldn't come right out and say), I must have stolen the money from Ansaldo, since Ansaldo pleaded guilty to making illegal campaign contributions. He knew I was precluded from telling what really happened, and he was taking full advantage of the fact that I was verbally handcuffed.

~

During the plea negotiations, Brodsky had told me that the prosecutor wanted me to plead to a tax charge, and he reported that he had answered "yes" for me. I couldn't believe what I heard. He did it without even consulting me. I asked, "Why? I wasn't indicted on tax charges!"

Bill told me that in a coordinated investigation of this kind, each of the participating agencies that had devoted man-hours to the case wants something: the FBI gets the false document count, and the IRS gets the tax count. But he told me not to worry, and also that it was too late. "The sentencing guidelines computation won't be affected by the addition of a tax count, and the judge will understand that the tax charge arose only as a result of improper payroll deductions for the campaign contribution reimbursements."

The bizarre thing about the supposed tax crime was that the government hadn't lost any money. We'd calculated that the taxes paid by the individual recipients of supposedly "illegal" bonuses were roughly equal to the increased corporate taxes Besicorp would have paid if the bonuses had never been given. But I learned that if the wrong person pays the tax, a technical tax crime has been committed, even if the government gets the same amount of money. This warped logic was further twisted when it was charged that I used the bonus funds I earned from Besicorp to give money to my own family. By some Gestapo logic, the government charged that I had "conspired" to pay myself a tax-deductible bonus from the company I controlled. So now I had to swallow becoming a "tax cheat" on top of everything else, a point the judge would not fail to mention in my sentencing.

~

Along with tax charges, my agreement to waive venue, not contesting the government's version of events, and agreeing that things which I denied I had done were nevertheless "relevant conduct" for sentencing, even more was piled on: the government reserved the right to ask the judge for an "upward departure" in sentencing if the prosecutor lost on his legal arguments. (An upward or downward departure refers to a judge's deviation from the sentencing guidelines based upon certain exceptions to the rules.)

But even that was not the end. Brodsky accepted the prosecutor's position that I agree not to seek a downward sentencing departure. We were unable to plead to the judge that the sentencing guidelines did not accurately reflect the seriousness of the crime, while the prosecutor vilified me as the enemy of democracy in America. Experienced criminal attorneys to whom I showed the plea agreement after the fact told me they had never seen a more one-sided deal in favor of the government.

30

The Scandal of Mandated Sentencing

L ike most Americans, I had no idea of how significantly the regulations called Federal Sentencing Guidelines violate the guarantees of democracy until I experienced the process firsthand.

Sentencing guidelines impose highly regimented rules that judges have to follow in determining sentencing, which force them to issue sentences no lower than certain minimum terms for specific crimes, even for first-time offenders in relatively minor cases. There is a complicated point system for each crime, with upward and downward adjustments based upon a series of statements that supposedly provide objectivity in weighing the seriousness of the offensive behavior. The manual for federal sentencing is over six inches thick. Each offense carries a basic point status—for example, eight points for the base offense of "conspiracy"; points are then added for such items as "number of people involved," (two points for three or more people), or "complexity of the scheme" (two to four added points), or "organizer and leader" (two to three points). The points are added together and the judge is then presented with a guideline calculation, which presents a minimum and maximum one. If the charges contain multiple counts, only the most severe points calculation applies, though the judge can take into account the totality of the behavior when weighing whether to sentence the defendant to the minimum, the maximum, or somewhere in between.

Sentencing guideline issues are addressed not only by the prosecution and the probation department, but by the defendant, and they are a major point of litigation in the sentencing phase of a defendant's case. Since the prosecutor is in control of determining what level of crime an offender is charged with, the prosecution in fact determines what the minimum sentence will be if the defendant is convicted. A harsh prosecutor may choose to prosecute a minor deviant act as a severe crime, precisely in order to force an onerous plea-bargain; if the party chooses to resist such overwhelming pressure to plea-bargain and goes to trial as accused, there may be a great disparity between the seriousness of the acts the offender actually committed and the way the case was charged, but a jury will not be able to discern the difference. Sentencing issues are not permitted to be presented to the jury during a trial. A jury will not know whether a defendant is facing thirty days or five years.

Even for the person who chooses, for whatever reason, to negotiate a plea bargain, the ultimate determination of sentence is no longer in the hands of the judge. No longer can a judge evaluate your life, your character, or the lack of venality of your actual behavior, except within a tight range of sentencing options, each with a mandatory minimum. Under many circumstances, for all but the most minor crimes, federal charges have a minimum sentence of incarceration attached, so even if the judge wants to be lenient and give a first offender home confinement or probation, the guidelines may prevent it.

The sentencing guidelines were developed to "level the playing field," by well-intentioned bureaucrats and politicians. Concerned that white-collar and drug offenders were being treated too leniently and inconsistently from judge to judge and circuit to circuit, they perceived disparities and lack of uniformity in sentences to be unjust, and to penalize minorities. Rather than lightening up on the harshness of the system toward first offenders and minor drug users, however, the guidelines have extended inhumanity to a broader spectrum of the population. Now, Americans are incarcerated at a far greater rate than in virtually any comparable civilized society. Today there are almost two million people incarcerated in our federal, state, and local jails and prisons. A large percentage of these people are nonviolent and/or first offenders serving long mandated sentences. Many of them are people who refused to testify against friends or loved ones, who were arrested on the premises where another person used drugs, or who otherwise were swept up into the government's prosecutorial engine and charged variously with conspiracy or other crimes. In a misguided response to political pressures, tremendous power has been transferred from the judiciary to the executive branch of the government. The sentencing guidelines are one of many tools that prosecutors, hell bent on racking up convictions, use to compel plea-bargain convictions. They accomplish their goal by working the charges and the enhancements to build up the guideline points so that the risks of going to trial become intolerable. A plea-bargain becomes almost inevitable. Statistics show that virtually all people currently indicted by the federal government plead guilty to something rather than go to trial. So awesome is the power of the federal government that of the few who do go to trial, only a fraction are acquitted. And so many formerly obscure regulations have been criminalized that a prosecutor now has a laundry list of ways to force a target into submission.

I understood none of this before my plea bargain, and I am sure that most American citizens are unaware of the dangers we face at the hands of a bureaucracy out of control.

31

UPPING THE ANTE

At the same time that I was agonizing over the prospect of plea-bargaining, the opportunity arose for Besicorp to finally make its fortune from almost two decades of effort as a power development company. It is incredibly ironic that the very provocateurs who tried to force the company to liquidate for so many years now stood to gain a great deal of money from my obstinate refusal to liquidate. Had I done as they had advocated, the projects in question would have earned only a small fraction of what was now possible for Besicorp. The next few pages summarize the beginnings of the complex story about how these values were achieved.

～

I've noted how Besicorp's opportunity as a power plant developer arose out of the energy crisis of 1973. In 1979, Congress passed legislation called the Public Utilities Regulatory Policy Act (PURPA). PURPA mandated that states establish plans to compel regulated electric utilities to purchase electric power from independent power producers (IPPs). Each state was left to work out the details. It took about ten years for the pace of activity in the newly forming IPP market to develop, and early in this period, a small IPP such as Besicorp found it easy to deal with the giant Niagara Mohawk Power Company (NIMO). NIMO was a giant utility. Its management controls were lax, but they wanted to follow the regulatory mandates in good faith. All an IPP had to do to obtain a long-term power contract with this powerful utility at government-mandated rates was walk in with a site and some basic information. With the aggressiveness of young and brash entrepreneurs, Besicorp marched into NIMO's offices with five power plant sites and walked away with contracts that would ultimately be worth hundreds of millions of dollars.

NIMO entered into dozens of contracts, continuing to act in good faith to comply with the regulatory mandate. As the years went on, this put them in what appeared to be a highly compromised position; they had a larger percentage of power purchase contracts than almost any utility in the nation, and the rates in the contracts at which they were to buy power escalated sharply over the long years of those obligations.

Many utilities fought tooth and nail against mandated power contracts, which they considered to be fostering unwanted competition. The contract terms seemed extraordinarily onerous to the power companies that considered the IPPs as unwanted competitors. This created inevitable conflicts between them and the IPPs. Thankfully we've done quite well despite this unsettled business environment.

In a vain attempt to put the IPPs out of business, some utilities (NIMO included) tried to make it impossible for these projects to obtain financing by forcing impossible contract terms on the IPPs. As a consequence, IPPs were forced to buy long-duration gas supply contracts that were not readily available and required major price concessions to fuel suppliers. There was still plenty of margin left for the developers, but these projects were saddled with long-term fixed price fuel contracts. When energy prices went down and stayed down during the 1990s, these long-term power contracts were seen as disasters.

In 1994, Besicorp and its partner, Kamine Development, Corp., completed a two-year process in which we voluntarily renegotiated our power contracts with NIMO. We initiated this massive effort (which required the reformation of dozens of contracts and refinancing of the projects to the tune of $500 million). When we completed this major accomplishment, NIMO announced that they were going to save hundreds of millions of dollars as a result. The financial prospects of our projects were enhanced; we had greatly strengthened our contracts and removed regulatory and litigation risks that our competitors continued to bear. But NIMO still had many other onerous IPP contracts, and partly as a result, they were facing a deteriorating financial condition.

In 1997, right in the middle of the criminal case that was grinding at me and Besicorp, NIMO unilaterally announced that they were going to renegotiate all of their IPP contracts, or to take care of the problem in court. As a lever to start the negotiating process, they even threatened to file bankruptcy. Despite our prior success in dealing with NIMO, we were caught up in this turmoil. Virtually our entire business was at stake. If NIMO was successful in court, Besicorp would be wiped out. It was now that the process began that ultimately delivered extraordinary value to our shareholders.

32

Putting in the Plea

At last it was June 19, 1997, the day I was to formally enter my guilty plea. It was early in the morning, long before the court would be in session, and I had hoped to arrive at the Federal courthouse in White Plains before the reporters. But there they were, cameras and video recorders in hand. I wanted to show them my best face and not hide my head. There was no way that I would walk in less than proud. So I moved on towards the courthouse, climbing the stairs with video and still cameras flashing and microphones thrust into my face, standing as tall as I could. With waves of trepidation, I entered the granite building and made my way to the courtroom with my attorneys.

My lawyers clustered around me at the defendant's table. Bill Brodsky and Doug Lobel tried to make the best of a bad situation. Steve Nachimson, Besicorp's general counsel, was also there at my side, ready to stand up for Besicorp and enter a guilty plea for the corporation. He hadn't been employed by Besicorp in 1992 when the "offenses" occurred, yet he placed himself voluntarily in that horrible space. One who hasn't been there can only imagine what it feels like to stand in court and say "guilty," even on behalf of a corporation. Here was a young man of fine character.

"All rise." Magistrate Lisa Smith entered the room. "Please be seated." Other cases were dealt with first and then came my turn. Bill Brodsky had previously consented on my behalf that a magistrate instead of the judge could take my plea. Brodsky stood up and announced my presence. We waived the reading of the charges and the plea agreement. Magistrate Smith informed me that she was going to ask a series of questions to determine if I had entered an acceptable guilty plea. "I understand," I said.

"Do you understand that you are waiving your constitutional rights to a trial by a jury?"

"I do, Your Honor!"

"Do you freely and voluntarily make this plea, and no one co-erced or threatened you, and you have no understandings other than as set forth in the plea agreement?"

I had a lot of thoughts I could not speak. "I do, Your Honor!"

"Did you knowingly commit the acts as set forth in the Government's information?"

"Yes, Your Honor."

"Did you know it was against the law at the time you did those acts?"

I looked over at Bill Brodsky as he sat next to me, unsure even at this point about the implications of these rapid fire questions, and of the answers I was about to give. I felt as if a piano wire was strung tight inside my chest. Bill shrugged, as if to say, "continue."

"I believe I did, Your Honor," I answered with a quizzical inflec-tion. But it appeared cut and dried in the transcript.

"How do you plead to the charges which have been filed against you?"

I stood before the magistrate and held myself erect, swallowed hard, and said to myself, "I know who I am. Nothing is going to take away my self worth. This is part of me now, and I will learn to live with it." I reached deep inside to find my positive spirit, searching for what remained after such a brutal siege. And in that horrible moment I heard myself say, "Guilty, Your Honor!"

On my way up to Judge Brieant's courtroom to receive a date for my sentencing, I had time to reflect on what was going on.

I was the president, CEO and chairman of the board of the com-pany I'd founded twenty years before, and I was entering a guilty plea to "settle" criminal charges that should never have been brought against me. And why? Because for a single, brief period in my life, I had thrust myself enthusiastically into something I knew nothing about, not cognizant of the difference between charity and politics. I couldn't believe this was happening.

I consoled myself with thoughts of how good my life was. To continue the course of the past year and a half by spending more months and months preparing for trial, and then enduring that agony only to risk conviction, a long appeal period, and then eventual incarceration, would have been sowing the seeds of my own destruction. I entered the plea, but while I held out my hand for the government to take a bite, I turned away inside, my faith in the American system of justice damaged forever.

It was all unremittingly bleak: the dark, wood-paneled walls inside the courtroom reflected little light. The prosecutor, Elliot Jacobson, eyeing me darkly up and down out of the corner of his eye, mindfully avoiding any eye contact. The FBI and IRS agents sharing the prosecutor's table, visibly relishing the satisfaction of bringing another target down. The reporters sitting on their benches, waiting to parlay any simple words into newspaper headlines. They were all vultures, I thought, hovering overhead, waiting for the kill, ready to pick at my bones. This was my life. To them it was just another meal.

33

PROBATION PATS ME DOWN

I prayed to get through what I knew was going to be a dehumanizing process without losing my mind or poisoning my heart.

I had always felt in control of my own destiny, but now I had to accept the loss of my independence, my autonomy, and control over my life. Entering the guilty plea was a desperate attempt to end the war that had engulfed me. I had taken a step backwards in order to move forward again, making a difficult but pragmatic decision. I hoped for the best.

After appearing before the magistrate and entering my plea, I began the process of pre-sentence screening by the U.S. Probation Department. It was June 1997; facing its upcoming summer vacation schedule, a late September sentencing date was set by the court. The probation prescreening was to take place as soon as possible, but I had to wait nearly a month before my first interview with the probation officer.

Most people are familiar with the monitoring and supervision of federal criminal offenders on parole or probation, but the Probation Department's lesser-known function is the pre-sentence screening of convicted offenders. A probation officer is an officer of the court and reports to the judge, not to the federal prosecutor; her role is to analyze the offender and the offense and then to make a report and sentencing recommendation based upon the sentencing guidelines. The objectives of the criminal justice system are supposed to be taken into account, and include not only punishment for the crime, but rehabilitation and deterrence. Deterrence was a concept with which I was destined to become very familiar.

~

Bill Brodsky and I had heated debates over how to deal with my upcoming interview. I was disturbed by the instructions he gave me: "Unequivocally, do not discuss the offenses with the probation officer. You are to refer only to the plea allocution and the statement you made in court. If any further questions come up about the offense, you are to defer to me." He told me this was common practice and that the probation officer would understand the constraint I was under, but it didn't make any sense to me, and characteristic of my approach to life, I vigorously questioned things that didn't make sense. I felt that I was skilled in communications and in human relations, and I felt it would be nearly impossible to restrain myself and follow the script that Brodsky was laying down for me. I wanted to be myself. I felt I had to tell my story the best way it could be told. How could the probation officer understand whether my offenses were the product of a criminal mind or were a mistake and a fiasco, unless I was allowed to talk about it?

But Bill was so insistent that I felt compelled to go along with him. "Probation officers are trained professionals," He said. "They are looking for things that you're not familiar with or prepared for." There was an extreme danger, he said, that I would say something, intentionally or inadvertently, that would cause the probation officer to conclude that I was not contrite and not "accepting responsibility."

Brodsky had represented me for over a year. He knew how indignant I was about the way I was used by Hinchey and how angry I was at the people who had instigated the government's investigation. Bill was afraid that I might appear to be backtracking on my guilty plea. He didn't want me to even come close to raising defenses and risk losing credit for acceptance of responsibility.

"If you make the wrong impression, the probation officer could recommend to the judge that you be denied the two-point reduction for 'Acceptance of Responsibility,'" he added. Those points, he explained, available to me in the sentencing guidelines calculation because I had given the government a plea bargain, could make the difference between my going to prison and being sentenced to home confinement. I needed no further convincing.

I was assigned to a probation office in Middletown, New York, over an hour's drive from my home and two hours away from New York City. The day of my first interview was a hot day at the end of August 1997. I met Bill Brodsky and Doug Lobel and we drove to a strange-looking building in the back of a strip mall in an ugly part of town. We walked up three flights and waited to enter through locked security doors.

Brodsky, Lobel, and I entered a sparsely furnished office and met Vicki Costanzi, the U.S. Probation Officer. She was a certified social worker and had her degree hanging on the wall; we sat around her desk, shifting in our seats and waiting for her to take the lead. She was obviously a professional.

Ms. Costanzi was trained in application of the federal sentencing guidelines. She meted out justice by referring to a giant book of complicated regulations published by the Federal Sentencing Commission. The ultimate sentence would be at the discretion of the judge, but the judge, busy with many cases, would rely heavily on the probation officer's recommendation. Armchair "experts" say that a judge will rarely sentence more leniently than what probation recommends. The odds were against you if you received a negative report from probation.

After exchanging pleasantries and dispensing with preliminaries, Ms. Costanzi looked straight at me and said, "I am an officer of the court, and I am primarily concerned with you, the offender. I will evaluate you for risks such as flight from sentencing, and I will recommend to the judge the terms of your release prior to the final disposition of your case. I will also evaluate you and all of the information I can gather about you and make sentencing recommendations to the judge. I will end up knowing more about you than almost anyone else on earth."

The interview began badly. Ms. Costanzi said right off that she would like me to discuss the offenses. Bill Brodsky immediately jumped in and cut me off, stating, as nicely as he could, that he'd instructed me not to discuss that subject. I picked up her sideways glance at me and shrugged my shoulders; I couldn't contradict my attorney, but I knew at that moment that she was not at all pleased at this. My stomach was churning. She said, "If that's the way you want it, Okay."

For the next four and one-half hours, we went into questions about my life and my business. She interrupted my narrative from time to time to ask questions she had assembled from the questionnaires and financial statements I had previously submitted.

I skirted as close as I could to discussing the case. Bill squirmed in his seat. Ms. Costanzi opened the door when she asked if the company had a history of giving bonus money to its management employees. Bill had told me to avoid that subject because it could be a trap (I still haven't figured out how), but I wanted to answer truthfully. It was precisely because of the extensive history of bonus compensation in Besicorp that I'd been able to rationalize the legality of what I did at the time. But Bill said that this could be misinterpreted to mean that I thought I hadn't broken the law, and if that got back to the prosecutor, he could petition the judge to take away my two-point benefit for plea-bargaining. Nevertheless, I used the question to open a peripheral discussion about my own compensation history and my financial support for my parents. I alluded to the history of giving bonuses to members of the Besicorp management team but stayed clear of details.

I tried to convey that I was remorseful for what had happened, and that I was not evading responsibility, but I stated emphatically that the offense did not arise out of a criminal thought process. It was a very difficult message to impart without discussing the case. I was biting my lips and my tongue.

A probation officer deals with hundreds of offenders and has to look at them all with a skeptical eye. Why should she look at me any differently than at an embezzler? In response to my denials of criminal intent, she replied, "Everybody says that they didn't do it, looking for sympathy." In a nutshell, her message was, "Save your breath." But what more could I expect when I couldn't tell her anything about the case?

~

She asked me if I had any scars, and I said, "No," but later on, in a moment of humor I tilted my head back and laughed. Quick as lightning, she asked, "You have a scar on your lip?" I said, "Well, yes I do, from a childhood accident, but it is under this mustache that I've worn for thirty years. I forgot about it." Holy Cow, she was serious. She jotted that tidbit of identifying information down on her questionnaire. Her observations about my scar were now in the official record; in case I skipped town they could add to the wanted picture in the post office, "has a tiny scar beneath his mustache."

At one point during the interview, I began to sob. I told Ms. Costanzi about my fears and my concern that I would be unable to remain with my family. My crying got to her, and her eyes teared up, but only for a brief moment. I knew she had a tough job and had to avoid empathy or she would lose her objectivity. But how I prayed for that empathy!

Suddenly, out of left field, she told me that she had received some negative letters about my character. All along, my worst fear was that the provocateurs would find a way to attack me even inside the depths of the criminal justice system. Kahn and Lichtenberg had been poisoning the waters even here, where my very life was at stake.

In the brief few minutes still available, I frantically tried to tell Ms. Costanzi as much as I could about the gang of litigious share-holders and the lawsuits we'd been facing. I begged her to con-sider the motives of those people, telling her how they were trying to force Besicorp into having no choice but to liquidate, and how they were trying to get me incarcerated to achieve their goal. She said that she would not take those letters into consideration in making her analysis and recommendations, but I didn't believe her. She was a human being, and I understood that she would determine what she wanted the outcome to be and then engineer her report to achieve that outcome.

Now I was in a waiting game, sitting on the edge of my seat again, hoping that Bill Brodsky knew what he was doing. My life was in Ms. Costanzi's hands.

34

ANOTHER SHAREHOLDER SUIT

Only five weeks after my guilty plea and right before the time of my probation interview, a "new" shareholder plaintiff emerged, represented by another practitioner of predatory litigation. Filed on August 10, 1997, this suit was brought by a "concerned" shareholder by the name of John Bansbach, and as a "derivative" lawsuit, it was similar in structure to the Lichtenberg suit and quoted extensively from the briefs presented in Lichtenberg. There was no doubt that the attorneys were in cahoots. They didn't even try to hide their collaboration. It demanded that I should be held responsible for financial damages that Besicorp incurred as a result of the "illegal" campaign contributions, and that I should repay Besicorp for the cost of my own criminal defense, repay all of Besicorp's legal fees incurred in its own defense, and repay all the fees paid for the representation of third parties.

The suit charged that Besicorp's board of directors was under my control and asked the court to allow Bansbach to represent Besicorp as its designated representative. Imagine. A predatory attorney attacks the company, seeking to screw the CEO who built the business, then tells the court that his "plaintiff" is the "true" representative of the company, because the board of directors has been corrupted by the CEO and chief wrongdoer. On that basis, the court was asked to excuse Bansbach from making a demand upon the board to deal with his complaint, which is otherwise required under New York State law. If the court accepted their premise, the complaining shareholder group would be designated as the representative of the public shareholders in a suit against the management on behalf of the corporation. They would have achieved the equivalent of "class action" status, a coveted position that had eluded our adversaries through all the years of their litigation against us. Of course, if Bansbach had made such a demand, he would have effectively transferred control of the complaint to the Besicorp board, something that would have defeated his purpose.

~

The New York State Business Corporation Law permits corporations to indemnify officers and directors for expenses in defending legal actions, including criminal cases. Without being too technical, there are limitations to that right if a director has acted in bad faith or knowingly violates the law; the board is left to determine the good faith and state of mind of the party seeking indemnification. The law is specific: a guilty plea or conviction does not preclude indemnification if the appropriate standards of behavior are met.

Like most corporations, Besicorp's by-laws go one step further and obligate the company to indemnify directors and officers. The indemnified party has a presumption of the right to indemnification; in my case, it was clear in my own mind that I did not know I was committing a crime when I made the mistakes that led to my plea of guilty.

But the litigants were leaving no stone unturned. They were determined to keep tremendous pressure on Besicorp and create a state of siege, as if we weren't under one already. Both Besicorp and I had already pleaded guilty to criminal charges, and we were holding the company together at this point with spit and baling wire. But our adversaries wanted the company to just give up and go into liquidation. Once again, they were figuring that Besicorp was worth more dead than alive, especially alive and with me at the helm.

In an attempt to add strength to Besicorp's position in the Bansbach lawsuit, Besicorp's outside counsel recommended that the independent members of the board demand that I pay back at least some of the money that the company had spent on my defense. I thought this was outrageous, that I had endured tremendous hardship on behalf of the company. By now, it was apparent to all involved that corporate raiders had instigated the federal investigation, and that I was their victim, so why were they adding this insult to my injury? Too exhausted to resist, I wasn't in the strongest frame of mind, so I reluctantly agreed, and gave Besicorp a promise that I would pay back at least $186,000. The board had half a heart, and was willing to wait and see what my sentence was going to be before they set the terms for payment. But the indemnification issue was not going to go away, and neither were John Bansbach, Alan Kahn, James Lichtenberg, or their attorneys.

35

"He Deserves No Leniency"

The date for my sentencing, September 20, 1997 was still weeks away when I'd first met with Vicki Costanzi. By late August, summer vacations were slowly drawing to an end and my legal team still needed to prepare the legal briefs addressing sentencing issues. I was assured by both Bill Brodsky and Doug Lobel that there was still plenty of time. In the meantime, Bill had written to Judge Brieant and received copies of all the hostile letters so we could know what we were dealing with.

One of the few remaining acts I could take on my own behalf was to get my own friends and associates to write reference letters to the judge. It is customary for a person about to be sentenced to submit a package of such letters, and Bill Brodsky assured me that the judge would consider them. With a human life in their hands, all federal judges take sentencing issues with utmost seriousness, he said. We wanted the judge to perceive me in the genuine totality of my life, not as the grotesque one-dimensional figure the prosecutor would present.

Sometimes crime victims and their families write a judge to plead that a severe sentence should be imposed on a convicted criminal, but an organized group of hostile shareholders in a corporate takeover battle? Bill and Doug told me that in their decades of criminal practice they had never seen anything like the letter-writing campaign that Kahn, Lichtenberg, Enowitz, and their collaborators had organized against me.

Alan Kahn wrote a hate-filled letter in which he veiled himself in a cloak of credibility, citing his many years as a Wall Street investment banker. The letter contained unsubstantiated accusations of a huge range of wrongdoing by me against the shareholders of Besicorp, insinuating that the present case was just the tip of the iceberg, and alluding to additional unspecified criminal activities of which I was guilty. Kahn wrote:

> I will testify in court, under oath, and under penalty of perjury, before any judge or magistrate, or sentencing officer, at my own expense, if requested to do so, on these topics which have relevance to the sentence to be given to Mr. Zinn by you next month. My testimony will go to the reasons why Mr. Zinn deserves no leniency, but rather deserves the maximum sentence which the law allows in the above-captioned case. The public welfare requires a full investigation of the civil, as well as criminal, elements surrounding Mr. Zinn's activities. Many of the charges in the past and currently-pending shareholder civil lawsuits which have been brought against Mr. Zinn have, of course, criminal aspects to them.

James Lichtenberg's letter also combined outright lies with a sentencing analysis that encouraged the judge to put me away for years. He argued how horribly venal my behavior was and also delivered a laundry list of additional unsubstantiated accusations that justified the most severe possible sentence. Lichtenberg actually wrote the judge that anyone at Besicorp who did not capitulate to my pressure and donate to the '92 Hinchey campaign would have been fired! He said that I breached my position of trust as CEO of Besicorp and hypothesized about the "victims" of my crime, speculating that Ansaldo (of all possible victims!) was defrauded out of $40,000. With a rhetorical flourish, he wrote:

> Perhaps the biggest victim is Congressman Hinchey. He received $27,000 and he believed it to be honest money. He spent it honorably and now, as a result of Mr. Zinn's felonies, he has pledged to repay it. That money is long gone and represents a significant loss to the congressman.

◇

Not surprisingly, Martin Enowitz, the person upon whose financially motivated testimony the government had based my indictment, had sent a letter as well. He wrote:

Sentence Michael Zinn to prison for the maximum amount of time allowed by law...Mr. Zinn should not be allowed to escape accountability and responsibility for his crimes by merely writing a check.... The only way for Mr. Zinn to pay the price is to serve time in an appropriate prison facility away from his home. With Besicorp offices a mere 5 minutes away from Mr. Zinn's home, it will be 'business as usual' for Mr. Zinn.

There were other letters written by Besicorp shareholders, people I didn't know and had never met. All followed the same pattern, imploring the judge to remove me from Besicorp and send me away for as long as possible, accusing me of the most egregious behavior. One shareholder wrote:

The Court is urged to issue the maximum criminal sentence available under the law and, at the very least, to remove Mr. Zinn as CEO....

Another requested:

Mr. Zinn should receive the maximum sentence allowed by law... it is my thought that he should be banned from ever holding office in a public company again...

Yet another said:

Please, throw the book at this man...

One wrote:

I am a shareholder of Besicorp Group Inc.... Mr. Zinn has used the assets of Besicorp for his own personal gain to the detriment of Besicorp shareholders.... Mr. Zinn's illegal campaign contribution scheme is only a part of the misuse of Besicorp money, employees and shareholders done by him over the years.... To protect the shareholders of Besicorp from Mr. Zinn, to punish him, and to discourage him or any other officer of a publicly traded corporation from doing what he has done. I ask that Mr. Zinn's sentence... prohibit him for at least ten years from holding corporate office in Besicorp.

Another shareholder wrote:

Please excuse me for writing this letter, but you are trying a case involving an individual who runs a company that my son's college savings is partially invested in, so I feel my letter is appropriate. Michael Zinn has undermined the value of the company by not divulging both positive information about the company's assets and concealing negative information about mis-activities while earning an exorbitant salary.... I hope you will bar Michael Zinn from involvement in his present company and any future companies he might try to take control of. If you don't unfortunately individuals investing in these companies will be negatively affected.

Another letter stated:

From my perspective I would like to see Michael Zinn, CEO... get the severest penalty, punishment, prison sentence possible for the way he has run BESI Corp. since I became a shareholder in 1989.... He has continually undervalued the share price from giving himself an outrageous compensation.... Such dishonest behavior in a CEO is unacceptable. To me... CEO's of companies should be working for the shareholders and to increase the value of the company and it's shares. I believe that the company and it's shareholders would be better off with him out of power and not associated with the running of BESI Corp. in any form or matter.

Yet another wrote:

I am writing to you because I understand that you will be sentencing Michael Zinn later this month and that you wanted to hear from victims of Mr. Zinn's actions. Mr. Zinn has damaged me as a shareholder of BESI Corp. in many ways, as follows: He consistently runs BESI Corp. as though it were his own private concern.... Because of the above mentioned actions, and others, I am requesting that you permanently bar Zinn from running a public company, and sentence him to the maximum sentence that your guidelines permit.

And two final excerpts:

> I would request your honor to consider stepping up the sentencing date to perhaps late August or early September in consideration of the damage and harm Mr. Zinn represents to the minority shareholders whose combined vote is still the minority.

And:

> It is my conclusion that directly or indirectly your decision as to the severity of the sentence you are about to give Michael Zinn, president and CEO of BESI Corp. will permanently and critically affect the condition of the patient, long suffering and economically exploited shareholders of BESICORP.... I am one of those shareholders... a victim of Mr. Zinn's financial and stock manipulations and of his fiduciary sleight of hand.... Over the last few years the gradual revelation of the fiduciary malfeasance of Mr. Zinn has been appalling. The most sobering point, however, is that so far he is almost getting away with it.

The people who wrote these and other such letters to a federal judge bought their Besicorp stock as part of a coordinated takeover group. The letters all followed the same pattern, libeling me on behalf of the aggrieved victims of my financial manipulation, and asking the judge to give me the maximum sentence. These people had all acquired their Besicorp stock for between one and ten dollars per share, and at the time they wrote these letters, Besicorp stock was trading at around $30.

36

The Probation Roller Coaster

By early September the probation report was still incomplete, and we still weren't very far along in preparing our own sentencing memorandum. I was nervous that my own legal presentation would be inadequate. It was clear that there was no way any of the parties would be ready for the late September sentencing date set by Judge Brieant. Jockeying began as to which party would ask the judge for a delay.

It fell to Brodsky and Lobel to make the request. Fortunately, it was September, and vacation schedules for the lawyers were reasonable explanations that we hoped would not annoy the judge. The new date was set for October 22, 1997.

Weeks had gone by with no word from Ms. Costanzi, and I was a nervous wreck. In mid-September Valerie and I left town for a week trying to take a break from the stress. It would be a working vacation; taking care of phone calls and faxes had always been part of my vacations.

We arrived in Cape Cod. Birds were singing, but I was not paying much attention to the outdoors. When Bill Brodsky called, he came right to the point: Ms. Costanzi had informed him of what was going to be in the probation report, and it was worse than our worst expectations. She had not only adopted the prosecutor's version of the offense, but had taken a cue from the hostile letters and had added two additional points to my guidelines calculation for "Breach of Trust." As the CEO of a public company, she maintained, I breached my fiduciary responsibility by causing Besicorp to break the law. She was recommending a sentence of eighteen to twenty-four months in prison, six months more than even the prosecutor wanted me to serve.

Bill added further bad news. If I were sentenced to twelve months, I would serve six months or so in prison and then be eligible to serve the balance of the sentence in a halfway house. But if I were sentenced to eighteen months or more, no part of the sentence could be served outside of prison. Under the rules in effect, with a sentence of eighteen months I would have to serve perhaps triple the jail time—a full one and one-half years away from my family.

I felt like I'd been hit by a truck. All Bill could do was groan and tell me that he was at a loss as to what to do. I'd known that going into the plea-bargain process was a risk, and I remembered Bill telling me that there were no guarantees, but he'd assured me that these things almost always went a certain way. I remembered his telling me that the judge would not want to see me go to prison.

There seemed to be no avenue of leniency open to me now. If the probation officer thought my acts were so egregious that she would actually enhance what the prosecution was demanding, why should the judge be more lenient?

∿

I was in a panic and didn't know where to turn. I needed to talk to Charlie Brown, my friend and attorney of twenty years. I called his office and was told that he was in California, ready to go to trial on a case. I took his hotel number and called him anyway.

Charlie picked up the phone in his hotel room. He was with a group of people, just leaving the war room. I burst into tears, wailing about what was going on, and he cleared the room. We talked, and I cried some more, but there was nothing he could do; he was three thousand miles away, involved in a case of his own, and wasn't experienced in criminal law. But he was there for me, and I was grateful.

I called other attorney friends, but no one could help me. By afternoon, I was a wreck. All I could think of was that dangerous criminals escape punishment in our society every day and that I was about to go to prison for giving bonuses to my employees. It made no sense.

∿

Bill Brodsky assumed that my plea allocution was sufficient for the limited purpose of getting two points off for "Acceptance of Responsibility." That may have been the case, but it hadn't been sufficient for eliminating the perception of willful and egregious criminal behavior. I made a decision. I would not go to prison without a fight. I would see the probation officer again, even over the objections of my attorneys, if need be. I felt they blew my opportunity the first time around, and now maybe, just maybe, if I told the story my way, the truthful way, I could reverse some of the damage that had been done. My best hope at that point was to get the probation officer to take the prosecutor's position, instead of going beyond it. As horrible as it was to consider, twelve months was better than eighteen months away from home.

I called Bill Brodsky that same afternoon and told him I wanted to see Ms. Costanzi as soon as possible. "I don't recommend it," he said. He strongly advised against such a meeting, telling me that if I blew it, I could lose the two points I'd earned for "Acceptance of Responsibility" and get an even more severe jail term than eighteen to twenty-four months. But I was firm in my decision. I said, "Bill, your strategy isn't working. It may have worked for your last twelve clients, walking them out the courtroom with probation or home confinement, and you think that you can apply that formula here. But I've told you from day one that my case is different. There are dark forces at work here. People are trying to take over my business, and they are succeeding. It is time for a change of plan. I want to see the probation officer now!"

Bill responded, "Mike, do you think you can sell anything to anybody? Do you think you are a snake-oil salesman?"

I was furious. My freedom was dangling by a thread and Bill Brodsky was reacting like a child with a bruised ego. To think that after more than a year and a half of intense representation, my attorney still didn't know me. How could he have made such an offensive remark?

I insisted on going to see Ms. Costanzi, and I took the bull by the horns with a full understanding of the risk. I couldn't be confident that I could achieve a positive outcome after so much damage had been done. But I knew that if I didn't try, I would go down, big time, and for a long time.

Bill called Ms. Costanzi and made the appointment for three the following afternoon. I flew to Newark Airport and took a car to Brooklyn to pick up Bill at the federal courthouse there. Then we drove the three hours to Middletown to meet with Ms. Costanzi.

~

Before the probation report is sent to the judge, a draft report is circulated to both the defense and the prosecution. Each side gets to comment. The probation officer responds to the comments and objections and makes the final recommendation in an addendum to the report. The entire file is then sent to the judge, so that he gets to see the evolution of the probation officer's thinking.

Ms. Costanzi explained that her report was already finished and had been approved by her manager. She'd agreed to my request for a second meeting only in reference to the addendum, she said. Time was short, so I started right in: I told her that from the beginning I knew she wanted to hear about the offense and about my conduct, but that I'd been advised that I was not to talk about it. I was uncomfortable at the time, and I knew that she was, and I was very appreciative of the opportunity to go into it now, I said.

I began with the story of my political involvement, the request by Hinchey to lead his finance committee, and my invitation for them to work out of our office. I described the pressure I was under to raise money. I told her that I now acknowledged that the bonuses that were given out were illegal reimbursement, but at that time, I considered the payments as compensation that was perfectly legal. (I had to put it that way as I had already pleaded guilty, even though I didn't feel morally culpable.) I showed her Besicorp's compensation worksheets for most of the individuals involved. I explained that I knew I had been close to the edge, but had never even imagined that I could be committing a criminal offense.

I used my own compensation as an example. We went over it line by line. I pointed out how the bonus I had received in September

1992 was in the same amount as the one I had received in 1991. Bill was visibly nervous, and, out of the corner of my eye I could see him squirm in his seat, but I didn't care. I was contemplating eighteen months in jail. What did I have to lose by finally telling my story?

We went over the money I had given to my parents, check by check, month by month. I pointed out the specific check that the prosecutor alleged was my parent's reimbursement, and I showed her how I had given them a similar amount almost every month, for years.

I showed her that Steve Eisenberg, the Besicorp executive with the second highest compensation, hadn't donated anything to the 1992 campaign, yet I had given him a personal loan for $15,000 in October 1992, right during the Hinchey campaign. I explained that though the loan was eventually repaid, it illustrated my custom of giving out funds, without quid-pro-quo for donations to the campaign.

I showed Ms. Costanzi Joyce DePietro's compensation spreadsheet. I pointed to the $10,000 raise on her first anniversary date, which the prosecutor had claimed was a reimbursement. But the following year, there was another $10,000 raise. I told Ms. Costanzi that I understood the law in 1992, but that in my naiveté, I did not act in a venal and conspiratorial manner. Through all of this I had to act contrite, even though I was burning up inside. What I was trying to accomplish could be blown if I displayed anger or resentment at the system.

There were some teary-eyed moments for me in this emotional fight for my life. Ms. Costanzi was a tough and experienced criminal justice professional. She had told me in the first interview that every offender comes in with a sob story. I explained once again that I had been a political novice. I told how professional politicians had pressured me, and that I had been unaware of the significance of what I was doing. Ms. Costanzi listened silently. Now she became animated and exclaimed to Bill, "That sounds like mitigating circumstances, and a potential issue for downward departure." Seeing the tide begin to turn, Bill pointed out that we were precluded from making that argument by the plea-bargain agreement, but we would appreciate it if she would make that recommendation to the judge.

∾

We ended the meeting at five. Despite her heavy workload, Ms. Costanzi took the time to delve into my case, to reach her own conclusions, and to try and make a cumbersome and bureaucratic criminal justice system work. Thank God, she was willing to try.

After the interview, when she and I were briefly alone. I broke down again and said, "I just want to be with my family, please. I'm not a criminal." She said, "You must be strong and get through this. Life will go on, whatever the outcome." Then, in a genuine attempt to comfort me, she said, "You should not forget that after this is all over, you will still have your wealth and your life waiting for you." This wasn't exactly what I was hoping to hear, and I heard myself saying, "What's wealth without my family and my freedom?"

∾

A few days later, the initial probation report from Ms. Costanzi came in the mail. It was as bad as we'd expected, and my only hope now was that she would lighten her recommendation in the addendum report.

The weeks went by, and we were hard at work preparing our own sentencing memorandum. I injected myself into this process, working closely with Bill on the narrative and the case law research. He wasn't accustomed to working with clients on their own defense, but I insisted. I had no desire to be marched off a gangplank, blindfolded, while my well-meaning lawyer told me I was just in a dark tunnel.

My attorney friends lent moral support, but nobody could assist me with the case at this point. At that late date, it was impractical to get a new lawyer up to speed, and the damage had already been done. My relationship with Bill Brodsky and our ability to work together for the next few weeks was critical to the effort, and he seemed sufficiently softened by my apparent success with Ms. Costanzi to be a little more flexible.

Given the downside to me, he dared not block my involvement at this point. I probed and pushed on every point that I thought important. It was far too late in the process, but finally Bill became receptive to my ideas in a way that he had resisted earlier.

Prior to preparing the addendum to her initial probation report, Ms. Costanzi was going to conduct an on-site visit to Besicorp and also to my home. Bill Brodsky warned me not to engage her in discussions without an attorney present. "Just show her around the office and around your home," he said. "Let her see where you work and live and show her that you're stable so she sees that you're not likely to commit further offenses. Then just leave it alone."

The day of her visit I walked into the office of Steve Nachimson, Besicorp's general counsel, and told him what I intended to do. "Steve, this is my life. I don't want to argue this issue with you, Bill, or anyone else. Don't pick up the phone and call Brodsky or Lobel. This is my last chance to avoid prison. I know what I have to do, whatever the risk." I was alone.

Ms. Costanzi arrived at Besicorp's office at the appointed time. I escorted her around our building, describing the different departments and how they operated. After the tour, we went to my office and I closed the door behind us. I told her how much I appreciated the opportunity to give her additional information. We reviewed the case in perspective, this time with additional financial spreadsheets at our fingertips. I showed her how Mike Daley had received a $4,600 bonus but had donated only $1,000. I showed her how he had received similar bonuses many times over the years. I showed her a compilation of total bonuses paid in various periods and how they correlated to the company's financial condition, that we didn't need Ansaldo's money, and routinely gave bonus money out in similar denominations, even though it was out of limited capital. Then I moved into the danger zone. My emotions were getting the better of me, and I knew it; I was getting hyper, risking statements that could work against me, but I couldn't stop—just what Bill Brodsky feared.

I pulled out the letter that Paul Shaheen, one of Lichtenberg's allies, had sent to the Federal Aviation Administration, accusing me of embezzling FAA funds, and showed her the FAA's letter of exoneration. This was only one example of the kind of accusations I'd been subjected to, I said. Ms. Costanzi asked me why a shareholder would file a lawsuit; I responded in depth about why and how a shareholder group gets organized and explained what a derivative shareholder lawsuit is. I told her what had really been going on inside Besicorp.

I pulled out the Ansaldo file, the solar energy business proposal of June 1992, and the thick file of work product. "Ansaldo had pleaded guilty to misdemeanors in the name of a minor corporate subsidiary, I told her. They'd reimbursed their own employees with phony expense accounts and were caught red-handed. But no personal prosecutions were launched, no felonies charged—they'd just blamed it all on me. We sent people to Italy; we spent the money they paid us. I solicited them for campaign contributions and some of their people contributed, but what they did was not under my direction. I was charged with crimes far out of proportion to what I'd actually done. I was then given a take-it-or-leave-it plea-bargain deal." Ms. Costanzi stood up and stared at me. "Are you raising a defense?" she asked. Tearfully, I whispered, "No, I'm just trying to let you know that I don't deserve a prison sentence. Please, please understand."

"Mr. Zinn, you must get a grip on yourself," Ms. Costanzi said, "You are going to have a nervous breakdown." I pulled myself together, and Ms. Costanzi and I left in my car to visit with Valerie at home.

～

Earlier, Ms. Costanzi had conducted a lengthy telephone interview with Valerie. I was supposed to let Val have space to conduct this conversation, but I was such a wreck that I kept sticking my head into the room she was in, trying to listen. Valerie waved me away, but I stood behind the door, trying to hear. When she was asked why I committed the "offenses," she answered, "He was lured," a remark I feared could have been construed as stating that I was not responsible for my own acts.

Val had also told Ms. Costanzi that when Hinchey asked me to be his Finance Chairman she was strongly resistant. Ms. Costanzi asked her why, and she answered, "My father taught me from early on to be suspicious of politicians. They lie and use people." Overall, their conversation had been a positive one, I thought, that had set the tone for a good face-to-face meeting. It turned out to be a very good thought to have planted in Ms. Costanzi's mind. The thought of my being lured clicked with my explanation of the events, without seeming like a denial of the facts of the case.

37

Into the Cauldron of State Politics

Now some of my best friends were counseling me to walk away from the company, to forget about money and just sell the business. But my life was being intentionally ruined, and I was determined not to lose more than necessary. If there was anything I could do about it, I would stay in control of Besicorp, even if I had to go to prison.

There were some unfortunate losses. I've described how after the indictment came down, Steve Eisenberg, my right-hand man, along with board member Gerry Habib, had tried to force me out of the company (for my own good!). I'd successfully beaten that back. Gerry had been able to lick his wounds and go back to being a serious board member, but Steve had been brooding continuously.

One day in June 1997, I walked into Steve's office and told him that it was clear that he was miserable. In just two months, he was due to vest his last installment of incentive stock. I wanted him to know that if he'd decided to leave, he should level with me; I told him I would not force him out to deprive him of his stock. He had paid his dues and more, working in Besicorp's hostile litigation environment. He was not my enemy, and I wasn't going to hurt him in any way.

Steve thanked me, and after a few days, told me he was going to leave. Although he had made a small fortune at Besicorp, people were telling him that the company was going to go down the tubes once I was convicted. As a "career" move, Steve decided to listen to these "advisers" and get out while the company was still functioning. I am grateful that most of the other Besicorp people had more confidence and stayed the course.

The environment within the company was tense and pessimistic. Most companies would have folded the tent. But there was also a tremendous reservoir of camaraderie and closeness that existed within these walls, and a determination by the people to keep the company going in spite of the adversity.

∾

In the middle of all this, yet another front opened. The New York State Attorney General served Besicorp with a new broad-reaching subpoena. The purported reason for this new investigation was to determine whether to bring a legal action to remove me from Besicorp. Leaving no doubt about who instigated it, the subjects the subpoenas covered were the very same issues being litigated by Lichtenberg. Press coverage was extensive, piling on even more stress. The local press treated it as a whole new scandal, as if Besicorp was now being run into the ground by an arch-criminal.

This was depressing, to say the least. Just after I thought I had "settled" with the federal government, the state's highest elected law enforcement officer had decided to make a move against me.

Dennis Vacco, then the state's Attorney General, was an elected politician from Buffalo, New York, and generally regarded as politically motivated. As far as I was concerned, he was extremely dangerous; this government law enforcement agency had the capability of bringing a new set of criminal charges against me.

Apart from whatever legitimate motivations Vacco's office may have had for responding to complaints, they must have regarded me as a politically valuable target. For years, Vacco had been putting out feelers about running for Governor of New York, but New York State Republicans had repeatedly rebuffed him. The local Republicans had portrayed me as the "villain" in their unsuccessful 1996 campaign to unseat Maurice Hinchey from Congress, and that was even before my plea-bargain.

Now Hinchey was making noises about seeking the Democratic gubernatorial nomination. His name began appearing in newspaper columns on short lists that speculated about who would run against incumbent Republican George Pataki or his successor, and prosecuting me could be a way for Vacco to score points with his party's political leadership and also knock Hinchey out of the box.

Rumors about Hinchey's possible run for governor stayed alive throughout the fall of 1997. Even if Hinchey declined to run, Vacco could still score points in his own quest for the nomination by using an "investigation" to force Hinchey out of his congressional seat. There was no doubt that the irregularities in the '92 campaign would be an issue again in the '98 campaign, and that Hinchey would deny any misconduct.

Besicorp's lawyers questioned whether the attorney general had the legal right to interfere in Besicorp's boardroom decisions. Under the New York State Business Corporation Law, the attorney general had the right to bring an action to remove any director or officer of a State corporation "for cause," but our case law research showed that this provision had never been utilized to remove an officer or director where there was an independent board of directors responsible for the business. The only cases ever brought under the statute were against private businesses that were being illegally stripped of assets.

I was still waiting to be sentenced. Now our legal team attended a meeting with the attorney general's investigator, Mr. Bill Mohr, at his office in New York City. The subject concerned the scope of the subpoena. In the course of the meeting, Steve Nachimson noticed a dog-eared Smith Barney letterhead in Mohr's file, with a fax number staring at him from the top of the page. He made a note of the number and as soon as he got back to the office, he confirmed that the letter was from Paul Vanucci's office. He was a Smith Barney stockbroker who had worked closely with Kahn and Lichtenberg in their campaign to pressure me out of Besicorp.

I had had numerous encounters with Vanucci over the years. For a period of time, he'd pretended to be neutral and had tried to lull me into complacency while he solicited information from me. During these conversations he had tried hard to convince me to put Besicorp into voluntarily liquidation, and I had consistently replied that the time wasn't right. Vanucci had regularly peppered me with questions that probed into Besicorp's supposed hidden value. He'd tried to get me to give him numbers and projections even though I'd repeatedly cautioned him not to pry inside information out of the company.

In those conversations, Vanucci had bragged to me that through the clients that he had placed into it, he controlled five percent of Besicorp stock. That fact would have required him to make a 13-D filing with the SEC, which he never did. He later went on to engage in a long campaign of harassing Besicorp's management with a series of demanding phone calls, which made it clear that he was working with Lichtenberg and Kahn. Eventually we asked the brokers who handled Besicorp's own Smith Barney accounts to contact their senior management and got them to order Vanucci to back off. They tried, but he didn't; he just slowed down for a while and got some of his broker friends to continue the harassment.

So I wasn't surprised to learn that Vanucci had apparently written—on official Smith Barney letterhead—to the New York State Attorney General. Vanucci represented that he spoke for the second largest brokerage firm in the world. What he didn't disclose was that he was part of an organized group that was trying to force me out of Besicorp, an event he knew would precipitate the liquidation of the company. It didn't take a genius to know that I wouldn't just walk away from my majority ownership of Besicorp and leave the business in the hands of others.

38

Litigating My Sentence

I t was now early October, and the October 22 sentencing date was looming. Bill Brodsky said he wanted to see the probation report and what the prosecutor would submit to the court before he completed our sentencing memorandum. In the meantime, his staff was pulling together the comparative sentencing information we needed in order to place my case in context against similar federal prosecutions and civil enforcement actions at the Federal Election Commission.

Bill and I were at loggerheads over how much information to put in my sentencing memo. I wanted to tell the judge as much as possible about what had happened, just as I'd told Ms. Costanzi in my second and third meetings with her. I wanted the judge to understand my state of mind during the '92 campaign, But, again, Bill told me that I couldn't go into these details, that the plea-bargain agreement I had executed forbade me from doing so.

Brodsky continued to insist that the only viable strategy open to me was to go before the judge and say, "I'm sorry" in as few words as possible, both in the sentencing memo and in my oral statement. With my life laid out before him and a showing of genuine remorse, he believed the judge would not want to put me in jail. Bill gave me no guarantees, but he believed that this approach would get me the shortest sentence, even if the judge did want me to serve time in prison. I wasn't convinced, but what were my options? What did I have to go on except my own instincts, which went against Brodsky's so often? I was moving through my life on adrenaline alone, keeping my family together with a combination of love and grief.

The plea-bargain agreement, as I kept finding out, tied my hands. After having been compelled by the circumstances and the severe risks of going to trial to sign a "contract" with the government that gave me virtually no concessions, I was obligated not to contest the "government version" of the case. And this meant I was precluded from seeking a "downward departure" in my sentencing before the judge. A "downward departure," as I have previously explained, comes into play when a judge finds that there are compelling reasons to hand down less than the mandatory minimum sentence called for under the federal sentencing guidelines. Even with the "guidelines" controlling sentencing, downward departures do sometimes happen, but the requirements are stringent and the process subjects the judge to appeal and reversal. Very few judges are willing to take that risk. I was cut off from even asking.

As I've noted, a key part of my sentencing submission would be letters of reference—the more the better at this stage.

I'd solicited such letters by mailing my friends and associates a "form" letter in which I asked the recipients to write from the heart to the judge and send the letters to Brodsky. I asked them to express their thoughts about my prosecution, my work, my life, anything at all they wanted to say. By the time we were ready, we had received more than fifty beautiful letters of support and encouragement. We'd forwarded these to the probation department for consideration by Ms. Costanzi, and now we included them in my sentencing memorandum, which we gave to the judge shortly before sentencing day.

In my darkest moments, I reread that outpouring of support and wept, sometimes just sitting and holding them and crying. I read how I had touched peoples' lives, often in ways I'd never realized—in time of need, or with a touch, a look of compassion, offering a shoulder to cry on, all the little things built up the good will I'd unconsciously carried through my life. I felt as if I were hearing the eulogies that would have been offered at my funeral, weighing the legacy that I had left behind. Later, it was this love from my friends that motivated me to go back to my life and not allow myself to be beaten down by the experience I'd endured.

The prosecutor submitted to the court a shrill, detailed sentencing brief in which he accused me of subverting the American electoral system and committing offenses worse than the most flagrant thievery. I had to pray that between findings of law on the Federal Sentencing Guidelines and the positive reference letters, the judge would disregard the hostility of the prosecutor, the negative recommendation of the probation officer, and the letters from the dissident shareholders. And I anxiously awaited what Ms. Costanzi was going to put in her addendum. If she didn't give me relief, the chance of the judge not sending me to prison was now remote.

I kept the business moving through merger and divestiture discussions, meetings with investment bankers and attorneys, and I searched for and found kernels of pleasure in little things to latch onto each day.

Bill Brodsky told me that the judge would probably disregard the negative letters. But the probation officer hadn't, so why would the judge? He might be smart, I reasoned, but could he be wise enough to recognize that this was an orchestrated campaign? Unlikely, I decided, unless I could tell my story. And I was finally convinced that I couldn't.

If I had any chance to avoid prison, I had to shake the "breach of trust" argument that Ms. Costanzi had added to the sentencing process. Notwithstanding what Brodsky said, I knew I had to earn the judge's trust, not just defeat the argument as a matter of law.

Under the "breach of trust" enhancement, I had a "special duty" to Besicorp's public shareholders not to commit a crime while CEO of a public company. The "breach of trust" I was accused of committing was pressuring subordinates to participate in the campaign while at the same time misusing the discretion that came with my position to pay bonuses as reimbursements for campaign donations. But this theory was clearly double jeopardy. The underlying "crime" was paying bonuses to employees to use for campaign contributions. Who else could do that but a person in authority? I was already being sentenced for that crime, yet I was in danger of having my sentence extended on the same set of facts.

Fortunately, Brodsky's research gave us one of my few shots to win a legal point. In another case, a Grumman Aerospace executive had falsified a document in a government contract. The prosecution had tried to stick him with the "breach of trust" enhancement, saying that he had a "special duty" as an executive not to commit a crime. He argued successfully on appeal that he had no "special duty" to the government or to his employer beyond the normal duty of a citizen or an executive to do business honestly and not break the law; he was already being punished for his crime. The appellate court found that to add "breach of trust" penalized him twice for the same offense. "Breach of trust" enhancements should apply only to situations where a "special trust" has truly been broken. An example would be the nephew who steals his elderly aunt's life savings after being entrusted with its safekeeping, or the doctor who rapes a patient while she is under anesthesia.

We submitted a reply to the initial probation report to Ms. Costanzi and gave a copy to the prosecutor (as is required). It was clear that I couldn't get a positive word in edgewise within the confines of the plea-bargain agreement, no matter what the prosecutor put in his brief. Jacobson seemed to be on a personal crusade.

We'd included in my submission to the probation department voluminous information on comparative sentencing outcomes, compiled from other cases from all over the country. This information showed virtually all other prosecutions of campaign financing violations resulted in no incarceration, and, tellingly, showed that many more egregious cases involving much more money were disposed of entirely with civil fines and enforcement actions by the Federal Election Commission. Moreover, virtually all of the criminal prosecutions were for misdemeanor charges. Still, ten days before my sentencing date, we had no word from Vicki Costanzi as to her final position in the addendum report. I was still facing eighteen to twenty-four months in prison.

The prosecutor responded to my probation reply with a scathing rebuttal in which he not only exaggerated the offensive conduct, but accused me of lying in my brief. His attacks were getting increasingly personal in response to the favorable references we submitted. For example, in a blatantly misleading statement designed to bait the judge, the prosecutor inserted into his brief unfavorable images of my wealth, as if in America success were a crime, and I had somehow made my fortune illegally.

In his rebuttal to my probation submission, the prosecutor tried to persuade the judge to disregard my guilty plea by arguing that I had put the government through an expensive investigation, and that I had pleaded guilty only when faced with overwhelming evidence of my crime. Jacobson even included innuendoes about alleged sexual affairs, trying to damage my credibility as a stable family man. At one point he actually called my attorney and threatened that he was going to do this unless I withdrew the fifty letters of character reference that I'd submitted in my behalf. My answer was, "Go to hell." Then, in response, when he included this attack in his memorandum, Valerie submitted her own letter, attesting to our long-term and very close relationship. Based on a completely false allegation from an unhappy ex-employee, Jacobson even accused me in writing of having a Swiss bank account in order to hide money from my wife. I was absolutely amazed that a federal prosecutor can get away with using bald-faced lies with no substantiation whatsoever in a sentencing brief. In a contention that enraged me almost as much, he disparaged how I had enabled Besicorp's survival by providing personal guarantees for the company debt. "Mr. Zinn makes much of his financial support of Besicorp," he asserted, "but that should be disregarded by the court. Mr. Zinn and Besicorp are interchangeable. He has made millions from his guarantees." Yes, my personal guarantees paid off. But had the company failed, I would have been left owing millions while the public shareholders would have shared none of that responsibility.

Less than a week before sentencing, Jacobson conceded in a conversation with Bill Brodsky that we were going to win on an important technical sentencing point that was being contested. The prosecutor had sought to increase my sentence with an argument that I should have even more points added to the guidelines calculation due to "fraud loss" as if I had committed a financial crime like embezzlement. This calculation is based upon the total amount of money involved in the alleged "fraud," in this case the amount contributed to the campaign. Under the sentencing guidelines, if he succeeded, this would have added a minimum of six more months to my sentence. Knowing that he thought we had a winning argument even on a single point was wind in my sails for a few precious days. I needed every bit I could get.

39

THE COUNTDOWN

R ight in the midst of these proceedings, Niagara Mohawk Power Corp.'s problems boiled to a head. As part of the independent power industry, Besicorp's objective was to build a new generation of clean, efficient power plants to compete with the regulated utility industry. I've noted how our valuable assets were created, and how in 1994 our contracts to sell electricity to NIMO had been renegotiated. In order to settle the differences between the independent power producers (IPPs) and NIMO once and for all, a process was set up during the spring of 1997 to negotiate a financial settlement with all of the IPPs. The process involved several major investment banking firms, several large law firms, and nineteen IPP companies, representing 42 power projects. Besicorp and our partner held five of those 42 projects, but we represented 24% of the total power generated by that group of projects.

NIMO claimed that they were facing bankruptcy within a few years if they didn't get out of the squeeze caused by escalating power purchase costs and regulatory pressure to keep retail prices in check. This was a severe threat to the very survival of Besicorp, as the bulk of our revenues and all of our earnings came from our NIMO projects.

Holding all nineteen companies together in the negotiation was a grueling task, and leadership fell to a small group of parties, first among them my partner Hal Kamine. He kept the parties focused on the big picture and prevented the greed factor from derailing the transaction. He also developed a relationship of trust with Bill Davis, NIMO's CEO, which kept the deal on course during difficult periods.

After months of grueling negotiation, NIMO and most of the independent power producers negotiated a Master Restructuring Agreement. ("MRA"). The MRA established the framework for a complex, long-term process by which each of the IPP's would undertake to try and "unwind" their projects, which required dealing with lenders to the projects and all the myriad underlying contractual relationships. NIMO's goal was to cancel all of their power sale contracts with IPPs. The MRA was only the beginning.

The negotiating process was far more complex than any of our prior project financings. If we signed the MRA, each of our five projects would have to be unraveled. We couldn't even start that process until after the MRA was signed, and the closing was contingent upon getting hundreds of parties to go along. This was going to be one of the largest voluntary restructurings in the history of American industry. It was a $4.8 billion transaction involving hundreds of companies. If the MRA failed to be consummated, it would precipitate the bankruptcy of one of the nation's largest utilities, and in all likelihood many of the IPP projects would end up in bankruptcy as well.

The closing also required NIMO to raise billions of dollars at less than "investment-grade" financing. (Most utilities were considered investment grade by the rating agencies, but NIMO had lost that coveted position as a consequence of their financial deterioration.) The entire enterprise would have to be approved by the Public Service Commission, New York State's regulatory body. A fortune of money would change hands if this deal could be consummated, as the IPPs were being asked to give up their business and cancel the long-term contracts that formed their entire basis. It was a very fragile situation, fraught with risk.

One of the provisions we negotiated into the MRA document obligated NIMO to enter into a tax-free merger transaction in order to cancel the power contracts for our projects, as long as certain conditions were met. This was of importance to Besicorp due to our ownership structure; we were one of the few independent companies that could benefit from a tax-free exchange of common stock, and we had to fight like hell to keep that provision in the documents. By saving taxes on the MRA proceeds, such a merger would be worth many tens of million dollars in benefit to Besicorp shareholders.

I was expecting to be there to get the deal done. As the architect of the merger strategy, I was probably the only one who could pressure NIMO to go along with what was admittedly a difficult transaction structure. Aside from the issue of my freedom, Besicorp itself had a lot riding on my getting a sentence of home confinement. But the dissident shareholders continued to agitate for my incarceration.

~

Beginning in November, 1997, a bizarre new twist in the campaign to pressure Besicorp into liquidation began to emerge. Hate mail began to arrive at the homes of various people associated with the company. The instigators were emboldened by their success in forcing my plea-bargained conviction. They were undoubtedly feeling close to achieving their goal of forcing Besicorp into liquidation. In a sense, they were correct. The environment within the company was so tense and pessimistic that they must have felt that adding a little fuel to the fire would bring about a grand scale implosion of the business, but there was a tremendous reservoir of strength within the walls, and a determination by the people to keep the company going in spite of the adversity.

The hate mail came in the form of packages intermittently arriving at the homes and offices of many people associated with the company—my wife and daughter, the Besicorp board members, senior employees of the company, and the owners of companies with which Besicorp did business. These packages contained odd compilations of material: press clippings with particularly negative or scandalous areas highlighted; public SEC filings; typewritten notes making veiled threats and nasty comments. The campaign was clearly intended to augment the intimidation that had already been taking place. The letters continued for months.

One of the most outrageous was an anonymous typewritten note to Valerie saying, "You're next." Another was addressed to my daughter at her college—a not so subtle message that the writer knew where my daughter was and that she was not safe.

Besicorp hired an independent investigation firm that was unable to trace the letters with any certainty. The packages were devoid of fingerprints. Besicorp tried to get the postal inspector involved, but the letters did not contain any overt threats, so they did not rise to the level that warranted government investigation. But there was no doubt what the message was: "Give up—or else!"

In mid-October, just a few days before my sentencing, the call we were waiting for came. Vicki Costanzi told Bill Brodsky that she was going to suggest to the judge that he consider a "downward departure" from the guidelines calculation. She had concluded that the offense conduct was not as serious as her original interpretation of the sentencing guidelines indicated. That was certainly good news. But, Ms. Costanzi said she was not changing her position on any of the sentencing guideline issues that we were contesting; she was standing firm on both the "fraud loss" enhancement and the "breach of trust," and had concluded that the proper sentence according to the guidelines was eighteen to twenty-four months. For us, everything depended upon how she qualified that view in her ultimate recommendation to the judge.

On the Friday before my sentencing, we received the probation officer's addendum report. Neither Bill Brodsky nor Doug Lobel, in their decades of experience as criminal defense attorneys had ever seen such a dramatic turnaround by a probation officer. Vicki Costanzi had understood my appeal not as a line of bullshit, but as a credible explanation of the offense. She concluded that there were mitigating circumstances and placed the offense conduct within the context of my life. She understood how I came to plea-bargain. She understood my lack of malice and bad intentions. I had achieved everything I could have hoped for. While Ms. Costanzi did not budge on her interpretation of the guidelines, she laced her report with clear signals of sympathy about the case, my life, and my family's suffering.

"There is zero probability of recidivism," she said "Mr. Zinn has been marked as a convicted felon." She recommended zero incarceration with six months home confinement. If the judge accepted it, I could be home and still be able to go to work!

It was awfully tempting to feel good that weekend and for the remaining days before the sentencing date, but I was not about to count my chickens. Everything was now in the judge's hands. There were many people praying for me. Ms. Costanzi had heard those prayers, I thought, and God had answered them through her compassion and wisdom. Now, at least, I had some hope for a compassionate sentence.

40

Sent Away

The day of sentencing was upon us, and I grimly anticipated the horrible moment. I wanted it over, and I wanted it never to happen. When the morning broke, I sullenly arose from bed, took my shower, and wished the clock would stop.

Valerie didn't come with me to the courthouse. She was unable to cope with any more stress or to deal with the reporters we knew would be there, and I told her to stay home and wait for word. Brodsky said it was preferable to have her by my side showing support, but that it was not essential to the outcome. Anyway, I knew she was with me spiritually and I was happy to relieve her of the burden of that day as much I could. She had already borne far too much on my account.

I was so anxious that I decided we should take two cars, in case one broke down on the way to White Plains. As much as I didn't want to be there, it was an appointment I could not miss.

We arrived early. Mike Daley, Steve Nachimson, and I advanced toward the courthouse to the snapping of cameras and rapid-fire questions by reporters with microphones. Josh Margolin, always the most hostile of the reporters, was particularly demanding, wanting comments even now, before anything had happened.

As we made our way to the courtroom, my entourage grew. Larry Fisher, my longtime friend and counselor arrived. Alan Epstein of Kelley, Drye, and Warren was also there. The three of us hugged on the courthouse steps. Bill Brodsky, Doug Lobel, and I embraced. Our hugs were captured and printed in the next day's newspapers. Two of my close friends, Steven Murphy and Dave Laskin, arrived to show their love and support.

We moved along to the courtroom of Judge Charles Brieant. I was still desperately hoping that underneath his hard, Teddy Roosevelt exterior there was compassion. But deep in my heart, I feared that the venomous letters he had received had poisoned his mind.

Elliot Jacobson was already there, along with the FBI agent who had run the investigation. There was a variety of reporters, including some I had never seen before. But the greatest surprise was the presence of Martin Enowitz. He had come to observe first hand the result of his ruinous campaign. Even if I had to spend ten years in jail, I thought, I would never exchange my life for his.

As I stood in the courtroom, I was intensely aware of Enowitz lurking in the background. I was determined not to look back at him to give him the satisfaction of an acknowledgment. No matter what pleasure he derived from being the architect of my difficulties, he was not worth a glance in his direction.

The tension between Bill Brodsky and me over the preparation of my sentencing memorandum had continued to the last moment and spilled into our deliberation over what I should say to the judge today before the sentencing—how much detail, how much explanation. In the end, I deferred again to Bill's experience and agreed to restrain myself and simply say "I'm sorry."

The court clerk announced the judge's entry. "All rise in the matter of the People versus Zinn and Besicorp."

In his first words from the bench, Judge Brieant cut the proceeding short by declaring he would rule on the legal points first. As he read his rulings on each of the points that we were litigating, our hopes rose. Yes! Each time he fired off a ruling, it was for us! I wanted to cheer but held my feelings in check. At last, after what seemed an interminable amount of time, we had won all the litigated points of law. The judge had established my sentencing guideline points into the range we had hoped for, without our even having to present an oral argument.

Now it was time to make my apology to the judge. Standing before him, I asked to remain with my family, and I told him that what had happened was the biggest mistake of my life. I was thinking how many mistakes I had made, but that wasn't what the judge was thinking; I knew I was pleading guilty to a trumped-up charge, and I couldn't tell him the truth. But I was short and sweet, the way Brodsky had said to do it.

Then Judge Brieant began to speak. He said, "The Court will disregard completely the derogatory letters which have come in. These letters go outside the offense behavior and are not appropriate in consideration, and the Court understands that any successful businessman will be expected to pick up a few detractors along the way." Judge Brieant also noted the large volume of support letters I had received. Then he dropped the bomb.

"As to Mr. Zinn, the sentence presents a difficult issue for the court, and the court is guided in the imposition of sentence by the need for general deterrence, which the court believes is important in this case, which involves serious violations.

"The Court believes that this crime is quite common and threatens the conduct of free election, which is at the heart of representative government. This is not a case of somebody who dipped into his own pocket, which he could have readily done and had his friends or relatives or employees mail him checks in excess of his emitt for hard money. That could have been done, that would be a simple violation, which might well be described as technical and relating to a rather poorly drafted statute.

"If the money was given in one lump sum of soft money to the county committee, that would have been lawful conduct under the circumstances. But here the Court ought to consider the entire behavior pattern. Mr. Zinn took advantage of the fact that he was the Chief Executive Officer of the public corporation and he dipped into the corporate treasury to pay for his own political goals at the expense of the minority shareholders, many of whom did not share his political interest or they didn't live in the district or they didn't have any benefit flowing to them out of the election; and in doing that, they also caused the commission of a tax fraud, and he condoned the twisting of arms of vendors. And when you do that, the vendors usually get theirs back by higher prices or reduced quality and service.

"So that this practice like the associated practice of stealing the money to make the campaign gifts from the corporation, violated the duty of undivided loyalty and good faith owed by a fiduciary to the corporation. And while a court cannot enhance the offense behavior for that as independent of the crime, the court can consider that in determining a sentence within the guidelines. The court finds that the representing interests of society to express its disapproval of this sort of conduct, a sentence has to be consistent with the conduct which occurred.

"We're a self-governing nation, and if we have silly or high technical requirements, it's our duty to obey the law until it's changed. This case is more than a simple election law violation caused by a person being a neophyte in politics. This is a case where in order to commit the election law violation, the person perpetrating the offense engaged in a fraud on his own shareholders and his own company and a breach of his duty of undivided loyalty and also in a tax fraud. And this Court's sentence ought not to be seen as trivializing serious misconduct by an otherwise talented person who had a very productive life. The Court can only say, neophyte or not, he knew better; and so, accordingly, Mr. Zinn, you are sentenced on counts one and two to the custody of the Bureau of Prisons for a term of imprisonment of six months on each count to run concurrently."

I was shocked and struck dumb. My friends surrounded me. The reporters descended, asking for comments. One, with a kinder face, came up to me and asked me gently if I had anything to say. I could do nothing but look him in the eye. (He departed to write a commentary piece in the Poughkeepsie Journal, describing the event as justice hitting me with an ax.) Enowitz edged closer to our group, lurking at the perimeter, a grin on his face as we moved out of the courtroom and into the hallway. All of us were stunned. I don't think anybody had expected that outcome. We moved to the bank of elevators, and Enowitz moved right along with us, as if he were with us; as the elevator doors opened and our group stepped in, Enowitz did too. I could not get into the same elevator with him; I waited. Brodsky stepped out to join me, and Enowitz stepped out as well. I decided to take the elevator since Enowitz had stepped out, but as soon as I stepped in again, Enowitz stepped in. We went down to the second floor, where the U.S. Probation Service was located, and when we all got out, Enowitz followed. I walked up to him and said, "Do you have something to say to me?" "Yes," He answered. Brodsky grabbed me by the scruff of the neck and pulled me away.

After processing by the Probation Department and being photographed and fingerprinted again, I went to a pay phone. I now had to tell Valerie. I had been dreading that moment, and here it was. Val was waiting impatiently at home, with Joyce DePietro keeping her company. Sadly, I gave her the bad news: I was going to prison in three weeks. The judge had cut off all avenues of appeal. She shrieked with grief. From that moment on, we had to accept that this was the harsh reality of our lives.

When I arrived home we were joined by some of my loyal team from Besicorp. Then I had to call my daughter at college and give her the bad news. She was waiting by the phone, sitting there and anxiously holding hands with a friend. She was inconsolable, at first. But I reminded her that she was a part of me, and that I knew she had intrinsic strength that she must find. I didn't want her to allow this horrible turn of events to affect her young life any more than necessary. When I found out that she cried in her room all day, I phoned the college counseling office, told them what had happened, and asked them to intervene. When they sent someone to be with her, she refused to open her door. I was grateful that her best friend on campus was able to comfort her.

The process of planning for my departure began. We sent out a press release from Besicorp. We planned management succession. I tried to put my personal affairs in order. It was almost as if I was dying, but I got to be an active participant in the preparation.

I thanked God that in just six months I would have my life back. It was long time, but I counted my blessings anyway; with the judge's mindset, I could have easily received twelve months and still been within the sentencing guidelines as he had ruled on them. If he had been so inclined, he could have disagreed with our guideline analysis and sentenced me to twenty-four months, or even longer with an upward departure. I didn't exactly feel gratitude, but I also understood that it could have been worse. In prison, I would meet many people who were serving far longer sentences than I, and I see how the injury more than doubled when the sentence doubled. For the company, six months was just a hiatus. Besicorp would be in good hands. Valerie could hold the fort for those six months, and then I'd be home, with nothing much changed.

I was determined to deal with prison and to come out stronger than ever. My enemies could take my body for a time, but I would never give up my spirit or my soul. I prayed for Valerie and my daughter to find similar strength.

41

To Prison

On the day I was sentenced, New York State Attorney General Dennis Vacco's investigators were still jousting with Besicorp's legal team over the scope of their subpoena. My surrender to the custody of the Bureau of Prisons was to take place in just three weeks.

In a decision I would later regret, I chose voluntarily to resign all my positions as officer or director of Besicorp and its subsidiaries, rather than take a leave of absence. I made the decision solely to make it easier for the board and management to cope with the NYS Attorney General while I was away.

I had the right to take a leave of absence and not resign, but that would have left the Attorney General in litigation mode. Michael Daley, who'd been such a loyal friend, would take on the role of president. Valerie, who had dealt with human resource issues in the past, would step up her involvement to the extent that she could handle it. The management team was in good shape, but they were not capable of handling an adversary proceeding with the AG without me there to lead the charge. If only as the majority shareholder, I wanted the company in as good shape as possible when I came out. I figured it would not be difficult to regain my position when I returned from prison, for I was confident that the board would want me back as Besicorp's CEO. If not, my majority ownership would still allow me the option of forcing my way back in.

So, after twenty years at the helm of Besicorp, I sadly resigned. Once the resignation was announced, Besicorp's outside counsel negotiated a suspension of the Attorney General's investigation. The Attorney General stipulated that the investigation would be reinstated if I returned to Besicorp. So be it. I would cross that bridge when I came to it.

Judge Brieant had granted me the privilege of self-surrender to a minimum-security prison camp to serve my sentence. He did this knowing my background, and making an informed decision that removal from my family and my life was punishment enough without the rigors of being among violent offenders and other aspects of harsh confinement. As opposed to being taken from the courthouse in chains, self-surrender is, in fact, a privilege. It allows the offender to transport himself to the gates of the prison and walk in voluntarily.

On Wednesday, November 12, 1997, I surrendered to the Fairton Prison Camp, a minimum-security facility adjacent to the Fairton Federal Correctional Institution in Southern New Jersey. Val cried as we had our final embrace. It was a chilly afternoon, and neither of us will ever forget that moment. Two correction officers ("CO's") patted me down, and all my belongings were handed back to Val; all I was allowed to take with me was a pair of white sneakers and a set of rubber earplugs.

Under the eyes of two correction officers armed with shotguns, I waved goodbye and walked through the gatehouse into the maximum security prison that processed inmates for the prison camp. I was sure I could survive six months no matter what was thrown at me. But what about my family? They were the true victims of those who did this dirty work.

On my first day of incarceration, I was inducted into the system at the maximum-security facility adjacent to the prison camp. I was medically processed and fingerprinted. After a wait in a holding cell, I was taken to a room, told to strip, and handed some old cotton fatigues; A CO asked me whether I wanted to donate my street clothes. Because I was more than a little rattled, I hesitated a moment too long, and the CO grabbed my clothes and threw them into a box. Then he then brought in one of his supervisors, who looked at my left hand and saw that I was wearing my wedding ring. "Take off that wedding band!" he barked. "That looks like a brass knuckle." I gave him the ring, and he threw it into the box.

Later, I had a quiet talk with that CO and told him that I wanted to donate my clothes. He said that they'd just wanted to give me a little lesson in how to deal in the prison system.

He opened the doors and pointed to the camp. "Go there," he said. I walked out of the gate of the maximum security facility, completely unsupervised, and ambled towards the steel warehouse that served as the barracks for the prison camp.

A group of friendly inmates made me feel welcome, and several of them went out of their way to ease the trauma of the first day of incarceration by providing me with small accessories that are taken for granted by people on the outside. One of the very nicest men actually had his wife call Valerie and tell her I was okay. Although it was a four-and-a-half-hour drive for my family and friends, at least I would be able to stay in phone contact and be among people who were going through the same experience.

The next day I met with Mr. Joyner, the camp administrator, a large black man with a booming voice. Several inmates had told me that he was tough but fair. Joyner looked me square in the eye and told me that I was a high-profile case. He said he wasn't going to give me any special treatment, I told him that I was just there to do my time.

Telephone access at the prison was by computerized access code, and it could take as much as a week to process a new inmate; I survived those first few days on calls that I made courtesy of the camp staff. The staff seemed to be reasonably nice under the circumstances—I imagine they go through the same thing each time a new inmate with strong family ties comes in.

I called home on the counselor's phone on Saturday morning and let Sunday go by without calling, hoping to get my phone system access code by Monday. I wanted very badly to talk to my wife and daughter, but I was also beginning to feel that I would be able to survive the six months there in the way I'd been anticipating—

without undermining my emotional stability. I hoped Val and my daughter would be able to do as well.

∼

On that first Monday at the camp, I woke up early with all the other inmates and took my shower. I was dressed by seven. The correction officer on duty at the barracks station told me to report to the Receiving and Discharge ("R&D") building at eight. I didn't ask why, figuring that I was going to be pushing a broom or performing some other redeeming task. I left my locker open and my clothes hanging over my bed rail. Little did I know what was in store.

The tall razor-wire double fence of the high-security Fairton Federal Correctional Facility loomed larger as I walked down the long concrete path in the cold morning air. Two white vans were parked in front of the double-lock entry gate, ringed by U.S. Marshals holding shotguns and assault rifles—dropping off a dangerous prisoner, I figured, so I assumed that I was supposed to walk on by and mind my own business. A marshal approached me and asked me to identify myself. I had barely learned my number but I managed to spit it out; I was ordered to stand still, frisked, and without further explanation, a federal police agent slapped me into handcuffs, wrapped me with a waist chain, and snapped on leg irons. I was being shipped! The marshal wouldn't tell me where I was being taken, but I had a pretty good idea what my ultimate destination was going to be. The previous Friday Valerie had told me that I had been served with a grand jury subpoena issued by Elliot Jacobson on the very day of my surrender!

I'd tried to call Brodsky that Friday to discuss the subpoena, but the counselor brushed me off until Monday. I told her that I needed to call my attorney, but she said to just wait, that she was too busy. I figured it was better not to make waves, and that I had better get used to waiting. I never got to speak to my attorney before being shipped.

∼

Being transported as a maximum-security prisoner is a never-to-be-forgotten experience. A chain was tied around my waist and tightened down fast; cuffs were slipped through a slotted link in the waist chain; my hands were pushed tight to my waist and then the "block" was installed, a metal clip that makes the handcuffs into a one-piece metal bar. My hands were bent and my arms pulled tight together and held at a right angle to my stomach. My wrists were bent and arms are immobilized. Cuffs were put on both my legs and linked by a chain that limits movement to a short and pathetic shuffle.

There I sat, in a van being driven by heavily armed U.S. marshals with an odd and angry-looking collection of federal prisoners. Over the course of a very long day, I was handed off time after time from one group of marshals to another. I became increasingly horrified at the behavior of the marshals, most of whom acted like jack-booted storm troopers. Over the course of the day to come, I asked several times for the cuffs to be loosened. At best, I was ignored. One marshal checked them and then tightened them further, squeezing and gouging my wrist bones even more than before. Then he grinned. Though I would occasionally capture a glimmer of compassion in a word or a look, never in a deed. There was camaraderie among the captors, however; we were human cargo considered no better than livestock by our handlers, and every day they had another load to move.

My first stop after departing Fairton was the Camden County Jail, outside of Philadelphia. I was dumped into a holding cell with a crowd of angry and disheveled people where I kept to myself, avoiding eye contact. Though all were black, I was bearded and dressed in prison garb, and I didn't stand out. Nobody bothered me. Eventually, my name was called and I was strip-searched, cuffed, chained, and blocked.

I was driven with a new group of inmates in a westerly direction. I had assumed by now that my destination was the federal courthouse at White Plains, New York, but that was to the northeast. None of the marshals would answer questions or make eye contact.

After a couple of hours of more driving, we arrived in Harrisburg, Pennsylvania. The van drove out onto the ramp of the Harrisburg International Airport, and over a two-hour period, vans, busses, and cars converged at the site. U.S. marshals with shotguns and submachine guns stood watch, ringing the site at 500 feet to make sure none of the inmates attempted to escape. A prisoner exchange was about to take place.

The number of vehicles and the confusion increased as we inmates were moved from the cars, vans, and buses and left standing on the ramp, lined up to be searched wearing only cotton tee-shirts in blustery twenty-degree winter weather. Jack-booted marshals wore black coats and parkas, moving their human cargo oblivious to the freezing conditions.

A jet loaded with prisoners arrived to rendezvous with all the vehicles. The prisoner exchange picked up speed with frenetic activity by the U.S. marshals and correction officers. I was watching it all sitting there in a van, still in handcuffs and leg irons. Finally, all the bodies were where they were supposed to be, and the vehicles began departing for points unknown.

I was put on a bus with three COs, heading north into the mountains of central Pennsylvania. The blocks were digging in and my wrists were sore as hell. I was in federal custody and I'd better get used to it. Darkness fell and the bus just kept on driving along as freeways became divided highways, which turned into quiet two-lane mountain roads. Late that night we arrived at the Lewisburg Federal Penitentiary.

Lewisburg is a maximum-security institution surrounded by giant stone walls, with immense brick buildings and gun towers ringing the perimeter. Giant motorized gates control entry beyond the twenty-foot-high walls. The bus drove through one gate, then another, and then another, pulling up in front of a basement door of what looked like the main building.

The very sight of Lewisburg would make anyone penitent.

One by one, each of us filed out to be frisked. At long last, the cuffs and shackles were removed; my arms were numb and my wrists were sore and inflamed. I looked back inside the bus. An armed guard rode in a cage in the back, and two others rode in the front. The windows were covered with steel mesh. The bus was followed by a van with more armed guards, all there to make sure the shackled, cuffed, and manacled prisoners arrived at their destination.

Still wearing only tee shirts, we were directed to an unheated basement room, where we were processed for strip search and medical clearing. Then we were given a new set of cotton prison clothes and shuttled into a freezing hallway. Our first meal of the day was brown bag baloney sandwiches.

~

We prisoners were taken away in small groups. We were in the bowels of the "Big House," as Lewisburg is proudly known to its guards. Among the last to depart, I shuffled through numerous iron gates into a basement corridor and was herded into a basement room with the fourteen other people in my group.

This was where we were staying the night. I looked around and noticed that there were no beds. We were given a box of bedrolls made of a sheet and torn wool blanket and pointed towards a pile of decrepit folded army cots.

One by one, each of us took a cot and dismantled it. The canvas was torn, without a level spot to lay our bodies down on. We were all in the same boat, and we made the best of it. We lined up the so-called bunks side by side and tried to sleep. Lying and staring at the dank ceiling, with plaster fallen all around, I wondered if something would drop on my head during the night. It didn't.

Five in the morning was wake-up call, and a box was passed into the room filled with brown bags containing a small carton of cereal, another of milk, and an apple. Once we ate, we were moved through a maze of the major hallways of this seemingly medieval monument; I marveled at the elaborate stonework and arches.

We entered a cell-block area, climbed stairs, and went through multiple-locked gates, finally arriving at an area marked "Special Housing Unit." If I'd hoped to be given decent accommodations as a "white-collar" offender, I was in for a shock. I was escorted down the hallway, passing door after door. Then the guard opened a metal door and told me to go inside. The cell was a putrid, filthy, welded steel box, no more that four feet wide by nine feet long. The door was solid steel plate with a hatch through which a food tray could be shoved. It had a tiny barred hole for the guard to look through.

Filth was everywhere. Garbage was strewn on the floor. I pointed the mess out to the guard, and he kindly brought me a broom. I removed and dumped what I could, but the encrusted filth wouldn't come off. As I worked, the door slammed at my back. How long would I be in this wretched place?

I moved the sodden piece of limp cotton provided for a mattress, I tucked and covered the mat with my sheet, hoping to avoid the odors and isolate myself from the bedbugs. Then I curled up under the blanket and went to sleep.

I was awakened by the sound of a food tray being shoved into the hatch. I jumped up and grabbed it before it crashed down and looked for somewhere to put it down. The only place was on the filthy toilet, so I balanced it on the steel latrine (there was no seat) and tried to eat. The meal was horrible-smelling porridge, but there was also boxed cereal. I stuck with what was in the box. At least I was safe.

Thankfully, some old paperbacks were lying around the cell, and I occupied my time by reading parts of junk novels. Shortly after dawn, a huge racket began, and the cell block was alive with screaming inmates, yelling back and forth and shouting continuously in jive or Spanish, arguing sports scores and making book.

Two black men occupied the cell directly across from mine. One tried desperately to get me to pass a note to the cell below mine through a hole in the floor. He screamed and screamed to get my attention, but I was determined to keep to myself. Eventually he resorted to having the inmate in the cell next to me kick repeatedly at the steel cell wall that separated us; it sounded like a cannon, and at that point, I could ignore him no longer.

I went to the tiny peephole in the door and looked across at him screaming at me as he tried to direct me to pick up the note he had passed. He stuck it on a metal mirror attached to a strip cut from a bedsheet that he flung towards my door along the floor. I pretended I was deaf so that he would leave me alone, pointing to my ears and saying, "I can't hear you, I'm deaf." The guy went berserk, stomping up and down and screaming at his cellmate, "The motherfucker is deaf." But from that point on, he left me alone. I prayed that I would remain locked in my cell for the duration of my stay in Lewisburg. All the putrid meals served on plastic trays smelled like septic waste when I lifted the covers, so I stayed with boxed cereal and milk.

After forty hours, my cell door opened. Thank God. I was again going to be processed and shipped. I had just seen hell on earth in the United States of America. It is hard to believe that the U.S. government houses human beings in such conditions.

Over the course of my incarceration, I would meet people who were in transit for months, moved from one institution to another with nothing but the cotton shirt on their backs. Inmates call this form of torture "diesel therapy" and, while not officially acknowledged, it's a form of punishment used by the Bureau of Prisons to "send a message" to troublesome inmates. What I've described is the standard method used to move the human cattle in the prison system, and those who go through it are usually cowed and grateful to finally be left in one place. It is one of the tools the system uses for getting "cooperation" from prisoners.

After a two-year investigation Assistant U.S. Attorney Elliot Jacobson had first served his subpoena for my grand jury appearance on the very day of my surrender into federal custody. My grand jury appearance was to take place at the federal courthouse in White Plains on December 15th, over thirty days after I was pulled out of camp. A trip by car from Fairton to White Plains would have taken two and one-half hours.

Elliot Jacobson had told Bill Brodsky that he wanted me in custody far longer than six months. He'd even said that he wanted me taken from the courthouse in chains, denied the opportunity to put my affairs in order and to say goodbye to my family. He'd wanted to put me in jail, not in a prison camp, and he'd found a way to do it, acting at my point of maximum vulnerability, subverting the will of the sentencing judge and abusing the power entrusted in him by the public. Wanting to be judge, jury, and executioner, he had wielded the awesome power of the federal government as his personal bludgeon.

～

Now I was taken by bus to the Otisville Federal Correctional Institution, located only one hour from my home. This time my cuffs weren't blocked; it seems that while the U.S. Marshal Service uses that sadistic tool, the Bureau of Prisons transports inmates within the system in regular cuffs.

After spending hours in a holding cell and undergoing another strip search, I was moved to Stewart Airport in Newburgh, New York to observe another airport prisoner exchange. In due course I was delivered to my ultimate destination, the Westchester County Jail near White Plains, New York. It was now Thursday, and I had spent more than three days in transport. Thank God for only three days. It could have been a month.

I was thrown into a holding pen with a dozen other prisoners. They were all in for a variety of drug and violent crime charges, and most had been arrested during the previous night. After processing at Westchester, I had my first access to a phone since the prior Saturday. I called Valerie collect, and she was distraught. By Tuesday, even Bill Brodsky hadn't been able to locate me through the Bureau of Prisons. I reassured her that I was okay and that my spirit was completely unbroken.

I couldn't know that the experience of worry and agony over my transport was only the beginning for Val. For me, the whole experience was eye-opening, not life-threatening, even enriching in a perverse sort of way. Most people don't get to experience what I just had and, thankfully, it was only a little over three days. I was certain that I would live to tell the tale. But every moment was hell for Valerie.

～

Fortunately, I ended up in a relatively new jail facility in White Plains, where I had a safe, private cell. I was able to receive two one-hour visits per week from my family, and visits from my attorneys. I played cards, scrabble, basketball, and worked out, and I was able to spend most of my time writing. I found out that most federal prisoners in the New York area are placed at Riker's Island or the infamous Metropolitan Correctional Facility—both hellholes. But I was lucky, in a manner of speaking.

In searching for me, Bill Brodsky had crossed swords again with Elliot Jacobson. Brodsky said he had called Jacobson a "prick" for doing what he did; in response, Jacobson replied that he thought my sentence wasn't harsh enough. I didn't know what horror would come at me next, but I did know that in the near future I would go eyeball-to-eyeball with Jacobson for the first time.

42

At the Grand Jury

For all this time, I hadn't had a single face-to-face encounter with Elliot Jacobson. The man with such awesome power knew me only through the eyes of Alan Kahn, James Lichtenberg, and Martin Enowitz. Now, a month after my surrender, I was to appear before the grand jury facing a hostile prosecutor.

Neither my "diesel therapy" nor my stay so far in Westchester County Jail had eroded my physical or psychological strength. I felt as capable as ever of withstanding what was coming. But this prosecutor believed that I wasn't being punished harshly enough, and I understood that once again I was in a highly dangerous situation.

Bill Brodsky had told Jacobson that I would plead the "Fifth" in front of the grand jury, so Jacobson arranged to force my testimony with a grant of "use immunity." Supposedly this would protect me from further prosecution on the subjects that I would testify about. The government grants this limited protection against self-incrimination to prevent witnesses from taking the Fifth Amendment, but despite the immunity grant, additional prosecution could follow, based upon an allegation of perjury or obstruction of justice.

Most people don't know that the Fifth Amendment right to remain silent and avoid self-incrimination is no longer absolute. The Supreme Court has allowed that witnesses granted immunity can be compelled to testify, a decision that has contributed to the gradual erosion of our civil liberties. The logic is that if the witness cannot be prosecuted based upon the particular testimony for which he is granted immunity, there is no breach of the constitutional right. "Use Immunity" satisfies the court's requirements, but it limits the witness's protection to assurances that subjects revealed by his or her testimony will not be prosecuted. There are exceptions, however. The government can still prosecute the individual on those subjects if it can show that it would have been able to obtain that information from other sources, and leads suggested by the testimony can be followed up, so that one is actually giving testimony against oneself. Of course, an indictment based on that tactic can be challenged on a technical basis, but the challenge could fail. Not exactly what we were taught in high school civics class.

My brief meeting with Bill Brodsky at Westchester County Jail gave me scant comfort. Brodsky had no idea how to de-escalate the conflict with Elliott Jacobson, and Brodsky's negative attitude continued to come out in his remarks. During one of our discussions, I criticized the performance of a new attorney working on the Bansbach shareholder suit. Brodsky jumped all over me, accusing me of criticizing her just because I disagreed with her conclusions. Well, why else would I criticize her?

From the beginning of the case, he and I had butted heads. I felt that the reason I was in prison was that my case had neither been understood nor presented properly by my counsel. I had always advocated the position that a prosecutor, probation officer, or judge would make decisions based on the outcome they wanted to obtain. Jacobson's mind had been poisoned from day one of his investigation, but instead of trying to change his mind-set, Brodsky had continued to employ a "circle-the-wagons" approach that perpetuated the prosecutor's hostility. The same mistakes had been made with the probation officer, I believed, and then again in what I was told to say to the judge.

I realized that I couldn't just walk into the grand jury and put my entire story out there without preparing the ground, but again I was being counseled not to volunteer anything, just to answer the questions in a minimalist fashion. It was the same bad strategy, being repeated one more time. It might get me through the grand jury appearance, but it wouldn't get Jacobson off my back. I made up my mind that I would not abide by it again.

〜

I was well prepared and knew the facts of my case like the back of my hand, but this was to be my first confrontation with Elliott Jacobson. The day I was to testify I awakened early at Westchester County jail. I showered, ate, and awaited my call to be processed for transport. I was escorted to the back of the jail, passed through metal detectors and motorized doors, and joined a group of other prisoners in the Receiving and Discharge area. I was handed my suit bag, and I reveled in unpacking my favorite olive double-breasted suit and a cotton dress shirt with my favorite tie. Even my sheepskin dress shoes! It was all the more satisfying knowing that these clothes had been packed by Valerie's loving hands. I don't wear suits to the office, but after a month in custody, prison fatigues and then jeans and sweats were grating on my nerves. It felt good to hang a business suit on my frame.

I trimmed my beard for the occasion and shaved around the edges. Although I cultivated the appearance of a wild man in jail so that the crazies would keep their distance, I intended to go into the grand jury facing Elliott Jacobson looking as much a professional as he was. I traveled the few miles to the federal courthouse in the custody of U.S. Marshals, wearing leg cuffs, a waist chain, and handcuffs, shackled to a chain with other inmates.

The van I rode in was driven directly into a basement entrance to the courthouse. I was anxious at the possibility of being photographed in cuffs and chains, but no photographers or reporters were waiting at the gate.

We moved into a holding cell, each prisoner to await his respective proceeding. During the wait, I heard some interesting stories. One fellow, who had been a crack dealer's courier, was appearing for sentencing (he got five years). Another was an accused bank robber who'd decided to go to trial even though he was facing twenty-to-life. He complained that the plea he was being offered gave him fifteen years; he would not cop a plea unless he could get down to ten. If he was going down, he said, he was going to go proud and fighting.

After a time, I was moved to an interview room to meet with Bill Brodsky. We were separated by a glass screen. Bill told me that the grand jury was being used by another Assistant U.S. Attorney to secure an indictment on another case. It was 11:30 a.m. before I was called up to the grand jury room.

I was escorted through the halls of the federal courthouse in shackles. Guided by the marshals, I passed through interior passageways into the hallway outside Judge Brieant's chambers. Bad memories of my sentencing day flooded my brain.

We arrived at the anteroom of the grand jury chamber. There was Elliott Jacobson and the FBI agent who worked with him on my prosecution. Amid the idle chatter as we waited for use of the room, the subject of my transport from Fairton came up, and I had my opportunity to tell Jacobson about my experience in graphic terms. He later told Brodsky he was sorry, but I didn't care how he felt after the fact, even if by odd chance he meant it. It is far too easy for bureaucrats to forget that they are dealing with human beings when they wield their swords. Real people feel pain and have families who suffer.

We entered the grand jury room, which was small, with amphitheater seating for about twenty-five people. Two ordinary-looking women were busy with paperwork: one was the chairwoman and the other was the sergeant-at-arms. I was led to an upholstered chair with a metal frame and watched with amazement as the marshal cuffed me to it. There I was, in a federal courthouse, in a business suit, handcuffed to a chair and being gazed upon by twenty-five people. There was only one exit door, and two federal marshals and an FBI agent were standing outside.

Jacobson began the session by asking me if I intended to invoke my Fifth Amendment privilege against self-incrimination. I replied "yes." He then proceeded to read into the record the immunity order signed by a federal judge.

The questioning began. Jacobson inquired into whether I intended to return to Besicorp as an officer or director when I finished my sentence. I had little question as to whom he had been speaking with and whose agenda he was pursuing.

I told him that Besicorp had been exploring a merger. The

company was at the point where serious discussions were underway with several major companies. I said that there may be a merger either in final stages or concluded before my release. I did not intend to make decisions until I saw what the conditions were at that time. Jacobson asked a series of further questions, but before we got into substance, he received an emergency phone call and adjourned our session until after lunch. I was taken to a holding cell to await my reappearance, but the call never came. I have learned how to chill out in a cell with nothing to do and nothing to read, just block walls to stare at. I was able to meditate, think about my family, my loved ones, and beautiful places. We accomplished virtually nothing in the brief session, and I was sent back to the county jail to await my next appearance.

Talking on the phone to Valerie and friends at the office was one of the few ways I could maintain my connection to the real world while I passed my time in the county jail. I called home and the office collect as often as possible, but when word reached the company's attorneys about my frequent calls, they became nervous about corporate employees being in contact with me. They were worried about possible allegations that I was somehow running the company from jail. But you could only make collect phone calls from Westchester County Jail, so I had no choice but availing myself of that method of payment. Reaching out for contact with my former life came from my deepest needs, but legal considerations were paramount, and Besicorp was still under siege. To protect the company from a possible lawsuit, the attorneys eventually pressured the company to cut me off by rejecting my calls! I must say that I was outraged.

The weeks passed. In due course I figured out how to maintain contact by bypassing the company's switchboard without the consent of Besicorp's upper management. The passage of time gradually brought some perspective that tempered my emotional reaction to being cut off. I was still calling into Besicorp to speak to Valerie, my friends, and my associates, but under greatly restricted conditions. I could see that Besicorp's board members had simply been given wrong-headed legal advice. They thought they were creating evidence of their "independence" to be used in a potential lawsuit, but all they were doing was causing me anguish and depriving themselves and the company of much-needed guidance.

The irony was that I was still personally guaranteeing Besicorp loans during my incarceration; nobody bothered to think about releasing me from my financial obligations when they cut me off from telephone contact. I felt wounded that, in the name of protecting Besicorp from possible future allegations of wrong, they were abandoning me.

The business was being litigated to death, and now it seemed to be going morally bankrupt. It seemed that the spiritual life had been sapped from Besicorp and it had become a shell consisting only of assets and liabilities, exactly what the raiders had wanted all along.

43

Toe-to-Toe With the Prosecutor

A second month went by at the county jail. My second day of grand jury testimony began. Jacobson challenged me, but this time he was armed with the transcript of my first session. Not content to hear me tell my story, he was angling to catch me in an inconsistency so that he could charge me with perjury.

If I told the truth and it didn't comport with his distorted view of reality, I might once again face a criminal prosecution, but this time for telling my story in an immunized grand jury appearance.

"Give him what he wants to hear and you're in and out," Brodsky had told me before my appearance. But the truth is gray, not black or white. When is a bonus a reimbursement? Why was it illegal? If some of the bonus payments I authorized turned out to be illegal in hindsight, did that make them all illegal just because Jacobson said so? I could not admit to things that had not happened.

So I walked Jacobson through the roster of Besicorp campaign contributors in excruciating detail. I told him and the grand jury the story of each person's campaign contribution. Even after Jacobson had succeeded in sending me to prison, it was now apparent to me that he still didn't really understand the case.

Jacobson repeatedly hammered me with probing questions. He kept asking over and over whether I ever did anything wrong, other than what I did during the campaign. I first replied, "In my life?" and the grand jury members laughed. I then replied, "Is this supposed to be a confessional?" and they laughed again.

Jacobson then asked whether it was wrong to "twist arms" to get campaign contributions. The judge had skewered me on this point in his sentencing as a result of the prosecutor's distortion of the factual record in his briefs. Jacobson had obtained notes of a campaign meeting kept by a secretary in which a reference to "twisting arms" to get money was noted. He had attributed those comments to me on no grounds whatsoever. But, in any case, whoever made them certainly didn't mean to convey that he or she condoned illegal activity.

I replied to his question, practically yelling, that nothing in that statement implied immoral, illegal, or coercive fund-raising methods. I said that what was immoral was Jacobson's lifting an innocent comment from a secretary's notes and using it to crucify me in front of the judge.

We had confrontation after confrontation. I challenged his theory of the case time after time as he questioned me about each donor. Finally, he asked me why I had pleaded guilty. I replied, "The way you charged this case, I was facing years in jail if I went to trial and was convicted. You forced me into being unable to defend myself." I added, "I recognize in hindsight that I facilitated some of the contributions. My attorney advised me that I broke the law even if I did so inadvertently. I had to plead guilty, but I did not reimburse anyone. I had no criminal intent." But I was talking to a brick wall.

Jacobson focused with particular intensity on Joyce DePietro. He was trying to drive a wedge between us. I told the grand jurors that the prosecution had ignored exculpatory evidence, had taken facts out of context, used hostile parties as witnesses, and had bought Ansaldo's testimony with a sweetheart deal.

Jacobson had come at me with his mind made up, but I was not going to be bulldozed, even if I was handcuffed to a chair. If he thought I was committing perjury and was determined to indict me, so be it. Let the chips fall where they must. I was already incarcerated for nothing, and if I had to tell my story in a perjury trial, then that's what I would do.

Finally, that horrible day wound to a close. We hadn't even touched on the politicians and their role in this nightmare. It seemed that Jacobson had actually concluded that Hinchey and his people had no responsibility for any of my transgressions.

At the end of the day, Jacobson asked me why I didn't come forward, if I had exculpatory evidence. I answered, "That is a very good question. My attorney would not allow it, and I don't blame you for that." This was our only moment of real communication in an otherwise intensely hostile confrontation. But the question remains in my mind: If I had come forward and told my story, would I have been indicted anyway? I'm pretty sure Jacobson would have used my own statements to screw me further to the wall, but I'll never know.

44

Trying to Cut a Deal

I was now awaiting my third grand jury appearance, still at the county jail, and my mind was working overtime. Even at this ridiculously late date, I still questioned whether Brodsky was able to represent me effectively, but I had stayed the course with him out of exhaustion and inertia. I did not question his sincerity. I did not question his experience. But I had serious and horribly belated reservations about his understanding of my case. The things that were so visible to me seemed to be inscrutable to him; he seemed never to take advantage of opportunities to deal effectively with Jacobson.

From day one, I'd tried to get Bill to negotiate a cooperation agreement with Jacobson in exchange for my help with his investigation of Hinchey and his top aides. But Brodsky had refused to take that approach. Jacobson should have been investigating the congressman, I maintained, and at least we should explore what kind of consideration I could receive for providing truthful information about what took place during the campaign.

Brodsky didn't think I had enough incriminating information to interest Jacobson in going after Hinchey's people, and therefore he consistently diminished the significance of that possibility, saying that Jacobson didn't want Hinchey or his top aides: "You're the fish he wants to fry." Brodsky even said to me on one occasion, "Wouldn't Hinchey and his people be grateful to you if you kept your mouth shut? They could find a way to help you in the future!" I was incredulous at this remark. "They will treat me like stinking fish for all time," I replied. "Beside, they lied to the prosecutor to protect themselves, so what do I owe them?"

Throughout the case, Bill was convinced that his strategy was the best way keep me out of jail. He reasoned that providing information to the government would only be opening a Pandora's box that would bring me more troubles.

~

By early February of 1998, I was busy waiting for my third appearance before the grand jury. I'd fantasized about the possibility of a sentence reduction if I really had something the government could use to prosecute others (I'd learned the disgusting game well by this point), but this was never a realistic hope.

I was miserable with my attorney. I went down the list of grievances against him in my mind, over and over again. What else did I have to do but write, talk on the phone, and let my mind run wild? Bill always told me not to talk to the press, with the result that press coverage of my case was universally bad. Each time I dealt directly with the press the outcome was much better. Our philosophies were so very different. How did I get stuck with him as an attorney and not know how to extricate myself? Valerie had told me during the investigation that she lacked confidence in Bill Brodsky, but again I didn't listen.

My mind was really going off the deep end. Sitting in jail stewing about this case was not the place to retain a balanced perspective. In my darker moments, I even imagined that Brodsky had a behind-the-scenes relationship with Lenefsky or other big-shot Democrats. Forgive me for even thinking such ugly thoughts; I was in jail and in the midst of grand jury proceedings, and my perception was that when I tried to fix what was broken, Bill Brodsky still got in the way.

My third grand jury appearance was at least another month down the road. It seemed that I was destined to spend over half my sentence in this maximum-security county jail, seeing my wife and daughter sitting across a table as I sat there helpless in a yellow jump suit; there was no hugging, no kissing, no contact allowed.

One day, when we were speaking on the pay phone in the cell block, Joyce DePietro said, "Hold your breath: Judge Bradley handed down his ruling. He dismissed the Lichtenberg lawsuit!" I came as close as I could to jumping for joy. What damage they had wrought, and what a little vindication could do!

~

With this little bit of wind in my sails, I made a move I should have made long before. I retained Stuart Abrams as a second attorney.

Stuart Abrams was a former Assistant U.S. Attorney from the Southern District of New York who had previously worked as Elliott Jacobson's supervisor. A mutual attorney friend introduced us. I didn't expect that he could accomplish a breakthrough, but I hoped that if Jacobson were inclined to continue grinding me, he would at least think twice if I were under the watchful eyes of someone whose opinion he respected. I spent the next several weeks educating Abrams about my case. I wanted to go forward and offer the government testimony about the campaign, which my previous appearances hadn't touched on. But I knew by then that Bill was right about one thing: Jacobson didn't seem to care about Hinchey, at least at this stage of the case.

Though the bargaining in information about another human being is disgusting to me, my decision to try and offer this testimony was an easy one to make. I would never give false testimony against anyone, and I wouldn't even consider giving truthful testimony against Hinchey and his people under ordinary circumstances. But I was in prison. I had two clear objectives. First, by cooperating I could avoid a perjury indictment, and second, I wanted to keep alive the hope of a modification of my sentence if my information proved valuable.

Brodsky told me I was dreaming, and Abrams was only slightly more encouraging, but I thought that by explaining how I was given manipulative advice by Lenefsky and then exposing his evasions, perhaps my situation would become more credible to Jacobson. That part of the story should have been told at the beginning, I believed; I'll never know whether Brodsky was right or wrong back then, because it's water under the bridge now.

Even though I don't give a damn for Hinchey or his people, I knew that I owed myself strict fidelity to the truth. I could not have lived with myself if I had tried to "buy" a sentence reduction with embellished or false testimony. I would serve out my six months, lick my wounds and go home rather than lie under oath, and there were other forums in which I could tell the story without risking further involvement with the FBI and the U.S. Attorney: But if I had been able to tell the absolute truth that should have come out at trial in the first place, and get relief from this horrible situation, I would have done so.

After I brought in Stuart Abrams as co-counsel, we began plotting a revised course. I understood that Jacobson still felt I was lying, and that he still believed the perjured testimony upon which he had based his prosecution. Although Abrams also recommended against what I wanted to do, at least he agreed to open discussions about a private office interview with Jacobson.

Stuart reported back that Jacobson would be interested in a deal if I could offer new information on the politicians. We made a list of the subjects we would cover in the interview and Stuart then made the meeting happen. He reported in our next phone call that Jacobson was particularly interested in the information about Eleanor Brown running the '92 Hinchey campaign while she was serving as a paid congressional staff member.

In preparation for the meeting, Brodsky, Abrams, and I went over what I was prepared to say. I repeated the story again: I went to Brown for help. I told her I was raising money from employees in a company that gives a lot of bonus funds away to employees. I was also approaching companies I do business with. I needed help. Brown called Lenefsky. I went over my concerns with him. He gave me specific guidelines to follow. I took his advice and went to Steve Levine, Besicorp's in-house attorney. Steve not only concurred with Lenefsky's advice, but he took a bonus and made his own donation to the campaign. He thought it was legal.

During one of our phone calls, Bill Brodsky asked if I hadn't read the FEC regulations myself. I replied that I'd scanned them, but with Lenefsky's advice under my belt, I'd handed them off to Levine and asked him to interpret them. I hadn't tried to come to my own legal conclusion, I said. Brodsky challenged me: "Michael, that's bullshit. Everyone knows you micro-manage everything at Besicorp."

At that point, I lost it. I had had it with Bill Brodsky. I saw now that he had actually convicted me in his own mind, even though he was supposed to be my defense attorney. Aside from all of the external forces working against me, he was one of the main reasons I was in jail. I shouted into the phone. "Bill, I'm sick and tired of hearing that attitude from you. What do you know about running a company? After almost two years, you still don't know shit about this case. Besicorp has thirty-six subsidiaries, projects all over the world, and six-hundred million in assets. We have twelve people working in the compliance and reporting department. I deal with inside counsel and outside law firms, and I'm involved in many litigations and business deals. There are an enormous number of decisions and issues that I delegate! How dare you imply that I'm lying? And besides, even if I'd studied the regulations, I would probably have done exactly the same thing based on the advice I was given."

I still didn't fire Brodsky. There was just too much vested knowledge in his head, and I didn't want to burn bridges. Besides, the damage had already been done.

~

I had my office interview with Elliot Jacobson. He opened it by saying, "I have no personal animosity toward you. As far as I am concerned, you are just another white-collar criminal."

I'd brought all of the compensation reports for the Besicorp employees that had contributed to the campaign; the entire file on the Ansaldo photovoltaic development effort; and the letter Dave Kulik had sent to the board that detailed his work on the venture, providing the testimonial evidence as to the sham allegations of impropriety regarding the use of Ansaldo's money. I also produced the phony disability claims that Enowitz had submitted to Social Security and to his private insurer. I even brought a pile of anonymous harassing letters that had been arriving at my home during my incarceration to show the continued hostile motivation of his witnesses towards me and my family. But Jacobson would receive none of this.

He wanted to jump right on what I could tell him about Hinchey, Brown, and Lenefsky. I obliged. After I finished reciting the story of the campaign, he said, "That's all you have?" He apparently expected me to directly implicate Hinchey or his people in my "crimes." But I refused to lie or embellish. It was as Bill Brodsky had said. Jacobson did not believe I was telling the truth. Jacobson turned to me and said, "If I was to ask Lenefsky what he said to you, he would tell me exactly the same thing you did. He would say, 'I told Mike Zinn that any bonuses you give have to be earned and cannot be a quid pro quo for a campaign contribution.'"

What Lenefsky wouldn't tell Jacobson was that he knew that Besicorp employees were getting bonus money and making donations. He wouldn't tell Jacobson that he'd told me this would be okay under certain circumstances, and then looked the other way while I dug myself into a pit. But in Jacobson's eyes, Lenefsky's advice was not illegal (although his knowledge of what was taking place made him at least equally culpable with me); my act was. The only thing that separated an innocent act from an illegal conspiracy was an accusation, combined with the perjured testimony and circumstantial evidence Jacobson had cobbled up. I was guilty by accusation.

Indeed, Jacobson was not interested in pursuing Hinchey, Lenefsky, or Brown based on the information I had. Why? Perhaps the case was stale by that time. The statute of limitations had expired long ago for the simple campaign finance charges. Maybe what Jacobson was after was not political corruption after all, but illegal corporate political contributions. Maybe Brodsky had been right all along.

Bill Brodsky and I reconciled and made up. He agreed never to accuse me of being full of BS, and I agreed that his advice, whatever the outcome, was not so far off the mark. Even so, I still believe that my case was mishandled, and that a more aggressive attorney could have achieved a different outcome. But I don't consider it productive to hold a grudge against Brodsky. I know who my real enemies are. And I can't turn back the clock.

45

FACING ANOTHER INVESTIGATION

My three-month journey through the maximum-security bowels of the prison system to give my grand jury testimony was about to come to an end. Except when I was locked down in my own cell, relatively safe and alone, I'd had to constantly maintain an elevated level of sensory awareness. Outwardly I was strong, confident, and tough, but in order to ensure my safety I knew I had to be ready to defend myself at all times. There'd been few moments of peace. Now I received another dose of "diesel therapy," this time in the reverse direction, and my bill of lading returned me to Fairton Prison Camp. Over the course of two weeks of travel through the system, I was placed for ten days in the general population of the medium-security Otisville Federal Correctional Institution. This was quite near home; I called Val as soon as I had access to a phone; and she practically ran the forty miles to visit me the next day. I got to hug her, and we got to cry together for the first time in almost four months. Next I did a brief stint in an ancient cell block in the maximum security Union County Jail in New Jersey, known to be one of the worst jails in the nation. In all these institutions I met many tragic people, living tragic lives. I managed to keep clear of violence, but sometimes only by a whisker; thankfully, I had been able to call on my street savvy from the old days in Brooklyn, so I had a certain understanding of how to deal with tough guys.

When I arrived back at Fairton, I was happy to find that all my abandoned belongings (toothpaste, sweat suits, etc.) were there in a duffel bag, waiting for me. In comparison with where I'd been, the silence was deafening. Val tells me that my telephone voice became different there: more relaxed, calmer, and no wonder; for over three months I had been in maximum security institutions or riding the awful circuit of the federal prison transport system, manacled with leg irons, and traveling again and again with the sad unfortunates and outcasts of our society.

Poor Valerie was still having a terribly hard time getting over the shock of what had been done to me. I was getting settled again, hoping to finish my time working on this book, and comforting her and my daughter from afar.

Just before I was scheduled to be released, a subpoena arrived at Besicorp from the office of the New York State Attorney General. Dennis Vacco's office wanted to know about every single contact Michael Daley (who had stepped into the role of president in my absence) had had with me since my incarceration began. Valerie was being ordered to provide the same information! They wanted details of every conversation we'd had concerning Besicorp, as well as copies of every letter, memo, or document sent by me or received by me while I was incarcerated. The issue being "investigated" was whether or not I was running Besicorp from jail. How preposterous! I was in a federal prison and had spent over three months in maximum security. Even when back at Fairton Camp, I was limited to fifteen minute phone calls. With only two phones for eighty-five inmates, the lines were long, and, at the end of a call, it was back to the end of the line. The Attorney General wanted to know if there were any "deals" to bring me back after my incarceration was over. Once again, I was being investigated as if I had committed terrible crimes.

As I was still fifty-seven percent owner of Besicorp, I was entitled to seek information and to be kept informed. And I was still entitled to give advice, solicited or unsolicited. But what amazed me most was the lack of plain common sense that this new investigation seemed rooted in: anyone with half a brain would know that my twenty-two years of experience would benefit the company. I was the architect of its successful strategy and the person responsible for its key contracts and relationships. I felt strongly that it would be irresponsible for the company's management to try and get through major business issues without seeking my advice and perspective. But that was what the company was once again being pressured into doing.

Once again I promised myself not to be intimidated, even though I was incarcerated. I was confident that Besicorp's attorneys could stop the Attorney General; they had absolutely no legal basis to invade the boardroom of Besicorp. The company's board retained the authority to decide whether to bring me back or not. I was hoping they would do the right thing.

I'm sure that there are readers who doubt that an organized campaign of destruction like the one I have described in this book could actually take place. I can appreciate such skepticism. Given that most of us live free of invasive litigation and prosecution by the criminal justice system, it would be surprising if my story doesn't seem exaggerated or embellished.

I've wondered myself why people would go to such lengths to make a "garden-variety" hostile takeover into such a personal assault. The only explanation I can find is that in the modern world of electronic communications, faxes, web pages, and computerized SEC filings, corporate raiders have come to expect instant gratification, and when they don't get what they want, they go ballistic. Be that as it may, the predators had not given up on their goal of removing me from Besicorp. Beside continuing to instigate criminal investigations against me, their campaign of hatred and intimidation was still in full swing.

Starting in November 1997, prior to my surrender to custody, this campaign had been extended to the Internet: a "chat room" had developed on the YAHOO.COM web site. Yahoo's stock quote service has a chat room for each company they quote, and as things heated up, the chat room focusing on Besicorp became increasingly active.

At first, the comments placed on the site were tentative, but soon they became downright inflammatory. Some messages spewed anti-Semitic venom and other anonymous attacks against me in the most graphic and violent language, charging me with thievery and justifying my personal destruction.

The board and management of Besicorp began scanning the

postings, which added to the feeling of fear and intimidation. Even while I was in prison, the raiders were posting their hostile diatribes and demanding threateningly that the board of Besicorp not bring me back. It was in this incredibly intimidating atmosphere that the Attorney General's subpoenas investigating whether I was running the company from prison arrived at Besicorp.

In late April, as the weeks prior to my release unfolded, calls had also been coming in to Mike Daley and his assistant who handled shareholder relations. Vee Hockmeyer, along with others, emboldened by their success with the Attorney General, had been questioning Mike Daley about whether I was running the company from jail. They were asking whether Valerie had been attending board meetings, and making threats about further litigation and accusations of insider trading. Unfortunately, there was nobody in command who was capable of dealing effectively with such pressure during this stressful period. Even Michael Daley was barely keeping his head above water as he devoted himself to dealing with the major business transactions of the company.

Just one week prior to my release, the Attorney General served a notice to take my deposition testimony under oath. The subpoena arrived at the office of my attorney Bill Brodsky. Adding insult to injury, the deposition was scheduled for just three days after I was scheduled to be released from prison. Any thoughts that the prison sentence would be the end of my horror were flying out the window. I wasn't even going to be allowed to get my feet on the ground and be with my family before facing a new barrage after spending six months in prison.

To my enormous relief, Bill Brodsky was able to obtain an extension of six weeks, based upon our need to prepare and on the fact that he was unavailable to accompany me on the scheduled date.

46

COMING HOME

My anxiety level as to whether the Besicorp board would vote to rehire me increased by the day as my departure from prison loomed near. My relationship with the individual board members ranged from good to tense, but there was no telling which way a vote would go. No matter how the board members felt about my past performance, they were still being faced with intimidation and threats of lawsuits by the raiders. I knew that bringing me back could precipitate a further confrontation with the New York State Attorney General.

Doug Lobel, Besicorp's attorney, was determined to oppose the Attorney General subpoena and he was confident of the outcome. Bill Brodsky was not going to allow Valerie to testify or provide information, citing spousal privilege. Letters had been exchanged between the attorneys, but the issue was still unresolved as my release approached.

∾

Though I was a "short-timer" in the jargon of my friends at the camp, and increasingly the butt of good-natured taunts from my fellow inmates, the final weeks at Fairton went by as slow as molasses. My body was strong. I was employed on the landscaping crew doing grounds maintenance, and I took it upon myself to prune overgrown hedges at the camp into beautiful "Bonsai" sculptures. At least I could leave that little legacy of beautification in this hostile and regimented environment. My heart went out to all the people I knew would still be there in prison, one month, one year, or three years after my release. And anticipation of my freedom grew day after day.

∾

Several of my "camp" friends actively participated in the early development of this book, and we spent many hours discussing it. This was especially true of Mike Thomas, a lanky forty-year-old black man who was serving sixty-day sentence for a crime he insisted he had not committed. The father of four wonderful children (I met the family on several visiting days), he was a career postal worker who functioned as an expediter in the central Philadelphia post office. He and his wife owned a home in Philadelphia, and he was one of the few people I met at Fairton with a sentence shorter than mine.

As I understood it, Mike was a troubleshooter. Like others who served in his position, he carried mail all over the building, moving it from the wrong place to the right one. On the day he was arrested, he had both hands full of boxes and had stuffed mail into several of his pockets, all on their way to be dropped off in the proper location. An inspector nabbed him, and he was charged with postal theft! He was offered a plea bargain but he could not accept it. He was even offered misdemeanor disposition, but he refused to plead guilty to a crime he had not committed.

Even though there was no evidence that he had intended to steal the mail, the government had to get its pound of flesh. Represented by a public defender, Mike went to trial. His attorney didn't even call any witnesses on his behalf. The prosecutor put Mike on the stand and asked him if he had the mail in his pocket. He answered, "Yes, but—" He was stopped right there and no ifs, ands or buts were allowed. Thank you. No further questions. Mike says that if he had known then what he knows now, he would have paid for a private attorney and called other postal workers as witnesses. He'd had the innocent idea that he could just tell the truth at trial and that the charges would be dropped. I told him that unfortunately this doesn't always work, that I'd had an expensive private attorney, and I still got six months.

Mike Thomas lost his job and had to start all over. He is an A-1 person who will undoubtedly land on his feet. But what a tragedy that our government is so vindictive with people charged as first offenders! A prosecutor should be ashamed to seek the incarceration of a person who, at worst, may have committed a minor first offense.

One day Mike and I were discussing the manuscript for this book, and he turned to me and said, "Why, you were guilty by accusation!" I thanked him for the best title I could conceive of so far. Thank you, Mike, for your friendship and support. I used Guilty by Accusation as a working title during the writing of this book.

There were others like Mike Thomas at Fairton, serving long sentences for crimes no reasonable person would think deserves prison. The lives destroyed, families torn apart, are terrible proof of how destructive our criminal justice system continues to be. I waited on the phone lines, listening to sad people on fifteen-minute, timed and recorded phone calls, rotating through their children to their wives, knowing that they were going to be imprisoned for years. It was heartbreaking. I learned again and again that first-time white-collar offenders and minor drug offenders are treated like armed robbers. In the federal system, a technical paper crime without an obvious victim can keep a first offender incarcerated for far longer than manslaughter in a state prosecution.

Finally, May 8, 1997, the day of my release, arrived. Joy and sadness engulfed me. Freedom for me, but those I left behind would be there for months or years. And new unfortunate victims of circumstance would keep arriving to fill the shoes of those who leave.

Arriving home at last, I took the first week and secluded myself with my family, but then it was time for action. A board meeting was scheduled for the week after my return. On the day of the meeting, the board members grilled me for quite some time about my intentions in handling the company if I was rehired. Given their fiduciary responsibilities, they were well justified in taking this approach. I assured them that I was not suddenly going to act like a wild-eyed maniac who would run Besicorp into a brick wall to pursue some kind of hidden agenda. I articulated my goals clearly. I was going to get the company running well and bring it to the finish line in the major transactions at hand. I was going to get a handle on all the outstanding litigation and lower the raging stress temperature within the company. I was going to take control of all of the lawyers who had been running Besicorp in circles, and, most importantly, I was going to deal with the New York State Attorney General. At the end of the meeting, the board deliberated privately. When they invited me back into the meeting they informed me that they were hiring me back. I was very very happy, to say the least.

∾

It wasn't surprising that fear of litigation, investigation, harassment, and management defections had been at the forefront of virtually every deliberation and decision the board and management had dealt with during my absence. It's a credit to the people like Mike Daley and Joyce DePietro, who stepped up and took responsibility while I was gone, that the company had held together at all. There were so many loyal people who cared about Valerie and me, and so many of them had showed Val wonderful support while I was gone. She couldn't have survived without them, and they'd hung in there, waiting for me to come back.

I was welcomed back with open arms by the people in the company. It seemed that everyone was just champing at the bit to get their arms around me. It felt wonderful to walk into the beautiful building that Valerie and I had designed. I felt that I was coming home, with my extended family there to welcome me. But the agony of the past months and the unrelenting pressure had taken its toll on all involved. The company was still operating in a state of siege and panic, especially on a corporate level, and I was determined to bring peace back to the business as quickly as I possibly could.

47

FAMILY PAIN

Lost in most discussions and debate about crime and prosecution is the question of what happens to family members caught in the crossfire. It can be worse for them than for the person who is incarcerated, as it was in my case. Valerie kept a journal to try and maintain some sort of equilibrium through the emotional trials of this time. With her permission, here are some excerpts.

I feel like things can never be the same. I will never feel like knowing the owners of my favorite restaurants, or being involved in an organization where I become known. Local charities and events are out. I want everyone to leave me alone.

The press has destroyed my life with lies and insulting attention to detail. My address has been in the local newspapers so that paranoia has seeped into every vessel of my being. I sleep at night with a burglar alarm on, my pocket phone next to me, and my bedroom door locked. Is this any way to live? And yet survive I must! I have a wonderful husband and daughter. I look forward to one day exposing the evil people who have crossed our paths and then healing my spirit. My spirit is a worthy one on this planet, and I know I was placed here to do good things. This political/legal upheaval in my life may turn into a great teacher.

∽

I can no longer take the simple things for granted, the every day delights I just expected on a daily basis. I rarely thought about not having a dinner mate except maybe on golf night or when Michael took an occasional business trip. Now just to have anyone to break bread with is a special treat.

I imagine how wonderful it will be when that guy I took for granted will be there every night again. I used to complain at night that he was on the phone too much or at his computer all the time. Now I'd give anything just to have his being in the same house with me. And the empty bed; need I say more!

One can't even imagine the feeling of not being able to call your spouse if there's an emergency. I will never take our freedom or our love for granted again.

I listen to friends now, couple friends with their little tiffs. I interrupt and say, "Imagine six months without one another. What's really so important here to fight about?" They look up and stop for a moment and then get right back into it. This experience has been mine. Only one who has felt this void can appreciate the lesson here.

What I want and deserve most is peace. Peace will also be the most difficult to attain. There is just plain old too much media attention on my husband. He will be released from prison on two years probation, still the target of sick shareholders and the NY Attorney General, but the author of a new book telling all.

I can only pray for sacred space and a way to escape all the public interest, sympathy, best wishes, concern and gossip. Part of survival is not putting more pressure on myself, like not making decisions I don't have to make today, putting stress on the back burner.

One of the last and final things I'd like to do is write

the judge a letter. I do hope he's in the midst of retiring because God knows these old-timers seem to have their heads screwed on the wrong way. If the judge that sentenced my husband thinks that he sent out a message and an example to the young folk, I can assure him it was the wrong one. People have cursed the judge for his lack of insight, gullibility, and insensitivity. Others have made comments about not wanting to live in this country anymore. I find it hard to believe that this was his desired outcome. What was the desired outcome anyway?

~

This will be over someday. There are wonderful people and things all around us, and that is what I need to focus on.

Michael was given three weeks to surrender and put his business and personal life in order. Many people were shoved into executive positions they could not handle; a board of directors is now responsible for making major decisions and all the employees are confused and depressed. Fears about losing jobs are now realistic questions.

The bad press surrounding every move the company makes continues and everyone is scared silly. We are without the creative entrepreneurial leadership we always had, and in fact some of the people in charge seem close to having nervous breakdowns.

~

One can never imagine what entering a prison is like. You are immediately treated like a prisoner yourself, a suspect for drug smuggling. I'll never forget my first prison visit as long as I live. No one knew where Michael was for almost four days. I finally received a call from him saying he was shook up and exhausted but was in Westchester, only 1-½ hours from home. My dear friend Carol was with me. Without a second thought we were in the car driving. After getting lost, in two hours we were on a huge line outside in the cold winter for a ½ hour wait just to check in at the first window.

When we finally entered the main building with a little white slip of paper, we had another wait for our number to be called. The next junction in the road was a big sign-in book, a log on to their slow computer system and the assignment of a locker key. Everything, absolutely everything, goes into the locker. Not even a tissue can enter the visiting room. The metal detector is the next obstacle. The belt and watch come off, then your shoes may set off the noisemaker. After this, you're given another sheet of paper to take into a holding room where you wait for the motorized doors to let you in. The holding room attendant calls upstairs to let a Correction Officer know you're there. You then enter the big visiting room with 50 or 60 plastic tables and chairs. Guards are everywhere. You hand over your white sheet of paper and get assigned a table. You are placed at the table so that the person considered the most likely to pass drugs (the wife) sits across and furthest away from the prisoner. And then you wait for the love of your life to come through that locked glass door.

Sometimes it takes only 10 minutes, and other times it takes 45 minutes. From the moment he walks out you have exactly one hour to hold hands with the man you've shared your life with.

∾

I never knew a friend or family member who went to prison before. This was never even a part of my possibilities. I married a kind and gentle man, who was good in business and always made me proud. I never knew the meaning of trouble.

No one in my life is prepared to help me. Guidance is scarce. My psychiatrist is a good reality check. He tells me I should be panic stricken. He's impressed with the fact that I'm surviving all this alone.

People say, "Call me if you need to talk." I don't need to talk. I need someone who understands this horror. I'd rather be alone these days than have to make conversation with an acquaintance with sad eyes. My real friends who have pushed through my emotional barrier are the only people I can handle.

I'm convinced after hearing stories from and about people on the inside that a large percent of the people are innocent or at least don't deserve the harsh punishment they received. People are trapped by a system where plea-bargaining is the only way to get a shorter sentence. If you go to trial the system gets pissed off, and does your family suffer! Six months is awful enough, but what about those poor souls that got 5 or 10-year prison terms? Think of all the people who could be supporting families, educating themselves, and helping others. They could teach poor kids who went astray to use a computer or even to read. There's no common sense to this system. The system needs some female input.

Just think, the government of the USA has the power to do this to anyone. When I was a kid we were taught to fear Russia. I think perhaps we were duped into trusting this country. At least the Russians are aware of the KGB and know to be careful. We are in the land of the free and feel a false sense of security.

I have 100 more days left. Of that the next 6 weeks will be the hardest. After 6 weeks spring will be showing its colors and days will be getting longer. I can begin a countdown in March. Taking this in smaller blocks of time and turning them into an accomplishment is a survival technique I have discovered.

~

A prison sentence is a sentence for the whole family. What did I do? I don't know the answer. I only know that I can't eat, I can't sleep without medication, and there's very little joy in my life right now. I am being punished by a system that cares nothing for family values where a regulatory and victimless crime of questionable origin has taken place. God help us all.

48

Clearing the Air

Now that I was back in the chair, running Besicorp again as CEO, I was determined to move quickly to bring peace to the company. We had big deals in the hopper, and the rewards of twenty years of work were within reach. But I knew how easily they could all be blown if I failed to get the company back on track.

I still had to deal with the Attorney General. Despite my bitter experience, I kept the legal team of Bill Brodsky and Doug Lobel. Their background working on the AG issue and their familiarity with the criminal case made this prudent. But Bill and Doug were in litigation mode, and I was preparing to pursue a different path. This time I was determined to do it my way.

Round and round we went. The attorneys were eager to litigate with the AG. They felt that he was way off base and had no legal grounds to interfere with boardroom decisions at Besicorp. Well and good, but I had a broad perspective now. The Attorney General had wide investigatory powers, and even the power to bring a criminal indictment. While the current inquest was presently a civil investigation, if we went into full-scale litigation mode, why wouldn't they retaliate with a criminal investigation, one that was manufactured just to force me out of the company? What made my attorneys think that couldn't happen?

I wanted the attorneys to set up a meeting with Bill Mohr, the principle investigator at the AG's office. In a replay of the past, Bill Brodsky said, "I don't recommend it." Déjà vu. All the reasons given were the same ones Brodsky gave me as to why I shouldn't talk with the federal prosecutor and shouldn't have talked with the probation officer. According to his theory, Bill Mohr would simply use such a meeting to take notes of everything I said. Then he would come down on me like a ton of bricks.

I objected to the strategy being advocated by the lawyers and, this time, I did something about it. I instructed Doug Lobel to set up a meeting with Bill Mohr. Bill Brodsky still was adamantly opposed, but I was willing to give him one assurance. "If we get the sense that this is a setup, feel free to interrupt the meeting any time for a caucus. If things are going bad, we will break up the meeting and go into litigation mode. But I will have the meeting."

~

Doug Lobel reported back that Mohr was decidedly hostile, to the point of asking why he should grant us a meeting when a deposition was scheduled. But Doug persisted. He eventually convinced Mohr that they had a lot to gain by having an informal discussion, and that, in any case, they still retained the right to seek a formal deposition if they weren't satisfied with the meeting.

We set about planning for the meeting. I assembled many of the documents I would have taken to trial, if only there had been a trial, in the criminal case. I assembled supporting material to explain and refute each and every allegation that had been made by the corporate raiders. To have issued such invasive subpoenas, I knew Mohr must have been instigated by these very same bogus allegations. I was prepared to go through the history of all of the litigations as well as to carefully address the complaints about the way the company was managed.

The meeting started off tensely. Bill Mohr and his assistant were probing and obviously suspicious. He even admonished me not to lie. I assured him that if I intended to lie, I wouldn't have asked for this meeting. We began the meeting at 10:30 a.m. From then on I spent four continuous hours presenting detailed information and explanations of every aspect of the history of Besicorp. We worked without breaking for lunch. I'm quite sure Bill Mohr hadn't expected to do that, but he became engrossed in my story.

I explained the financial guarantees that I'd provided for Besicorp, with detailed numbers charted out against the financial history of the company. I explained how some of the very people who had benefited so handsomely as a result were the ones who were leveling horrible and vicious diatribes in every possible forum. I explained that by engineering my personal destruction, what these people where really seeking was the liquidation of the company. I used a stock price history chart to show how these people had bought their shares for a small fraction of their present value and explained why their theory of creating value by forcing the company to liquidate was just plain wrong. I laid out the facts to justify the stock issued to me and to the other members of the management team, and I explained the Special Litigation Committee process and the procedural history of the shareholder litigations.

I'd brought examples of the kind of unjustified charges that had been leveled at me. For example, I showed Mohr the bogus complaint to the Federal Aviation Administration, written by one of the instigators, that alleged criminal collusion and embezzlement between Besicorp and me concerning federal funding of the airport I owned. Then I showed him how the FAA had resolved the complaint after an audit, with a finding of no wrongdoing. We went through each of the issues in turn until I had shown him everything.

At this point things began to warm up considerably. I think Bill Mohr began to see the depth of my understanding of the business and how I had created significant shareholder value from virtually nothing.

Then I showed the legal files of the Enowitz disability case and how Enowitz had made fraudulent disability claims pre-dating his employment with Besicorp, explaining that he was the primary government witness against me. I think it became clear to Mr. Mohr how Enowitz was motivated to get me out of Besicorp to get his hands on what was now $3 million worth of disputed Besicorp stock. I showed the anonymous harassing letters that had been arriving at my home and those of other people associated with Besicorp during my incarceration.

Bill Brodsky tried to stop me, but I raised my hand to keep him quiet. I launched into a detailed explanation of the 1992 Hinchey campaign, armed with all the spreadsheets, facts, and figures to explain each of the donations by Besicorp employees and my family. I explained in detail how Hinchey and his people had used me, and how they'd lied to avoid taking any responsibility for what went wrong.

Bill Mohr was visibly moved by my stories about the terror of prosecution and incarceration. He eventually asked why I pleaded guilty, and I replied in the following way: "Mr. Mohr, as someone who sits in the prosecutor's chair, I understand how you couldn't possibly relate to what it's like to be on the receiving end. I can tell you that the circumstances that led me to plead guilty were horribly unjust and painful, but it was the only practical course. It seemed to be the only way to avoid the risks of a long jail term for what you have now seen was virtually nothing."

Mohr then asked why I had been prosecuted at all, and I said it was because the same people who had instigated him to come after me had instigated the federal government, but the difference was that I had no knowledge of the system at the time or any ability to sit down with the prosecutor as I was doing with him now. Perhaps if I had, I wouldn't have been prosecuted. Or perhaps if I had been, I wouldn't have been incarcerated.

Mohr conversed quietly with his assistant and then asked about the outstanding subpoenas and interrogatories. Bill Brodsky began to answer, but I again raised my hand and asked him to let me explain.

I told him that Besicorp had been brutalized by the federal government. It had cost us $250,000 just to deal with the federal subpoenas in legal fees and copying costs alone. That didn't count the cost of defending the cases or the total disruption of the business. The federal government had already investigated every single allegation of these hostile shareholders. How could this small company survive being put through this again? "I will sit with you anytime, any place, and answer your questions informally," I said. "I'll give you whatever information you need to understand the issues, but I can't allow Besicorp to get into an expensive, legally intensive process with your office at this point. If that is the way it's going to go, we're going to litigate over your right to pursue this at all."

I could see that Mohr was surprised. "You mean to say that the federal government has already investigated these complaints?" he asked.

"They most certainly have," I said. "They even had my personal accountants grilled under a hot light and they found nothing to indict me on. If they had, you can be sure they would have brought charges."

Bill Mohr and his assistant went out of the room to caucus. When they came back some time later, Mohr announced that we could consider the depositions and subpoenas to be indefinitely adjourned. He told me that I still needed to supply certain supplemental information that I didn't have with me to answer some of the questions that came up in the meeting, but that if the information checked out and I was on the level, there would be no further proceedings.

Mohr now raised another subject. He said he had just received new complaints. A Besicorp shareholder was alleging that we were hiding information about a major development involving a large power project that Besicorp was co-developing in India. (This project was a proposed 500-megawatt power plant that would cost about $800 million to build. We were initially the lead developer, but over time we'd transferred that responsibility to our co-developer. We'd retained a share in the ownership and turned our attention to other markets closer to home.) Mohr said the complaint alleged that the project had received clearance from the Indian Central Electricity Authority (CEA), and that we hadn't sent out a press release. The implication was that we were deliberately withholding information to depress the price of the stock as part of some sort of scheme to cheat the public shareholders.

His query couldn't have come at a better moment. I had planted the seed of doubt in his mind about the veracity and motivations of the corporate raiders. Now he had in his hands a real example of their tactics. Several days prior, we had obtained a wire service release from Reuters indicating that the project had CEA clearance. I immediately dispatched a congratulatory note to our partner, but I received a note in reply saying that the Reuters release was in error and that no such clearance had been granted. We verified this with the engineering firm that was designing the project. We checked with sources in the Indian government and got the same message. The Reuters release was in error.

We referred the matter to our outside counsel, and we were working on a clarifying press release on the day I sat there with Bill Mohr. I explained this all and asked if he needed further example of the bogus complaints that had been the cause of these problems. "But this is from Vee Hockmeyer!" Mr. Mohr exclaimed. "What makes you think Hockmeyer is an ethical person?" I asked. "Just because he wears a suit and works as a stockbroker for a large brokerage firm? He's been one of the most hostile, aggressive, and nasty people I have ever been associated with."

Mohr was amazed. He was holding in his hands exactly the kind of evidence I'd been telling him about.

I promised to send along all the additional supporting information to document everything I'd said about this and all the other issues.

As we all left the room, I noticed that Mr. Mohr's demeanor and attitude had remarkably changed. We shook hands firmly, and he looked me in the eye and said, "Go out there and do a good job for the shareholders."

Looking him back in the eye, I replied, "I will, and I always have. Thank you for the opportunity to have this meeting."

On the way back, Bill Brodsky and Doug Lobel shared their elation with me at the meeting, but I couldn't stop shaking my head. Why couldn't I have done the same thing with the feds? I'd spent six months in jail, and my family had endured all that pain, and for what?

Afterwards, Bill Brodsky wrote me, "I think you did very well today, and I have to eat some crow. Nevertheless, I'm glad that it turned out so well."

49

Putting Humpty Dumpty Back Together

Firmly in control again at Besicorp, I brought the management team together and helped them get to work on priorities with focus and motivation. I was doing what I do best, setting the goals, providing the big picture, and moving the process along by tactical intervention. The temperature was being lowered each day, and I could feel the relief among the staff.

While I was in prison, all of the many parties involved had been hard at work through the winter of 1998 on the NIMO Master Restructuring ("MRA") deal, but there was just nobody at Besicorp who was capable of managing the process of restructuring our interests in those plants, participating in the MRA process itself, and forcing NIMO to go through with the additional complicating factor of a tax-free merger. These were very complex considerations, even in normal times, and even for the very large companies that were involved; for Besicorp in those troubled times, the load was overwhelming. Consequently, by the time I was released, the possibility of our implementing the MRA by having Besicorp enter into a tax-free merger with Niagara Mohawk Power Corp. was a dead issue.

Mike Daley did a commendable job keeping the company together, and I'm not certain that even I would have been able to get a merger with NIMO through, but I would have tried like hell.

During my incarceration, the Besicorp board had put off dealing with the question of indemnification for legal fees incurred in the criminal case. (Besicorp and I were both being sued by "John Bansbach" to force me to pay the company for the costs of legal defense and damages). Once I returned, I brought the subject to the top of the pile. The Bansbach lawsuit had been dismissed but was still on appeal by the plaintiff. If the dismissal was reversed, it would be back to square one, and perhaps a trial on the merits would then be required.

Over time, the board had three different law firms study the issue of indemnification. Two gave opinions that I was not entitled to be indemnified for my legal defense costs, and one decided that I was. But none of those firms could qualify as independent, and none had conducted any type of actual investigation or interviewed any of the people involved in the 1992 Hinchey campaign. Besides, I wasn't prepared to accept any decision that denied me indemnification without a knock-down, drag-out fight. This was not simply a matter of money; for me, it was a matter of principle. I'd suffered enough personally at the hands of these predatory shareholders. No way was I going to let the corporation off the hook. In any event, by virtue of my shareholding in Besicorp, it was, in fact, fifty-seven percent my money.

I suggested to the board that outside counsel retain a law firm to conduct a truly independent investigation, similar to what would be done to prepare for trial. This way the board could make a determination on the issue of indemnification and rely on a report done by a true expert.

A law firm was hired by a special committee of the board in September 1998, and they took a full five months to complete their report. They reviewed the pertinent legislation, looked at volumes of documents and interviewed many witnesses, including Dave Lenefsky, Hinchey's lawyer. Lenefsky acknowledged to them that he and I had discussed the issue of campaign contribution reimbursement relative to bonuses given to employees, but when he was asked specifically whether he and I had discussed the issue of Besicorp's people donating their own bonuses, he declined to answer. He and I know what his answer should have been.

The law firm that did the investigation found (i) that there were reasonable grounds for the board to indemnify me, based upon a conclusion that I had a plausible defense had I taken my case to trial, and (ii) that there was significant and credible evidence that I didn't know that what I was doing was against the law at the time I committed the "offenses." The attorney in charge made an offhand remark to me in one of our interviews that, if he had defended me, he would have recommended that the case go to trial. How I wish I could turn back the clock! The board eventually granted me the indemnification I was entitled to, and now I had an independent investigation of what really took place to refer to in the future.

50

MOVING AHEAD

In due course, the Niagara Mohawk Master Restructuring Agreement closed, and Besicorp received over $130 million dollars. The power purchase contracts with NIMO were canceled. Twelve years of stress, aggravation, and risk had finally paid off. We sold off our interests in the power plants that remained in New York State and closed that chapter in our corporate life. Unfortunately, as we didn't get to merge with NIMO, we had to create alternative means of getting all this wealth into the hands of our shareholders.

In July, 1998, Besicorp hired Josephthal & Co. to help the company maximize shareholder value. Over the summer of 1998, Bob Wien (Josephthal's investment banker) and I strategized, considering that there was all that cash, on how we could deliver the value of the company to the shareholders. After much investigating, we found a merger partner offshore who would pay the highest after-tax value for the company, and Besicorp signed a merger agreement, put a proxy statement in front of the SEC for review, and put the merger to a shareholder vote. During the pendency of the merger and proxy, two new "class action" lawsuits were filed. The first sought to enjoin the merger, claiming that the board had wasted Besicorp's value and that the price wasn't high enough. The second filed by Lichtenberg and Bansbach under the sponsorship of their contingency fee attorneys didn't try to enjoin the merger, but wanted the federal court to preserve their shareholder suits after the merger, contending that my own money should be put in escrow. Those claims are still to be litigated.

Despite the agitation of a small group of shareholders, the vote passed overwhelmingly. More than 99% of the votes were cast in favor of the merger and Besicorp shareholders received over $110 million in cash. I was proud of this accomplishment. Less than $4 million had been invested in this company since its inception. This payday was earned through the sweat and blood of my management team. I'd paid a heavy price to get there. As part of this activity, we spun off to the shareholders a small company to continue in business. Where that will go, I don't know, but I'm too young to retire. Whether I'll be willing to run a company for the long term with shareholders like Alan Kahn, James Lichtenberg, and Vee Hockmeyer remains to be seen.

In the middle of all this, I was able to bring Besicorp into a new and exciting project. We negotiated a fifty-fifty partnership to develop a major newsprint recycling plant and a co-located 500-megawatt cogeneration plant. The project will be developed only two miles from our corporate headquarters! This is an environmental project of the highest order and will require $700 million in new financing.

51

"COLLATERAL" DAMAGE

V al has had a hard time getting back to her life. She becomes terribly anxious when we go out in our own community. I understand how she feels; because of the press coverage, I now have one of the most recognized faces in our region. But the vast majority of people in the area, especially those who know how to read between the lines, know that I was cynically used and then punished, first by Hinchey, and then by the government.

Today I go proudly into the community with my head up. Perhaps the government prosecutors wanted something else: but where is the deterrent if its target isn't cowed and ashamed, and then goes out and tells his story of how the prosecutors used self-motivated witnesses in a corrupted process that forced a plea-bargained conviction out of me?

After my return from prison, Val wrote:

> Its now been 8 months after the fact. I haven't written anything since the early days of Michael's incarceration. As the six-month sentence passed, I became more and more paranoid and closer to a nervous breakdown. I hired an armed guard to be on my driveway every night from 10 PM to 6 AM so that I could sleep at all. The hate mail and anonymous threats from sick people kept coming in on a regular basis to my home, the office, the homes of our employees, and even to my daughter in college.

> Many well-meaning acquaintances said I'd be stronger for getting through all this. Well, I disagree with that theory. I'm more than bitter, having seen the most evil side of business and politics, and I'm much more beaten up in my soul. I don't yet feel 50% of the way to the top of the mountain where normalcy returns.

I pray for peace and understanding every day. I pray that all the people who used to be my friends forgive the unreturned phone calls and unanswered invitations. Life did not return to normal the day my husband came home. Did anyone return from Auschwitz the same? Not to compare, but just to make a point.

52

Before It's Too Late

I've survived the barrage of assaults directed at me by those who sought the destruction of Besicorp, But I didn't begin to understand the implications of what had taken place until the damage was done. I believe that what happened was a crime, as surely as if intentional extortion had been employed. Even though I can recover some of the lost ground, I can never undo the damage done to my family and to the business.

Once I understood the true nature of what happened, I became determined to shine the spotlight of scrutiny on those who are responsible for these acts. I hope I can help stop similar campaigns of destruction that have yet to be unleashed against other targets. At the time of my release from prison, friends advised me not to return to Besicorp. I confess that I never seriously considered that option. The corporate raiders who organized the assault against Besicorp, and the criminal justice system that unleashed an ambitious prosecutor in a campaign of destruction have taken quite a lot from me. But they won't deprive me of my business.

I want to raise an alarm with this book. Most of us are concerned primarily about our public and private safety, which provides fertile ground for those demagogues who are driven to pursue a politically motivated anti-crime agenda. When the apparatus is turned on one's enemies, it's easy to cheer the process on. But when one's enemies have the power to turn the situation around, woe on those who seek to inflict punishment as an example to others, or to justify their budgets, or to rise in the bureaucracy of the criminal justice system, or who believe in the severity of the law but accept the word of the most personally motivated "witnesses" to enforce it.

Over time, non-elected bureaucrats have come to wield great power in our government. Partly as a result, the government has dramatically increased the size of the federal prison system at a cost of billions of dollars. Tax money continues to pour into prison infrastructure and massive increases in law enforcement-related employment. Billions more are spent on halfway houses, food services, and medical care, and now there are even private prisons, run by corporate entities making a profit! A veritable prison industry is in place and it has a vested interest in maintaining and steadily increasing the rate of incarceration. This industry employs lobbyists and seeks to expand its influence. Our prisons are being filled with white-collar first offenders and nonviolent drug offenders, while all across America, dangerous criminals are being released to the streets due to the severe shortage of prison space this creates.

The system needs to be fed, and only new inmates keep the beast satiated. So incarceration has become the punishment of choice, accepted as a way of life in our society. This spells doom for freedom. America is on the verge of losing its humanity.

I feel a great sense of urgency about proposing the following correctives, all of which are within our power to undertake:

√ End the rhetoric of "The War on Crime."

This recommendation may seem heretical, but it should be understood that a war on crime means a war on citizens of the United States. In war, anything goes. Those in law enforcement can justify excesses and abuses in the name of achieving victory. Unless they receive unusual press attention, the errors and the ruined lives stay invisible.

The "civilians" caught in this web of conviction quotas and gung-ho prosecutions are the innocents who are set up, non-violent first offenders who are harshly prosecuted and incarcerated for lengthy periods. The "collateral damage" is what happens to the families of these unfortunates, and what happens to a society that brutalizes its own citizens. This "state of war" provides a rationale for the loss of civil liberties and the sacrifice of our constitutional rights.

What is the alternative? In the first place, commentators, legislators, and politicians must cool down the rhetoric. We must confront the demagogues. If we don't, it won't be long before we live in an environment where nobody can speak out; elected officials and candidates for elected office will be unwilling or unable to criticize the growing power of the state for fear or getting a soft on crime label. When critics of the criminal justice system become the targets of investigation, we will have lost our precious democratic heritage. It's time to address the ugly truth and to make the abuses in our legal system part of the political dialogue. Before we run out of time, we can still stop this runaway train.

√ Change course in "The War on Drugs."

More than sixty percent of our federal prisoners are incarcerated for drug-related crimes. A large percentage of these are nonviolent first offenders. In my journey through the world of courts and prisons, I have seen many formerly productive men whose family lives have been destroyed by a criminal justice system that was set up to protect society. Our drug policies are producing unintended tragedies.

Our destructive drug laws are particularly ruinous for the families of minorities. Whites are incarcerated far less often than others for drug offenses, and the penalties for the drugs that white people seem to prefer are far less than those that govern crack, for example, still a scourge in our inner cities. As I've learned, the powerful law enforcement bureaucracy presides over a system in which these harsh sentences for minor drug offenses produce systematic plea-bargain abuses. The pattern is that deals are made in exchange for "information," so informers, usually witnesses seeking to escape severe charges themselves, provide deal-driven testimony. In this way, the next victim down the line is convicted, and the chain stops when someone refuses to capitulate—or has nobody to turn in. Prisoners solve this problem by implicating people they don't even know, and some prosecutors willingly oblige them. This system works especially well on a relatively defenseless minority population, that cannot afford private legal representation. Busy public defenders handle masses of cases, sometimes meeting defendants for the first time a moment before their plea-bargain is entered. As a result, there has been a huge increase in minorities in federal custody.

√ Lighten-up on white-collar crime.

In an attempt to appear "even-handed" and deflect charges of racism, the government has expanded the "war on drugs" to include "white-collar" crime. The attempt to create the appearance of class and racial equality before the law has caused new and unanticipated problems. The "system" has been targeting otherwise productive people for criminal prosecution and meting out long periods of incarceration to people who clearly do not belong in prison.

Over the past generation, criminal sanctions have increasingly been attached to thousands of federal regulations. People are prosecuted for minor violations. "Derivative" crime laws, such as conspiracy, have exponentially exploded the number of acts that can be charged as criminal and have escalated the seriousness of the sanctions to extraordinary levels. Virtually anyone in business is vulnerable to being prosecuted for violating some law or regulation. As the criminal justice system has expanded, its appetite has become voracious. Virtually all federal agencies now have "criminal enforcement" divisions, and they all work together with the FBI and the Justice Department. There is now in place a massive network of people whose livelihood depends upon ferreting out "wrongdoing," people whose careers depend upon identifying "offenders" and prosecuting them. One need not be guilty of wrongdoing at all, let alone serious wrongdoing, to be criminally prosecuted. Just draw the attention of an overzealous investigator, or step on the wrong toes, and you might find yourself propelled as I was into a relentless whirlpool with no exit.

A generation ago, the FBI stood as the bastion of law enforcement. Federal agencies had auditors, not criminal enforcers; when a crime was discovered, a referral was made to the proper authorities. No longer: violating administrative rules often gives rise to criminal prosecution. Filing a false document or making a false statement can lead to prosecution, even if there was no criminal intent, no loss to the government and no gain for the "perpetrator."

Nonviolent first offenders are being made into felons and incarcerated for technical crimes that were not even criminal offenses just a decade or two ago. It's time to put an end to this madness.

√ Stop plea-bargain abuses and end mandatory sentences.

The Constitution provides us with the presumption of innocence and the right to trial by jury. Each of us educated in American history can explain what these rights are supposed to mean, but every day they are being denied to more American citizens. The erosion is gradual and almost invisible, but it is doing us great harm.

If a prosecutor were to say, "I am going to charge you with a crime, and I'm going to penalize you severely if you plead 'not guilty' and insist on having a trial," most people would instantly say, "That's unconstitutional!" But this is exactly what's happening.

If convicted at trial or by "voluntary" plea bargain, a person charged with a federal crime may be faced with a mandatory prison sentence. Under the Federal Mandatory Sentencing Guidelines, there are "incentives" to induce a person charged with a crime to plead guilty and not go to trial. If you "accept responsibility" by plea-bargaining, you are entitled to a guaranteed sentence reduction. In addition to the guideline incentive, prosecutors will very often reduce the charges and eliminate "derivative crimes" for a "voluntary" conviction, which further reduces the exposure in sentencing. Most people, scared out of their wits and going broke, will do as I did and take the deal.

In the end, penalizing a defendant for going to trial and giving "incentives" to plea bargain instead of going to trial have exactly the same effect. Is not the absence of an incentive the equivalent of a penalty? In both cases, the defendant has been muscled by the government to give up a trial by jury, and the presumption of innocence until proven guilty has gone out the window so that prosecutors can accumulate convictions.

The Supreme Court has upheld the constitutionality of mandatory sentencing guidelines and plea-bargain-reduced charges. The Court has also accepted that testimony by a prosecution witness who has had criminal charges reduced for "cooperation" is not inherently tainted. So while the use of biased and, in all likelihood, perjured testimony has now become commonplace, defendants have no effective remedy against the government.

This crisis is reversible only if enough people demand an end to mandatory sentences, put an end to plea-bargaining, and give judges back the power to judge. Let prosecutors charge a crime, and force them to actually prove their case. The courts may be crowded, but is not expanding the court system better than expanding the prison system? This process will undoubtedly produce far fewer abusive prosecutions, and renew law enforcement focus on incarcerating only those people who are truly threats to the community.

√ Develop alternative sentences.

I believe that the criminal justice system's proper role is to remove dangerous people from society for as long as possible. But in order to prevent the irreversible transformation of our society into a kind of police state, we must get the government off the backs of nonviolent first offenders of all types. Prison must no longer be the penalty of first recourse for minor drug and white-collar first offenders. Alternative sanctions that involve no incarceration must be created. As a side benefit, our society will actually save money, for incarceration is the most expensive punishment of all. Furthermore, the immoral spectacle of a "prison industry" is expanding to accommodate the thousands who might repay their debt to society far better in other venues.

What good does it do for society to remove people who pose no further threat to their community? Those first offenders who pose a possible but remote chance of recidivism, who have committed nonviolent offenses, should be sentenced from a combination of alternate sentences, fines, and restitution, along with suspended sentences and close supervision, including electronic monitoring. For those without family responsibilities, imposing some form of community service might better serve the interests of both justice and society at large.

For such a person with familial responsibilities, it should be adequate punishment after a first conviction to say: "You have a sentence of one year of incarceration and five years probation. Your one year of incarceration is suspended. If you are convicted of a crime again within five years, your sentence will be served consecutively with whatever new sentence you receive. You will also pay out of your earnings towards the cost of your supervision."

How much would our society improve by compassionate sentencing? Do we need such harshness against minor offenders, and such power in the hands of the law enforcement bureaucracy that innocent people can be beaten into submission? I say no.

√ Remove prosecutor immunity.

Why should police corruption generate public outcry, but prosecutorial abuse be swept under the rug? It is already a serious criminal offense for any law enforcement person to procure false testimony by inducement (by offering a favorable plea bargain or a reduced sentence), but many prosecutors nonetheless fail to follow clear rules of fair and open dealing during the prosecution process.

"Zero-tolerance" for crime should also extend to prosecutorial abuse. Strengthening the power of the government has meant gradual dictatorship by the bureaucracy. Police power and the apparatus of government have become so strong that it seemingly cannot be challenged. Even without a powerful demagogue at the top of the government, this is the beginning of dictatorship in America.

It will not be enough to strengthen internal oversight within the U.S. Department of Justice. In the event that a prosecutor engages in abuse of due process, prosecutors must be subject to court sanction. Deliberate and egregious misuse of the government's authority must be made a crime, and the law must be enforced. We must assume that the safeguards that presently exist within the law enforcement bureaucracy for self-policing are simply never going to be effective, and that society must provide an independent means to address grievances by citizens.

Yes, there may be more lawsuits against law enforcement personnel as a result, but that is far preferable to the alternative—a police state by gradual erosion of civil liberties.

√ Implement civil litigation reform.

Our litigation-crazy world must be tranquilized. But how can this happen when the Trial Lawyers Association remains one of the most powerful lobbies in Congress? The task will require dedication, because most legislators are lawyers. But we must put an end to one-sided, predatory litigation that is based upon phony allegations. How? Certainly we cannot legislate that charges and complaints must be true in order to be brought to court; that would be the end of due process in the civil justice system. There is no objective way before the fact to screen frivolous litigation out of the system. But we can implement specific changes to correct the abuses that presently exist by emulating features of the legal system that have been widely adopted in Europe. We can legislate that losers in such litigation pay the legal fees of the prevailing party, and we can mandate that lawyers who bring frivolous litigation have stronger sanctions.

Each and every reader should understand that the kind of experience I've described here doesn't happen only to CEO's, drug offenders, or people who "must have done something wrong." The truth is that if we fail to undertake corrective measures, what happened to me can happen to any one of us.

EPILOGUE

Maurice Hinchey has gone on to become an entrenched member of Congress. He has been re-elected three times. He has consistently and publicly (and understandably) denied all knowledge of or involvement in wrongdoing with respect to his 1992 campaign. Sadly, in all the years since my legal entanglements began, he never once reached out to my family or me to express his remorse or his empathy. Long after the events I've described here, I learned through an attorney who happened to represent an involved party that Hinchey had been a government witness in a federal investigation of organized crime and the garbage-hauling industry. It finally makes sense to me why the government pursued neither Hinchey nor any of his key people for their involvement in the supposedly "illegal" 1992 campaign, for an accusation of illegal campaign practices would have destroyed Hinchey's credibility in the other case. And I understand all too well now that once the prosecutors had committed themselves to an investigation, they had to move ahead with it and have their victim.

David Lenefsky rode Maurice Hinchey's coattails to Washington and obtained some blue-chip clients as a result. During the Senate impeachment trial of President Clinton, I observed Lenefsky escorting the President's pollster, Dick Morris, into a grand jury hearing.

Eleanor Brown resigned her position running Hinchey's Washington office shortly after my release from prison. Newspaper coverage of my release was extensive, and for the first time since the investigation was made public, I was no longer under the gag-order imposed by my attorneys. I told the story to the newspapers as it really happened (of course without the detail provided in this book), and suddenly Brown decided to leave the political world. I imagine her departure from Washington reflected her loyalty to Hinchey; if the information that ultimately came out should reflect badly on him, he could always point his finger at Brown and say, "She did it, and she resigned."

The claims by and against Martin Enowitz continue to wend their way through the courts. Discovery proceedings have confirmed that

Besicorp was not the first company he had left "disabled": he had submitted disability claims to his prior employer, stating in writing that he was totally disabled and not capable of working, while he was, in fact, working for Besicorp!

A five judge panel of the appellate division of the New York State court system unanimously affirmed Judge Bradley's dismissal of the Lichtenberg suit, concurring with Judge Bradley that the plaintiff's position consisted primarily of "ad-hominem" attacks.

But the war of attrition with Kahn, Lichtenberg, the contingency-fee attorneys, and their stockbroker allies goes on with no end in sight. Perhaps that ongoing saga will make for a sequel to this book.

Many questions remain in my mind. Would Judge Brieant have sent me to prison if he had heard the full story of the 1992 Hinchey campaign? Would he have been so influenced by the letters from the raiders had I been able to present him with the full story of Besicorp, the way I was able to with Bill Mohr of the New York State Attorney General's office?

In making the agonizing decision to plea-bargain, I was greatly influenced by the anecdotal information from my lawyer that Judge Brieant was particularly hard on defendants who went to trial. Having experienced the results of my personal interaction with my probation officer and the investigator for the New York State Attorney General however, I am convinced he would have executed the sentencing with greater compassion and understanding had he truly understood this case. If I had to do it over again, I would go to trial.

The senior supervising probation officer in charge of my case told me long after my release from prison, that I could have asked for a "bench trial" and presented the case directly to the judge. This was an alternative I didn't know existed at the time I plea-bargained.

Another question: If I had been represented by another defense lawyer, would there have been a different outcome?

My plea-agreement was certainly a total disaster. Only my lawyer could have prevented such a fiasco, but I didn't know enough at the time to influence the process. Perhaps another attorney might have been able to arrange a meeting with the government earlier in the process, before the prosecutor had hardened his position. I now know that prosecutors hate going to trial if they can negotiate a deal to get a conviction. Perhaps with a more effective advocate, I could have held out for a better plea-agreement, even if I had to continue preparing for trial while trying to get better terms.

Observers have asked me why I didn't hire another lawyer once I became dissatisfied with the one I had. They always remark that someone with my business experience should have been able to choose his own attorney and control the strategy employed. I ask myself that same question all the time. I don't have a good answer. Perhaps it was inertia. We were too far along in the process before I realized that there was something really wrong. At times, I rationalized that Brodsky's experience and knowledge of the case outweighed our lack of strategic alignment, and finally, I liked Brodsky personally. Yet I know that none of these reasons suffice. The truth is that it's not easy for anyone to know when to override the professional advice of counsel, and I only know that I am far from being the only person ever to have suffered grievously from the overwhelming complexity of the criminal justice system. This in itself is a reason for more leniency and compassion in the prosecutorial process. While incarcerated, I found dissatisfaction with counsel to be a constant theme among the people I met, usually because they couldn't afford an attorney, or were unfamiliar with the legal process. How many people targeted by the criminal justice system are innocent and unable, for one reason or another, to avail themselves of their "inalienable" rights to trial by jury and the presumption of innocence?

For those unfortunate people who end up on the receiving end of predatory litigation or a government investigation, I hope this book will provide the road map that I didn't have when I went through that agony. GODSPEED to you. You'll need it.